195 Centre Street, P-51 Mustangs, and, Me

Reflections of a Semi-Famous Writer

RALPH JOSEPH FERRUSI

195 CENTRE STREET, P-51 MUSTANGS, AND, ME
REFLECTIONS OF A SEMI-FAMOUS WRITER

iUniverse books may be ordered through booksellers or by contacting:

iUniverse
1663 Liberty Drive
Bloomington, IN 47403
www.iuniverse.com
844-349-9409

Because of the dynamic nature of the Internet, any web addresses or links contained in this book may have changed since publication and may no longer be valid. The views expressed in this work are solely those of the author and do not necessarily reflect the views of the publisher, and the publisher hereby disclaims any responsibility for them.

Any people depicted in stock imagery provided by Getty Images are models, and such images are being used for illustrative purposes only.
Certain stock imagery © Getty Images.

ISBN: 978-1-6632-2764-5 (sc)
ISBN: 978-1-6632-2765-2 (e)

Library of Congress Control Number: 2021916609

Print information available on the last page.

iUniverse rev. date: 09/24/2021

CONTENTS

Foreword v

Acknowledgements.. xv

195 CENTRE STREET

195 Centre Street, October 11, 2004 1

    Mom, Pop, And 195 Centre Street... 4

        Mom 4

        Pop 6

    Grams-isms.. 7

    Pop's Favorite Joke, plus... 8

    2 North 9

    Pop's Last Anniversary Card For Mom 12

P-51 MUSTANGS

    Don Gentile on the P-51 Mustang: 17

    In My Opinion... 17

    Mustangs I've Sat In! 20

    A Tale Of Two Mustangs.. 21

    A World Without P-51 Mustangs..25

    The Last Mustang???...27

    Let's Talk About the P-82/F-82 Twin Mustang 29

    Back to 1943 30

    Some Facts and Figures 31

    Surviving F-82's.. 31

    The F-82 and Me 32

    A Twin Mustang in the Sky Again 33

    A Tale of Four Old Crows 33

    U.S.A.A.F Captain Don Gentile 36

    The *NINE O NINE* 40

    The *NINE O NINE* Revisited 44

The *NINE-O-NINE*..46

Let's Talk About B-24 Liberators 48

Tondelayo!!!...52

My All-time Favorite Airplanes 56

AND, ME

Summations And Ruminations 59

    Summing It Up At 60 59

    "Summin' It Up At 60"...60

    This could be called "Summing It Up At 70...".................63

        Me, Then...63

        Scourges, Etc That Didn't Exist Then 64

    "Turning Points" 64

    Life Changers 69

    "Magic" 69

        Non Travel 69

        Travel Related 70

    I Took Another Pass At This In December 2015, and Here's
What Came Up 72

        Moments... 72

    Things I've Let Go Of..73

    Things I Hate...73

    Things I love 74

    2015 additions, written *before* I found the 2000 document 75

    "The Golden Years"..75

    Ralph J. Ferrusi Author Profile 75

    50 Years: Written for my 50th Hendrick Hudson High School
reunion: 2005...76

    A Friend Jim's 50th birthday 77

    Writers/Authors/Books...79

    A Bill Bryson Funny Story 81

Writing/Essays/"Profound Thoughts" 82

    "Writing", From Sometime In 2007???:................................82

    Meet The Author 86

    If Anybody *Had* Come...86

Luna..87
Small Pleasures 88
Heroes/Persons I Admire 89
Men That Changed My Life..89
The Cruelest Word in the English Language......................89
Thoughts on "Winning" 90
Happy/Not So Happy...91
That Picture, right over there... 92
US Presidential Qualifications..92
Christmas "update" Note Goof...93
Twin (From *Catskill Tales and Trails*)...............................94
"Other News"...94
Affluence... 95
"Squirrel-Proof" Bird Feeders..98
Pop Music, 1966 To 2009 99
Nothing Left to Ooze; My Life as a Leper and Other Career Moves...100
Henry Hudson...102
It Doesn't Get Much Better'n This 104
Mort..104
March 30,2015 Terrifying Moments................................105
And, While We're At It, How's About The Using Up Of
Eight Of My Nine Lives???..106
Poems..107
#47, Sat. July 20, 1985..108
On Being 78...109
Wednesday Morning, December 9, 2015 109
2016 110
The Canyon of Heroes, 2009...113
"Local Boy Makes Good"...114
"Grown Up" 118
Lucy Jordan..118
Kath's Retirement 121
The Unicorn of Assateague Island...................................123
Then And Now: April 1, 2013 125
Scourges, etc..125
The River, and, The City 126

Eulogies 128

Pure Christine 128

Meme Biourd: March 16, 1911-February 15, 2016 129

Johnny Rit, Sonny, and Patty..129

My Cousin Johnny..130

A Few Good Words...133

Some Words Of True Wisdom, And, Some Funny Things.....................134

A magazine ad 144

From my 70's "Nothing Book"...144

Country Music Wisdom...150

One of my IBM "Out of the Office" e-mail notifications 152

And what do YOU do, Ralph???...153

My All-time Favorite Limerick 153

Farts..154

Paper Clips..154

Travel/Adventure 155

Our Vacations, 1985 To 2020..155

A Tale of Two 777's...156

My New Favorite Place in the World 158

Boating in the Azores: Paradise Found..158

Getting to Scotland, September 2013 163

Alitalia 165

Ten Guardian Angels; in Belize??? 166

An Extraordinary Day..171

Saranac May 2015 176

Hello, Goodbye, Please, and Thank You..178

Auschwitz, Birkenau..179

A Single Drop of Water??? Or Rum???...179

A Tale of Ten Cities..183

In Defense of "Real" B&B's..186

Scotland..187

Goal: More American Tourists To Scotland 189

Scotland/Ireland Similarities...189

Differences..190

So........Let's Talk About Scotland: 190

CARS: My Recollections of Each One 192

My First Car: a 1950 Plymouth fastback 193

1936 Ford coupe 195

1958 Plymouth Belvedere two-door hardtop 196

1934 Ford convertible 198

1963 Chevrolet Corvette Sting Ray Split Window Coupe............201

Fiat 600.. 204

Fiat 600 (for parts)...205

1964 Dodge Dart two-door hardtop 206

1972 Ford Pinto fastback... 207

1974? Fiat X 1/9.. 208

1962 Chevy Impala two-door hardtop.................................... 209

1985 Honda CRX.. 209

1986 Honda CRX Si..210

1991 Honda Civic Si hatchback..210

1996 Dodge Neon four-door 211

1996 BMW 328i convertible 212

2006 Chevy Aveo hatchback..213

2009 Smart FourTwo Passion Coupe......................................213

The Appalachian Trail..216

Ode to the Appalachian Trail:

Rediscovered in November 2020...219

ALDHA Gathering, October 2011 221

Kath AT thoughts: October 2016...223

Little Claire And The Flamingos... 224

Appalachian Trail Timeline 226

Appalachian Trail Quotes...229

Planting Seeds: Trail Magic Becomes A Two-Way Street 229

Taking a Step Back...231

My Appalachian Trail Favorites

1971-1975, 1979-2000 First Pass...232

My Appalachian Trail Favorites

1971-1975, 1979-2000 Second Pass..233

The Last Mountain 235

Cairn Memories: In Defense Of Cairns 236

War/The Military 239
    Land Mines in Vietnam..239
    Lieutenant General Hal Moore on "War" 239
    I Was A Soldier Once, And Young.. 240
    9/11 241
    9/11, Vindicated 243
    Lieutenant Colonel Geoffrey Slack.. 244
    HudsonValley Honor Flight Mission #5, September 27, 2014........245
    HudsonValley Honor Flight Mission #22, April 13, 2019 249
    My Saturday, April 13, 2019 words at the "farewell" dinner
    in Washington, DC 249
    POLSKA... 251

Health/Medical 252
    Vegetarianism, Meditation, Fitness, And, Cancer 252
    Carpal Tunnel Release:..253
    Happy Birthday, Sis!...255
    A Thousand (Or So) Things You Don't Know About Heart
    Attacks, or, Open Heart Surgery 260
    Hospitals → Surgery 261
    ICU → Discharge 263
    Discharge → Home: The Long Road to "Recovery" 265
    Some Heart Attack Information To Ponder 267

29 Years at 34 Kim La.. 268
    The Early Days 269
    Home Improvements 270
    The Pool..271
    Buttoning Up..273
    Thoughts While Splitting Firewood At 34 Kim Lane On A
    Cold, Damp, Dreary October 2016 Morning.................................276
    24 Years Later...277
    Raking Leaves, November 2015 277
    "Feedback"..278

Miscellany 279
    Lists 279
    Countries... 279

Places I would like to get to in the future............................282

While we're at it, let's do Border Crossings 282

And, we might as well do states I've been to 284

Movie Scenes/Songs..286

Close Encounters With The Rich And Famous 287

Les Mis, and movies... 289

Food and Drink 290

The Eight Greats..290

The Seven Dwarfs..291

Numbers...292

Principal 1998 New York Yankees 293

Friday, October 29, 1999 294

My Mona Lisa 295

The Library Announcement 297

"Jackson-isms"...298

A 1997 "Status Report"..298

IBM and Alessandro Botticelli..299

"Fabulous"..300

Global Warming, or, Naturally Occurring Cycles??? 302

My Obituary...304

Epilogue..307

ACKNOWLEDGEMENTS

To Mom and Pop, Josephine Theresa and Ralph Joseph Ferrusi, who instilled in me—by word and by example—their Polish and Italian "Old Country" values:

> Respect your elders.
> Respect women.
> Be honest.
> Work hard: keep your nose to the grindstone.

These became deeply ingrained in me at an early age, and I've strived to live by these basics all my life.

195 CENTRE STREET

195 CENTRE STREET, OCTOBER 11, 2004

It's summertime, and the kitchen windows are open and a warm, gentle breeze is blowing the spotless white lace curtains into the room. The sun is shining through the window over by the sink, and everything is fresh and clean and smells good. Mom keeps it that way.

The house is small: the kitchen is tiny, smaller than the bathrooms in most modern houses. The two bedrooms upstairs aren't much bigger than modern walk-in closets. The living room/dining room area is tiny, and in the winter the only heat comes up through a heavy yard-square iron grate in the middle of the downstairs hall floor. Beneath the grate is a coal-burning furnace.

I am 7 years old, my sister is 5. Mom is in the kitchen. Pop is at work at the vinyl wall-covering factory. He's there 10 to 12 hours a day, 6 days a week, and brings home something like 50 dollars on a good week. Mom keeps the house clean and orderly, and Pop works long, long hours.

They both grew up in small, cold, electricity-less houses in Greentown, a community of Polish and Italian immigrant factory workers, on the "other side" of the New York Central Railroad tracks. They both feel fortunate to be living the American dream in this small house on 195 Centre Street,

Buchanan, New York, USA. Me, I just can't wait to finish my tasteless bowl of shredded wheat so that I can run outside and play in the summer sunshine.

60 years fly by. Pop has been retired for 30 years, since the vinyl wall-covering company pulled out and moved to somewhere in Pennsylvania. He lives alone in the tiny house. Mom has been in an Alzheimer's ward in a nursing home for over 2 years. At 92, Pop is not the housekeeper Mom always was. To give him the benefit of the doubt, he was quite abruptly thrust into the role of sole housekeeper at age 90.

Earlier, Mom and Pop shared the load in the traditional "old country" manner: he never complained about the long hours at the factory, and kept the outside of the house, the roof, the yard, the garage, and the car in good repair, while Mom cooked, put food on the table, cleaned the house, did the laundry, and looked after us kids. Pop does give it a try: he vacuums occasionally, washes some of his clothes in cold water in the bathtub, and ties up stacks of newspapers to be recycled, but somewhere along the line, on his way to 90+, his overall perceptions of order and neatness slowly, gradually moved far to the left of center.

Everything in the house remains where it was when we tricked Mom into the nursing home: the furniture, the curtains, the rugs, the pictures, the books and knick-knacks. They are all either threadbare, dusty, and/or faded, and buried in unbelievable clutter: Pop's clothes, shoes, laundry, stacks and piles of newspapers, flyers, and junk mail, tissues, discarded tissues, loose change, paper, plastic bags, empty VA pill bottles…

The house is an assault on the senses. It smells: must, dampness, mold. The bathroom and the kitchen are the worst. As hard as my sister and I and various housekeepers try to keep the house and the yard clean, neat, and orderly, Pop somehow stays 'way ahead of us, circumventing our efforts. We wonder how he manages to accumulate so much clutter and junk and paper and plastic in such short periods of time.

The lace curtains are still hanging in the kitchen. They are gray, spotted, stained, and limp. They don't billow in the summer breezes anymore; the kitchen windows haven't been opened in years. The sunshine has a hard time penetrating the dingy gray-ness of the curtains. Mom will never live in this house again, and for whatever reasons, the newspaper piles and mayhem have become "normal" for Pop.

When I walk into the kitchen I flinch at the food and fruit – uneaten, half eaten, and to-be-eaten—wrappers, utensils, dishes, glasses, cups, and crusted pots and pans piled on the table, in the sink, and on the stove and the small counters. Over the years I have grown to accept all of this, but there are times when I look over at the small window by the sink and try to picture it wide open, a warm, gentle breeze blowing the white lace curtains into the room, the sun shining through them, everything spotless and clean, just the way Mom kept it. And I try to imagine what it was like to have nothing more to do than force down the dry shredded wheat, before running outside to play in the small, neat, trim, uncluttered yard.

MOM AND POP

Mom and Pop each lived to 94.They were born to Polish and Italian immigrants in 1912 and 1913. They lived the American middle class dream: a little house on a quiet street in a typical middle class American small town. Both drove, but they never had more than one car.

Pop worked long hours in a factory. Mom cooked, made the beds, washed the dishes, and took care of their two kids. They passed along "Old World" values to them: work hard—"nose to the grindstone", be honest, respect your elders, respect women.

Their life-long diets were typical middle class "meat and potatoes". Every once in a while Mom cooked an apple pie. They never "dieted" or experimented with their diets. They were never concerned with calories and never read food labels/ingredients. They just ate: Mom cooked, the family ate what Mom bought at the town's within-walking-distance little grocery store, and, cooked.

They were healthy most of their long lives in spite of never "running", going to a gym, or having "personal trainers". Pop sat in his favorite chair in the small living room evenings and read the newspapers. I don't think Mom ever did (or had the time to). I don't think either finished high school.

They did their best with what they had and what they knew. They worked hard and brought us up right. They were good parents, good people, good neighbors, and good citizens.

Pop had as serious stroke on April 3, 2016, and died in a rehab center on July 5th. He always said he "wanted to go out kicking and screaming": no DNR. Mom lived the final years of her life in a VA Alzheimers ward. She died September 11, 2017, the day *before* my birthday.

I shall forever be indebted and thankful for their guidance, love and care, and for the fine examples they set and passed along.

November 2020

Mom, Pop, And 195 Centre Street

Mom

Mom was a great Mom. She was a fine lady.

She nourished, encouraged, educated, and inspired us, with quiet strength, determination, and her strong intuition, both by example and by deed.

When I began to travel the world, she told me to keep my eyes wide open and "To see, and see what I saw": to soak it all up and take it all in.

She always told waitresses they were beautiful, no matter how un-beautiful they might have been.

She could never resist little jokes, and would always tell people that she was "polish Polish".

When we drove down to the Croton Dam on our Friday rides in the Neon, she would remind Pop and I that it was not the Croton Dam, it was "the Croton Darn".

Mom and Pop were inseparable. It's hard to find a photograph of just Mom; it was always Mom and Pop. On February 23, 2006, their 70th anniversary, Pop handed Mom a card. One word was written on the envelope, in Pop's squiggly, 93-year-old handwriting: "Us". It said it all.

I truly hope that they are now together again, in some nice place, and they are both 22–23 years old, and will be there forever.

With: Aunt Lil and Uncle Pete,
          Aunt Mary and Uncle John,
          Uncle Pat and Aunt Mary,
          Aunt Ann and Uncle Harry,
          Uncle John and Aunt Helen,
          Cousin Nita,
          Bob McGinnis,
          Cousin Henry,
          Cousin Ronald, and
          Cousin Peter.

The last words I ever said to Mom, just last Friday, were the words I always said to her before I reluctantly walked out of the Fairhaven ward in the VA:

"Love you a bunch, Mom."
"Pop loves you too."
"You're The Best."

She was a great Mom.

She was a fine lady.

Pop

He's tall and strong, standing at ease in his Army khakis: Fort Belvoir, Virginia, 1945. He's my dad: a good soldier, a good man. I'm proud of him.

As I come through the front door he glances at his watch: 10:45 AM Friday: right on time. He greets me in his soft, quiet voice, and extends his right hand—a big, workingman's hand, with long, strong fingers. The skin on the back of his hands is thin, the blood vessels purple and prominent, but his grip is firm. On the ring finger of his left hand is a small, worn, gold wedding band. Mom put it there 67 years ago.

He's sitting in his chair in the tiny living room of his tiny house in small-town Buchanan, New York. The chair is worn and sagging. It's old, and looks it. Pop does too. His hair is pure white and a little on the longish side, as are his sideburns. The skin on his face and neck sags; he has dark age spots. His eyebrows, and the hairs in his nose and ears are dark, long, and unruly, in need of a trim. A close shave is impossible anymore—the skin on his face and neck is too loose. His eyes though, are clear, bright, and curious. Alert and attentive, at age 92 he rarely smiles. When he does, his eyes and his face light up. Laughter is a rare gift, as when he speaks Italian.

He's a thin and frail 130 pounds. His body is stooped and worn. His once-broad shoulders slump forward, his chest is caved in. His limbs are thin and bony. A grayish undershirt peaks out the top of his threadbare dark grey/green cotton shirt. All the super-duty laundry detergent in the world will never get it white again. A pair of dark green, permanently soiled factory-worker pants are precariously held up by an antique black leather belt.

He pulls on his beat-up black faux running shoes. This everyday task is a major struggle, and takes forever. I watch, and don't interfere: I respect his dignity. He doesn't tie the laces. He glances at his watch, and begins the slow, laborious process of standing up. It's time to go to the diner for lunch. Getting up out of the chair is a fight with gravity; a struggle. He is determined. Walking is not a simple task anymore: he shuffles, stooped over. He is very unsteady on his feet at times. A cane has appeared from somewhere. I ask him about this. He doesn't answer.

When the bill comes at the diner, I hand it to him. He studies it, calculates a generous tip, reaches into his pocket, and puts it on the table. We visit mom in the Alzheimer's ward at the nursing home. I watch him sitting next to her, holding her hand, looking at her the same as he did 67 years ago.

He's tall and strong. A good man. A very good man...

Grams-isms

Mom loved little puns; she could not resist them. One of her favorites was "I'm polish Polish!"

Here's some more:

Faster than a herd of turtles
Take a sit
Bass-ackwards
She cooks her carrots and pees in the same pot.
Glad to see your back (if you were standing in front of Grams)
Sewer/sewer (Mom worked as a sewer in the little place in Buchanan by the circle. The sewer was out front on Tate Avenue...)

Some Grams sayings:

Ah hah, she cried, as she waved her wooden leg. Ah hah...
I'll give you back to the Indians.
I'll kick you in the ankle.
Three men in a boat and the oars leaked.

I hate to see you go,
I hate to see you go,

I hope to hell you never come back
I hate to see you go.

The apple doesn't fall far from the tree.
Don't take any wooden nickels.
He's working steady. (An actor in a movie or on the TV)
Better out than in (burps and farts)
Go play in traffic (to Danielle and Emily Berta)
I think he/she has a couple of pages stuck together.
Love hurts.

Pop's Favorite Joke, plus

Some people tell jokes, but for the life of me right now I can't think of a single relative, friend, acquaintance, co-worker, etc who "tells jokes": "Did you hear the one about...???" I don't tell jokes: I get nervous and self conscious. Pop didn't tell jokes either, but there's one that I remember him telling. It went something like this:

Four moles were crawling through a tunnel.
The first mole said "I smell carrots."
The second mole said "I smell turnips."
The third mole said "I smell radishes."
The last mole said "I smell mole asses."

Pop also told the story about a co-worker who injured his arm on the job and was staying home collecting Workman's Comp.
One day he came in to show his boss how badly injured he still was.
He said to the boss, "Before I was injured I was able to raise my arm this high.", and he raised his arm straight up over his head.
"Now I can only raise it this high.", and he raised his arm straight out from his shoulder.....

Pops and I once "repaired" a cement porch on the house on Old Hopewell Road. Both of us had only layman's experiential with cement, but we forged ahead and the end result was passable, but pretty much a "cob job". Pop summed it all up with this statement, that I very often quote: "It may not be perfect, but it's a helluva lot better than when we started." He also often greeted up with, "Where the hell have you been???", and also had a phrase that I don't recall anyone else ever saying: "Shit, piss, and corruption."

2 North

a.k.a. The Alzheimer's Ward, Autumn 2002

The door to the ward is locked. It's a punch-in-the-combination lock, and the combination is 1234*. None of the patients on the ward can figure this out. There are about 40 patients on the ward, and most of them are in wheelchairs. They have forgotten how to walk. A majority of them are propped up in the wheelchairs, with their heads lolled to one side or the other, dozing or staring at nothing. Most of the few that aren't wheelchair-bound are sitting in chairs, many of them are dozing.

There are always a dozen or more patients lined up in the room with the TV. It drones away, but no one is paying any attention to it. Some of the patients talk to themselves, or to someone we can't see—in English or in foreign languages. One lady SCREAMS for long periods of time. This is terribly unsettling to everyone—other patients, staff, visitors. There is only one guy on the ward—he sits in a chair, nodding off, every time I've been there. I have caught his eye a couple of times, and have said "Hi" to him. Some of the women always try to catch my eye, and if it works, I smile at them and wave, to give them a little bit of attention.

There are only a few patients that are ambulatory. Mom is one of them, and the people who work on the ward often don't know exactly where she is. When they do find her, and we are walking towards each other, it takes a little while before a glimmer of recognition comes into her eyes (sometimes it doesn't—this is hard to get used to), and she will usually break into a big smile, but sometimes she cries.

One day she was wearing a nice, faded pair of blue jeans. Mom is 89 years old, and it took a while to register on me that she was wearing jeans, and that this was the first time I had ever seen her wearing jeans. There is a lot of "trading", clothes and possessions, that goes on this ward. Patients wander (or more correctly, wheel...) in and out of each other's rooms, and somehow Mom ended up with a pair of jeans. A lot of Mom's "stuff"—clothes, jewelry— disappear from her room.

Mom's room: we've tried to make it a little "homey", with photographs, quilts, Mom's chair from home—but, it is basically a hospital room; two people in a room, very sterile and stark. The stuff we brought in doesn't really do a hell of a lot to disguise this starkness.

The people who work on the ward: all of the nurse / attendants are black women, 20 to 30 something, and most of them are pretty "jive", and many of them have "attitudes", that infer that they don't really care all that much about the mostly 70-90 year old white women patients.

The supervisors are white women, 30, 40, 50, and are generally hassled. They really have their hands full with the patients, and the who-the-hell-else-would-DO-this-job black women. And that kind of sums this situation up— it's a tough, dirty, thankless job. None of the patients can wash themselves, or dress themselves, or take care of basic bathroom functions. I don't think I could stand up to something like this, 40 or so hours a week, and I'm sure the people that have to aren't making Big Bucks...

Every time I punch in the 1234* and walk in, it's a brick between the eyes. Every time I have been there, I have "become emotional" at some time or other in the course of my visit. Every time: from a few tears rolling down my cheeks to full-on racking sobs when my kids and I and my nephews brought Mom back on Christmas day.

Mom sometimes looks pretty good when I get there, but sometimes she looks awful. Very old, tired, eyes red and sunken, hair in wild disarray. But as bad as this is sometimes, she just about always comes around when she gets in the front seat of the Neon, I buckle her seat belt and lock and close the door on her side, and we go off on one of our "Friday adventures".

She talks quite a bit, and makes little jokes, and seems to relax and enjoy the ride and the adventure. She always speaks Polish at some time or other, and I now know the Polish words for "red" and "green" (traffic lights—I can't seem to retain the word for "yellow"—Polish has not been easy for me to pick up on.), and, as Mom often counts stairs while we are going up and/or down, I can count to five in Polish—yedden, dvah, trezzsh, shditty, pee-yench. I'm working on "6". Mom sometimes says an entire phrase, and I'll ask her what it means, but as of now I have no hope of mastering complexities like this—languages aren't "my thing".

When we are in diners or restaurants, a lot of people look at Mom and seem to be frightened, or put off. On the other hand, just about the same amount of people "get it", and smile at her with caring and respect. Mom always tells waitresses that they are "beautiful": whether they are Polish, Czech, Guatemalan, inner city Peekskill, whatever—they are "beautiful". Some of them have the wherewithal to tell Mom she is beautiful also, and she is, but many of them don't know how to respond to this kind of attention from an 89 year old woman accompanied by a 90 year old man and a 65 year old guy with bleached hair.

It's always hard when our little adventure is over—the diner (most often) / restaurant (less often) has been visited and the little ride to Croton Dam, or the Bear Mountain Bridge, or around Verplanck Point is over—and we have to return to the nursing home.

Pop and I dreaded this at first, because Mom would ask "What is this place??? Why are you taking me here???". Now she pretty much accepts it, as "the place where she lives". I'm not sure if I think this is good or bad. I pull up to the door, and Pop helps Mom into the lobby and up to 2 North. I park the Neon and hustle back over, and by that time Pop has pretty much brought Mom back to her room, and is convincing her to lie down and take a nap after all of the exertion of sitting in a car and looking at the scenery.

Mom pretty much buys into the lying down part, but when I leave she often starts crying and asks why she has to stay here and we can go. I tell her that we are "working on it", and that we will be back to see her as soon as we can: Pop is down there just about every day, and I am a Friday regular. It's hard to tear myself away, but I do, and walk away misty-eyed, and feeling like homemade shit....

Pop's Last Anniversary Card For Mom

February, 2006

Mom and Pop were both in the Montrose VA hospital, and had been for quite a while, Mom in the Alzheimer's ward, Pop in room 122A in the Catskill Wing. They were both wheelchair-bound.

When I visited Pop on the Friday before their Anniversary, he told me he had wheeled down to the VA gift shop/store and bought an anniversary card for Mom.

I wheeled him over to the Alzheimer's ward and we found Mom and he gave her the card. When Mom handed it to me I opened it up and looked inside, and Pop had written a single word, in his now-squiggley/shaky script: *"US"*

After Pop died in July the hospital packed up his few possessions and gave them to us. They included several cards that had been tacked on the corkboard in C122A. Somehow the anniversary card had not been included....

March 1, 2016

May 10, 2017

Yesterday (or today, I've never gotten it right recently) woulda been Pop's 105th.

It was a typical grey, dreary day—there've been a lot of them in the last couple of weeks—so instead of moping around doing nuthin', I decided to mow the lawn, even though it really didn't need it yet.

Our Poulin PRO wouldn't start—the engine is probably ruined because of the ethanol in all the gasoline now—so I dragged Pop's Poulin PRO out of the shed. I hadn't started it, or used it, in a long, longgggg time. The last time I recall trying to use it it wouldn't start.

It fired up on the third or fourth pull—thanks Pop—and I mowed the lawn with it, all the while thinking back to when I mowed the Centre Street lawn with it, and Pop would sit there on the back steps watching me.

When I finished the lawn, I washed Pop's mower, and put it back in the shed, in the middle, where it'll be handy to use next time.

P-51 MUSTANGS

Don Gentile on the P-51 Mustang:

"It could go in the front door of the enemy's home and blow down the back door and beat up all the furniture in between."

In My Opinion...

It is my opinion that the P-51D Mustang is the sweetest, most perfect airplane ever conceived and devised by man. I love the looks, and the proportions of them: not too big, not too small; 37-foot wing span, 33-foot length; in-line engine, 4-bladed prop; bubble canopy; 6 50-calibre machine guns. It is a graceful, elegant aircraft, both in the air and on the ground.

I love the sound, and the snarl, of the Rolls Royce V-1650 Merlin engine. I used to dash out of the house when I was a kid in the late 40's and the 50's whenever I heard a flight of Mustangs in the sky over my parent's house. The sound of the Merlin engine was unmistakable to me. I would watch them until they flew out of sight.

In the 50's, the Air National Guard flew F-51H's (they were *F-51*'s by then) at the Westchester County Airport, and my Dad would take us down there on weekends and I would be enthralled by the Mustangs. I must admit that I never liked the "H" anywhere near as much as I liked the "D": the tail was taller, the distinctive radiator scoop had a different shape, and the bubble canopy was longer and less graceful. The whole plane was not as well proportioned as the "D". It was a faster, more powerful, more aerodynamic evolution, but it wasn't anywhere near as classic as the P-51D. That didn't stop me from wanting to see them, though.

They would take off two-by-two; the wingman would be a little behind the lead Mustang, and they would both open their throttles at the same time, and start rolling down the runway. They would pick up speed, and lift their tails. When they were airborne they would pull up their flaps and landing gear, and then the pilots would point the noses to the sky and they would climb; the Mustangs had a great rate of climb. It was impressive to watch.

They would join up, and then disappear over the horizon. Often, we would wait for them to return. When they did, they would gracefully peal off one by one, drop their flaps and gear, and circle in the landing pattern.

The Mustang looked as good with it's gear and flaps down as it did when it was "clean". As an aside, I think the Mustangs looked *very very* cool with their black and white "invasion stripes". The Mustangs were eventually replaced by jets: first by F-80 Shooting Stars, and then by F-84 Thunderjets. We used to go down to watch the jets, but it was not the same for me as watching, and listening to, the F-51's.

Once the ANG Mustangs were replaced by jets, I didn't see or hear one until over 40 years later. Honestly, I truly never did expect to see or hear one ever again. Then the newspapers announced that "The Warbirds" were coming to Dutchess County Airport, about 10 miles from here. There would be an assortment of WW I and WWII aircraft, included several Mustangs.

The air show would be over the weekend, but planes would start arriving the Friday before. I drove over to the airport after I left work, and as I was coming up to the end of the runway, I heard the sound of a Merlin engine in the sky. I hadn't heard that sound in almost a half a century, but it was unmistakable. I quickly pulled off the road and jumped out of the car. Up in the sky, in a landing pattern, were 3 Mustangs, gear and flaps down. They came in right over my head as they landed. How sweet... The first one was an olive drab P-51B or C, and did not have a bubble canopy. The next two were silver P-51D's.

There were six Mustangs lined up at the show. The Credit Union had a booth at the show, and Kath and I were allowed in early, before the general public arrived. We went right over to the Mustangs, and were admiring "The Jackie C". Kath climbed up on the wing and sat in the cockpit!!! No one said you couldn't, so she did! I had never occurred to me to do this, and I didn't believe my eyes at first. I took some pictures, and she got out of the cockpit and told me to get in. I hesitated, looked around, climbed up, and climbed in. I didn't stay long, just long enough for a few pictures – after all, this was someone else's airplane, and a cool million dollar one at that.

Years later, when I sat down one day and wrote down what I thought were some of the most interesting, memorable things I had ever done in my life, the first thing I wrote down was "Sat in the cockpit of a P-51 Mustang".

Every once in a while I dream that I am flying a Mustang. It is a very natural thing in the dream, and it feels very very real. I think that this is a very important, unfulfilled wish in my life: to actually fly in a P-51. It used to be doable: I have heard of Mustangs that were converted to two-seaters by removing the military radio equipment from behind the pilot's seat and installing a small jump seat. I'm pretty sure The Jackie C had had this done to it. I've never been sure how to go about getting a ride, or how to find a Mustang and owner that would be willing to take me up.

Along this line, there never have been that many air-worthy Mustangs around in the first place in modern times, and as time goes by there are less and less. Several years ago I read in a book that there were only 33(?) air-worthy Mustangs in the whole world. And, realistically, the D's are now 60-year-old airplanes, so the odds of finding one to get a ride in, slim at best in the first place, are less and less each year. A few years ago I just happened to see a little article in a newspaper that said that 3 Mustangs had crashed that year. This saddened me, but, they are man-made, and they are aging flying machines, so these things are going to happen, through accident, pilot error, the weather, mechanical failure.

Sad to say, but a day will come when no one will ever again hear the sound of a 1944-1945 Packard-built Rolls Royce Merlin engine up in the sky, or be able to look up and see a Mustang gracefully slicing through the air. I'm very glad that I did, both as a wide-eyed young kid and as an adult... ... ...

Mustangs I've Sat In!

As of Friday, September 9, 2016 I have sat in the cockpits of three P-51 and/or F-51 Mustangs:

1) *The Jackie C*, a P-51D, on September 2, 1994 (???) at Dutchess County Airport, New York

2) The **FRAGILE** *but* **AGILE**, on August 29, 2015, at Stewart Airport, Newburgh, New York

3) The Collings Foundation *Toulouse Nuts*, a TF-51D two-seater, on September 9, 2016 at Dutchess County Airport, New York.

A Tale Of Two Mustangs

I read Sarina Houston's *Why the P-51 is Still the Most Beloved Airplane at the Air Show* (*Boating on the Hudson and Beyond*, August 2015, pp. 74, 75) with great interest. Sarina nailed it. I've been a "Mustang nut" for as far back as I can remember. In my opinion, it's the most perfect airplane ever to take to the skies. Sure, the Corsair's cool, and I admire 747's, C-130 Hercules, C-47/DC-3's, B-17's/B-24's, but, for whatever reasons, the North American P-51D Mustang holds a very special place in my heart, and in my mind. A thought: whenever any of the above admirable planes take off, balls to the wall, they **ROAR**, very loudly. Big radial engines, or big jet engines, ROAR. The short-stacked V-12 Merlin growls and *snarls*... It's a sound like no other that I have ever heard, and a sound, for whatever deep, mysterious reasons, I can't get enough of... You Mustang nuts know what I'm talking about.

On his way to the Philippines in 1945, my Dad spent some time in Hawaii, and though he was in the US Army, somehow ended up at Hickam Field attached to the Seventh Air Force. He told me that he once took the carburetor off a P-51...

Years later, the New York State Air National Guard 137th Fighter Interceptor Squadron based at Westchester County Airport (now the 105th Airlift Wing based at Stewart International Airport) flew F-51H Mustangs. The "H" was a "lightweight" Mustang, thicker around the middle, and with a thin, taller tail and a less visually aesthetic bubble canopy than the "D": to me, it never had the "mystique" of the "D".

Pop would load us up in his old black Plymouth and we'd go down to the airport to watch the Mustangs fly. They would take off two-by-two, and when they finally returned from wherever they went (we would wait patiently for them), they would gracefully peel off and enter the landing pattern, gear and flaps down. They would taxi by on the way back to the hangars, but were always quite a distance away. I took dozens of pictures of them with my old-fashioned fixed-focus little camera, but they were always pretty much specks in the distance. They were eventually replaced by jets (F-80's???). Once the Mustangs were gone, we stopped going to the airport.

About four decades went by before I again heard the sound of a Merlin in the sky. In 1994 the Dutchess County Airport hosted a bunch of warbirds. The day before the airshow, I bicycled over to the end of the main runway on Route 376, and watched four Mustangs arrive, enter the landing pattern, and, flaps and gear down, land right over my head. It was the first time I realized the Merlin sounds like a popcorn popper as it backs off while landing.

My recollection is that eventually *seven* (I only have photos of four. Hmmmm...) Mustangs were lined up on the tarmac. And, besides the Mustangs, there was a very impressive turnout: a natural-aluminum B-17G, *FUDDY DUDDY*, with a yellow tail and yellow cowlings; an oddly camouflaged P-47D Thunderbolt; a Corsair; and an F7F Tigercat. Maybe a Hellcat, an Avenger??? No B-24, that I recall.

Kath and I got to the airport before the big crowds arrived, and we wandered among the not-yet-cordoned-off Mustangs. At some point, I looked up and Kath was sitting in the cockpit of *The Jackie C*, a beautiful red-nosed, invasion-striped P-51D!!! Holy s**t!!! I took a couple of pictures, and thought, "If Kath can do it, so can I", and clambered up on the left wing (avoiding NO STEP areas), and clambered into the cockpit. It was a dream come true: *I was actually sitting in the cockpit of a Mustang.* I got out pronto, staying only long enough for Kath to take a couple of pictures: this *was* somebody else's million-dollar airplane.

The warbirds returned in 1995: three Mustangs, including *Moonbeam McSWINE, Baby Duck,* and *BALD EAGLE*; an olive drab B-17G, *909*; a natural aluminum B-24H *Golden Girl*; a mean-looking MARINE F8F Bearcat; a Hellcat; and a B-25.

In 1996 *The Jackie C* was now a shark-mouthed P-40, and the former *Jackie C* P-51D was now the (ill-fated) *Big Beautiful Doll*. An F-86 and a P-38 showed up. Sadly, '96 was the last warbird appearance at Dutchess County Airport. No more Merlins in the sky.

In 2009 I heard the Collings Foundation B-17G *909*, B-24H *Witchcraft*, and the two-seater TP-51C *Betty Jane* were going to be at the Westchester County Airport. I skootched down, and clambered through the bombers, and then some lucky guy forked over the $2400.00 or so for a ride in the TP-51C. I was mesmerized as it fired up, then taxied to the far end of the runway. I stood by the fence with another Mustang-nut and we both had goose bumps as the Merlin hit full throttle and lifted off the runway, and we both watched it, wide-eyed, until it was a tiny dot in the sky, and, patiently awaited its return.

In 2014 the Collings Foundation trio returned to Dutchess County Airport. I called the airport to ask approximately when they were going to arrive, and hustled over to the end of the runway across 376. There were about a dozen other people there. I half expected the planes to arrive together, but the *909* arrived first, alone. The *Witchcraft* arrived next (the *only* B-24 (out of 18,188 built during World War II)) still flying, and a few of us got braver and walked to a point just about directly across the road from the end of the runway. It was an experience I'll never forget, watching that huge, powerful, last-one-flying Liberator coming just about right at us, gear and flaps down, roaring about 20 feet over our heads, clearing the chain-link fence and touching down right across the highway.

The Collings planes returned in 2015, and I again hustled over to 376, eagerly anticipating a repeat of my 2014 *Witchcraft* experience, but the wind was, unusually, from the east, and the B-17 and B-24 landed at the western end of the runway: quite a disappointment.

The 2015 New York Air Show at Stewart was a week after the Collings planes were at Dutchess. On-line, I learned the Bremont Horsemen—pilots Steve Hinton, Dan Friedkin, and Ed Shipley—the world's only P-51 aerobatic team, and the Air Force Flight Foundation Heritage Flight (AFHFF)—this year an F-22 Raptor and a P-51 Mustang—were going to be there. WOW!!!

(Check out this 7:28 Bremont Horsemen video: it's The Best Mustang video I've ever seen; incredibly, impossibly, smooth, graceful precision flying, three Merlins snarling: https://www.youtube.com/watch?v=RXvxnE4PDVQ)

We ended up in a VIP tent, and were very disappointed to learn the Horsemen would not be performing: one of the pilots was ill. But, at some point Kath noticed two guys with AFHFF flight suits on. One of them had "Mustang" written on it. She called me over. Tommy Williams was piloting the Dallas-built P-51K *FRAGILE BUT AGILE*. He sat down at our table, and I was awed: I was having lunch with a guy who actually flies a Mustang!!! I was babbling my Mustang stories: Pop and the carburetor, the differences between the Inglewood-built P-51D's and the Dallas-built P-51K's, etc, etc. Tommy said, "Would you like to come out and see the plane close up?" I damn near fainted... He gets on his phone.

Brian Lilley, Director of the show, picks Kath and I up in a golf cart and scoots us down right across from where the *FRAGILE...* is sitting all by itself, on the other side of the fence, unapproachable by the masses, and opens up the fence, and we are escorted out to the *FRAGILE...* where Tommy greets us, and asks if we'd like to sit in the cockpit. I glance at Kath, and she says to starry-eyed me, "Why don't you go ahead..."

Tommy then demonstrates the right way to climb up on the wing of a Mustang and get into the cockpit: right foot on the tire, left foot on the strut, right foot on the wing; step over the side and stand on the seat, then sit.... My gawd, I'm in the cockpit, feet on the rudder pedals, hand on the stick, looking out over the OD anti-glare panel at the long nose... It's surprisingly roomy. Tommy has me wiggle the rudder, and move the ailerons up and down. I'm acting casual, but my head is spinning...

When the Heritage Flight takes to the air, the ***FRAGILE BUT AGILE*** takes off first, and does a high-speed low-level fly-by along the runway. I *know* the guy flying that plane, and I just sat in it.......... I watch it got by, slack-jawed; the snarl of the Merlin gives me goose-bumps.

Tommy told us this particular P-51 flew in the Pacific during World War II. Mmm, the Seventh Air Force: could it just possibly be the self-same plane that Pop took the carburetor off of???? Yuppers, it's just possible.....

This first appeared in John Vargo's Boating on the Hudson and Beyond *2015 Holiday issue.*

A World Without P-51 Mustangs

I have several P-51 Mustang books, and I occasionally take one off the shelf and browse through it, usually for the umpteenth time. On Sunday, March 8, 2020 I picked out one of my favorites, Martin Bowman's 2013 *P-51 MUSTANG COMBAT MISSIONS: FIRST-HAND ACCOUNTS OF P-51 MUSTANG OPS OVER NAZI GERMANY.*

Thumbing through it, A Really Profound Thought hit me like a ton of bricks: if it wasn't for the Nazi's and Nazi Germany, the P-51 Mustang wouldn't have been needed, and, the Most Perfect Airplane, Ever, would not have been created. And, for the millions of us who love it, and, the sound of the Packard-built V-1650 Rolls Royce Merlins, life would be different: a world without P-51D Mustangs in the sky...

I'm a "Mustang Nut": I've loved the P-51D for as far back as I can remember: since I was a seven- or eight-year-old kid. Mustangs used to fly over our house at 195 Centre Street, in Buchanan, New York, and when I heard the snarl of their Merlins I would run out of the house and into the back yard and watch them until they were out of sight.

Later, Pop would take us down to Westchester County Airport and I'd watch the New York State Air National Guard F-51H's taxi by and then take off, and we'd wait until they returned, circled the field, and peeled off and landed. I took pictures of them taxiing with my little Kodak Brownie camera.

Back to March 2020: I imagined a world without Don Gentile's "Shangri-La", "Ratsy" Preddie's "CRIPES A' MIGHTY", "Kit" Carson's "Nooky Booky IV", John Lander's "Big Beautiful Doll".

John Godfrey, Gentile's ever-faithful wingman; Glenn Eagleston; Don Blakeslee, John Meyer, and Duane Beeson of the 4th Fighter Group would never have flown in combat. These men were all Captains, Majors, light Colonels, or full Colonels.

"Moonbeam McSWINE", "ALABAMA RAMMER JAMMER", "JERSEY JERK", "Ferocious Frankie", "Fragile but Agile", "Toulouse Nuts" would never have existed.

My world, and, the world in general, would be very very different.

While we're at this, let's not leave out the 56th Fighter Group's P-47 Thunderbolt pilot Francis Gabreski, World War II's top USAAF European Theatre fighter ace. The 56th is the only fighter group that stuck with the rugged, dependable Thunderbolt the entire war: all other fighter groups either switched to, or were originally equipped with, the P-51. Quite a while back I actually met, and talked to Francis Gabreski at a Warbirds air show at Dutchess County Airport.

Nope, like the Mustang, P-47's wouldn't have been needed either without World War II. Or, Corsairs and Hellcats, B-24's and B-17's. And, the world might not have morphed into Korea, and/or Vietnam... And, maybe now we'd all have Peace flags in our front yards, and be waking up singing zippity do dah every morning.

Dream on...........

March 11, 2020
483 Words

The Last Mustang???

Sunday, July 2, 2017 could well be the last day that I will ever see—or hear—a P-51D Mustang in the sky.

The 2016 New York Air Show at Stewart Airport was a Mustang Miracle. Kath had VIP passes, and we ended up having lunch with Tommy Williams, who was going to fly the P-51K FRAGILE *but* AGILE in the Heritage Flight. He invited us to sit in the Mustang, that was on display on the far side of the spectator barrier. During the fly-bys, I thought "We were just talking to the guy *flying* that Mustang!"

July 2, 2017, I did *not* have a VIP pass, and I experienced first-hand the ordeal—yup, ordeal—that NIP's: Non Important Persons—experience in order to view this hugely popular air show. Traffic was backed up just about to the I-84 exit ramp. I had expected this, but was truly stunned at how bad it really was, creeping along in low gear for miles and miles. It got worse past the left turn for VIP parking. We crept over the hill, then crept down the other side, where we were directed to turn right, *away* from the flight line. We were ultimately directed to turn left, where I handed out a twenty-dollar-bill for parking, and eventually was directed across a rutted grassy field, where I parked amongst several thousand other cars.

We then walked, about a quarter-mile, to stand in long lines waiting to board school buses, finally being driven another half-mile (or more), where we were herded out onto the tarmac, towards long lines at ticket booths: another thirty bucks!!! From there it was a long, long, long walk, through huge crowds—people were seated 20-30 deep along the fence—as I looked for the Mustang that had been promised for this year's Heritage Flight.

There wasn't a Mustang parked where the FRAGILE *but* AGILE had been parked last year. I kept walking through the crowds, looking all over the place for a Mustang, all the way to the very distant VIP area: *no* Mustang. I asked one of the volunteers guarding the VIP area if she could find me a program, so I could see if a Mustang was still supposed to be flying.

She—bless her—scrounged up a program, and, sure enough, a Mustang was still scheduled to be part of the 2017 Flight, along with a jet (or two).

Last year I was able to watch the FRAGILE *but* AGILE fire up, taxi out to the main runway, and take off. This year, the mystery Mustang just appeared in the sky, heading west. It was a highly-polished "D": I couldn't see if it had a name on it, and don't recall, for example, if it had invasion stripes or not. It eventually teamed up with the jet, and they flew formation—tiny dots well to the south—for a long time as the F-16 performed.

By now I had starting heading back towards the entrance, and was standing at the back of 20-30 rows of seated NIP's. It was hot as hell, I was tired of standing, and hadn't had any fluid, or food, since breakfast. I was leaning against as big blue plastic trash can...

The F-16 had done a whole bunch of wonderfully ear-splitting fly-bys, and finally the Mustang showed up with the F-22 (???) on its wing. They made several passes, and were joined by the F-16. Finally, the jets peeled off and landed, and the (mysterious) Mustang made several anti-climactic solo passes.

But, the thunderous roar of the jets were a very tough act to follow. In my weary, glazed condition, the Merlin—for the first time that I can remember—did not give me goose bumps. I just wanted to get on a school bus, find my car, and get the hell out of there. Several thousand other people had the same idea. Getting the hell outta there was a reverse of the long, long arrival ordeal.

I can't imagine ever going back to the New York Air Show—definitely not as a NIP—so right now, sadly, there's a damned good chance that July 2, 2017 will be the last time I ever see—or hear—a Mustang in the sky.

Whoops, I was so disappointed with the New York Air Show experience— hell, it was something I was (somewhat) looking forward to, and, it was supposed to be enjoyable—that, while writing this, I overlooked a strong possibility that might allow me to see—and hear—Mustangs in the sky again: the Collings Foundation TP-51C *Betty Jane*, and/or their recently-acquired TF-51D *Toulouse Nuts*. The Collings Foundation has been a regular at the Dutchess County (and Westchester County) Airports the last couple of years (but, neither are on their 2017 on-line schedule...).

So, if and when they show up again at either of these nearby airports, and if the *Betty Jane* and/or *Toulouse Nuts* are still able to get airborne, I'll have some kind of a fighting chance to see them in the sky. But, I must admit, neither of these planes are favorites of mine: they're both "T's": two-seaters. And, the *Betty Jane* is a "C"; my heart belongs to the "D's". And, for whatever reasons, I just can't cotton to the *Toulouse Nuts*; it's an *F*-51, and my passion is World War II, red-nosed, invasion-striped, P-51D's (K's are OK also).

To be continued????

July 8, 2017
892 Words

July 20, 2021: A P-51D flew in the Heritage Flight in the Ocean City, Maryland Air Show in July, with an F-22 Raptor on it's wing. On Sunday, I saw, and heard, it heading south, right overhead of where I was parked on Ocean Parkway, in Ocean Pines, Maryland. It was tail number 44-73420, owned (and flown???) by Andrew McKenna, of Arlington, Virginia.

To be continued...???

Let's Talk About the P-82/F-82 Twin Mustang

I've been a "Mustang nut" since I was a kid: more specifically, the Rolls Royce Merlin-engined P-51D/F-51D Mustang. None of the other variants particularly charmed me: the Allison-engined "A" and "B" models, nor, the Merlin-engined "C" model with a conventional early World War II P-40-like cockpit canopy. I'm not alone: there are zillions of Mustang nuts out there; I've talked to quite a few of them. I/we love the sound of the Merlin: the rumble/roar/whine of it is like no other sound.

Hold the phone: near the end of World War II another Mustang appeared out there: the P-82 Twin Mustang. Two Mustangs stuck together: pretty much joined at the hip!!! Hadda be twice as good, right??? Nope... Let's do some digging to find out why.

First things first, I've always—as a World War II aviation "enthusiast"—been aware of the P/F-82. But, a lot of other WW II planes trumped it: the Corsair, the B-17's, the—yup—B-24 Liberator, the Douglas Dauntless. Probably, I must admit, even the FW-190. Irregardless (I love this non-word), I do have an F-82 story to tell.

But first, here's a "Reader's Digest" version of the Twin Mustang's Story:

The North American F-82 Twin Mustang was the last American piston-engined fighter ordered into production by the U.S. Air Force. Based on the P-51H, it was originally designed as a very-long-range World War II escort fighter—able to travel over 2,000 miles without refueling—and intended to escort B-29's on 2,000+ mile missions from bases in the Solomons or the Philippines to the Japanese mainland that was at the time beyond the range of the P-51. Both cockpits of some P-82's were fully equipped so they could be flown from either position, allowing alternate control on long flights, but later night fighter versions had controls in the left cockpit only, with a radar operator on the right. World War II ended before the first production P-82's became operational.

But, during the Korean War, Japan-based F-82s were among the first USAF aircraft to operate over Korea. And, the first three North Korean aircraft destroyed by U.S. forces were shot down by F-82's, the first being a North-Korean Yak-11, by a 68th Fighter Squadron Twin Mustang. F-82's accounted for 20 enemy aircraft: four air, 16 ground. Ten F-82's were lost in Korea.

Back to 1943

In October, the North American Aircraft design team began working on slapping two P-51's together. Early P-82's were powered by the Mustang's Packard-built Rolls Royce Merlin V-1650. But, the Packard plants were dismantled when the War ended, so later models were powered by the Allison V-1710-100, resulting—surprise, surprise—in a lower top speed and poorer high-altitude performance. This gave the P-82 the dubious distinction of being one of the few aircraft in U.S. Military history where the earlier versions (made trainers) were faster than the fighter version...

And...the left propeller turned opposite to the right propeller, turning upward approaching the center wing, but...during it's first flight (attempt...) the aircraft *refused* to become airborne!!! After a month of "head scratching", the engines and props were exchanged, their rotation meeting on the downward turn. And, the plane took off...

Some Facts and Figures

Cruising speed: 286 mph.
Maximum speed: 461 mph.
Range: 2,240 miles!
Service ceiling: 38,900 feet.
Armament: six .50 caliber M3 Browning machine guns.
Cost per plane: $215,154.00

The Air Force accepted a total of 272 P/F-82's between 1945 and 1949. They were all manufactured at North American's Inglewood, California plant. There were eight production variants, A-H. In 1948 all P-82's were re-designated F-82.

All in all, the Twin Mustang had a very short operational life, being phased out of service by Republic F-84 Thunderjets and in Korean combat by Lockheed F-94 Starfires. Then they were either scrapped, declared "excess" and/or sent to storage or disposal. The last Twin Mustang (46–377) was officially retired on November 12, 1953.

Surviving F-82's

Airworthy:

XP-82 44-83887 was restored to flying status by aircraft restorer Tom Reilly, at Douglas Municipal Airport in Douglas, Georgia. After ten years,

207,000 man-hours and (nobody's saying how many) $$$$$, its first post-restoration flight took place New Years Eve 2018. It was the first time it flew since December 14, 1949. Half of this plane were found on a farm in Ohio. The other half—an entire wing and fuselage—were fabricated. A left-turning V-1650 Merlin was found in a shed in Mexico City, and a woman in Tampa Florida (somehow) possessed a unique-to-F-82's cockpit canopy!!!

On display:

F-82B 44-65162 is on display at the National Museum of the United States Air Force at Wright-Patterson AFB in Dayton, Ohio. It had been a "gate guard" outside Lackland AFB for many years, was acquired by the Commemorative Air Force in 1966, and stalled while landing in 1987. It arrived at the museum in 2009 and was restored to the appearance of the F-82G that shot down a North Korean La-7 on June 27, 1950, near Kimpo Air Base in South Korea.

F-82B 44-65168 *Betty Jo* - Displayed at the same Museum. It was delivered to the museum on June 21, 1957. On February 27, 1947, P-82B *Betty Jo*, flown by Colonel Robert E. Thacker made history when it flew nonstop from Hawaii to New York, 5,051 miles (!!!) without refueling, in 14 hours and 32 minutes, averaging 347.5 mph. WOW!!!

F-82E 46-0262 – is on display as a "gate guard" at Lackland AFB.

Under Restoration:

F-82E 46-0256, an intact airframe formerly located on the same farm in Ohio the XP-82 was at (somebody in Ohio collected Twin Mustangs???!!!), is currently under restoration to flying status by James Harker in Anoka, Minnesota.

The F-82 and Me

From Boating on the Hudson and Beyond, June 2018, Pages 45-46:

"I once sat in the radio operator's seat in a Stewart Air Force Base 105th Airlift Wing C-5A heading for Lackland AFB, a Brigadier General in the left seat, a full bird Colonel in the right. I was like a kid on Christmas morning when they pushed those throttles forward on Stewart's LONG runway."

In Lackland I sat next to the General on our Air Force tour bus, and, spotting a static-displayed F-82, I excitedly poked him in the ribs and exclaimed, *"There's a Twin Mustang*!!!" After he recovered his breath, he said "You know more about planes than I do."

A Twin Mustang in the Sky Again

I watched a video of XP-82 44-83887 airborne (Google "F-82 Twin Mustangs"). I expected to be thrilled by the sight, and sound, of two Mustangs stuck together. Oddly, I must admit, I wasn't: Allisons, not Merlins??? To me, the P-51D is still The Most Perfect Airplane, Ever. A tough act to follow, even by a "twin". The F-82 served nobly in Korea, and beyond, and I'm very glad there is, finally, one flying again. I truly hope, someday, to actually see this now-very-rare aircraft in the skies, and, be thrilled.

1159 Words

This first appeared in John Vargo's Boating on the Hudson and Beyond *Nov/ Dec/Jan 2018 issue.*

A Tale of Four Old Crows

Some people are "natural born" collectors: think stamps, and coins. And, I've known people who collect bricks, and, barbed wire: OUCH!!!

I've never considered myself a "collector"; ummm, I *do* have a half dozen or so 1/24th scale model NASCAR Dodges. But, this isn't like having a roomful—or an attic full—of them. Right!!!???

Uhhhh, and, as I've mentioned in these pages several times, I do "collect" P-51 Mustangs: I've sat in the cockpits of three of them now, a P-51D, a P-51K, and, a TF-51D. But, none of them are in our attic, or, driveway. Yet....

Recently I came across a beautiful, all-metal scale model P-51D in a consignment store in Milton, Delaware. $29.00... It was perfectly proportioned, had a really nice heft, and a 9 1/2" wingspan. It was silver with a yellow tail with a big "V" on it, tail number 472777, a red nose/spinner, and a dark green anti-glare panel in front of the cockpit. It said "Doc Watson" on the left side of the fuselage below the canopy. The landing gear retracted, and the canopy came off. It said "Liberty Classics, Libertyville, IL, LIMITED EDITION" under the wings. I just *had* to have it. It sits in a Place of Pride in our living room. I love gazing at it.

I Googled "P-51 472777": the "Doc Watson" Mustang flew in the 52nd Fighter Group, 5th Fighter Squadron, 15th Air Force in the Mediterranean Theatre of Operations in World War II.

A couple of days ago we returned to Milton. My wife enjoys browsing in this unique store. I had a mission: back when I bought the "Doc Watson" model, I had seen there was also a model of the famous olive drab "OLD CROW" P-51D, tail number 414450. I knew of this airplane, and way way back had seen an actual P-51D "OLD CROW" at a warbirds air show at Dutchess County Airport. I just had to add it to my Mustang model "collection". I bought it, and tail number 414450 now sits next to tail number 472777.

Let's talk a little bit about the World War II "OLD CROW" P-51D.

This P-51 was flown by Triple Ace—16 1/4 enemy aircraft downed— Colonel Clarence E. "Bud" Anderson. A native of Newcastle, California he flew two tours, 116 missions—without ever being hit by enemy fire, and, never having to turn back from any mission for any reason—with the 363rd Fighter Squadron of the 357th Fighter Group, the "Yoxford Boys", based in Leiston, England.

He originally flew OLD CROW P-51B tail number 324824. The OLD CROW's were named after Old Crow 86-proof Kentucky Bourbon Whiskey!!! The 357th Fighter Group produced 42 aces, and was credited with downing 609 ½ enemy aircraft in 15 months, a score unequaled by any other fighter group.

Leonard "Kit" Carson was the leading ace of the 357th, with 18.5 kills, flying P-51D "Nooky Booky II", and P-51K "Nooky Booky IV". Chuck Yeager also flew for the 357th, and was credited with 11.5 victories, in *three* Mustangs: P-51B "GLAMOROUS GLEN", P-51D "GLAMOROUS GLEN II", and P-51D "GLAMOROUS GLEN III". Yeager described Bud Anderson as "the best fighter pilot I ever saw".

The 357th favored the Olive Drab/Grey paint job that is on "my" OLD CROW but eventually switched to bare aluminum. The 357th was also one of the last outfits to remove the black and white D-Day "invasion stripes" from their Mustangs.

Colonel Anderson flew "over 150" airplanes and logged over 7,500 flight hours. Asked in an interview to name his favorite airplane, he commented "If an airplane looks good, it flies good", and noted that the P-51 is "A beautiful airplane, and, flies very nice." It's his favorite. Number two was the North American F-86 Sabre. Number three was the F-15 Eagle.

He wrote a book: "To Fly and Fight, Memoirs of a Triple Ace". I found it on-line, and bought a September 1991 Bantam Books paperback version of it! It's a remarkable book, beautifully written, with a Forward by Brig. Gen. Chuck Yeager, USAF, Ret., who eventually became his best friend.

I devoured it, and highly recommend it to anyone who is a "reader" interested in aviation, fighter pilots in general, and, especially P-51 Mustangs. It describes, in being-right-there detail the day-to-day life of World War II Mustang pilots flying missions from Leiston, England, with the Yoxford Boys over "the continent", escorting "heavies" and dealing with ME-109's and FW-190's. Descriptions of touch-and-go encounters with talented Messerschmitt pilots were gripping, and stories of losing squadron mates and seeing B-17's blown out of the skies were disturbing.

Anderson had a policy of never doing victory rolls over Leiston when returning from a mission: just in case his P-51 had battle damage he wasn't aware of. But...his description of finally doing a victory roll in 1989 (or so) in an "OLD CROW" replica, and his "wingmate" Chuck Yeager "obediently following" in a "Glamorous Glen" replica, gave me goose bumps, and choked me up.

Anderson originally flew P-39's in the late 30's, flew 26 missions in F-105 "Thuds" in Vietnam, and had a remarkable career as a test pilot at Wright-Patterson and Edwards AFB. I was mainly interested in his exploits in P-51's, but also became very absorbed in all of his flying. This book was the best couple of bucks I have spent in a <u>long</u> time....

Let's quickly talk about other famous Eighth Air Force Mustang aces:

The 352nd Fighter Group, "The Blue Nosed Bastards of Bodney's", George "Ratsy" Preddy, 25.83 victories in three "CRIPES A'MIGHTY's", and John Meyer, 24 victories with his "PETIE 2ND and 3RD".

The 4th Fighter Group's Don Gentile and his famous P-51B "Shangri-La", 19.83, Duane Beeson, 17.33, John Godfrey, 16.3, Don Blakslee, 11.5.

I hope Liberty Classics produces a LIMITED EDITION of one of these Mustangs, particularly Preddie's or Gentile's...

June 26, 2021
981 WORDS

This first appeared in John Vargo's Boating on the Hudson and Beyond *Feb/Mar 2021 issue.*

U.S.A.A.F Captain Don Gentile

Piqua, Ohio-born Don Salvatore Gentile has been a World War II Mustang pilot/ace hero of mine for as long as I can remember. First flying Spitfires with a Royal Canadian Air Force Eagle Squadron, then P-47 Thunderbolts with the 336th Fighter Squadron, 4th Fighter Group in Debden, England, at 23 years of age he hit his stride flying an olive-drab P-51B *Shangri La*. Surprisingly, at least to me, he never flew the iconic bare-aluminum P-51D in combat.

He is credited with 30 German aircraft destroyed air-to-air and on the ground—equivalent to nearly two full Luftwaffe squadrons—prompting Allied Supreme Commander, Europe, General Dwight D. Eisenhower, when presenting him with a Distinguished Service Cross, to refer to him as a "one-man air force".

44-page *ONE-MAN AIR FORCE, THE PERSONAL ACCOUNT OF A LEGENDARY WORLD WAR II ACE*, 1944, L.B. Fischer Publishing Corp., all-too-briefly tells, in his own, air-combat-graphic, often gut-wrenching, words, his story, as told to squadron mate/editor Ira Wolfert.

A long-time "Mustang friend" from Michigan found a copy of this book and shipped it to me in September 2020, and I just picked it up and reread parts of it, prompting me to sit down and write this summary of Don Gentile's early life, love of flying, and his often-quite-detailed memories of going head-to-head with the Luftwaffe's yellow-nosed FW-190's *Abbeville Kids*. Strap yourself in, fire up that V-1650 Rolls Royce Merlin, and hang unto your seats.

I'm going to start at the beginning of the book, and summarize it, either interpreting it or directly quoting from it: *italicized*. Don Gentile doesn't pull any punches when he talks about going head-to-head with the Abbeville Kids or less formidable, or experienced, Luftwaffe pilots. In fact he shows admirable sympathy for the "green" pilots—he can tell, from experience, their inexperience—he shoots out of the sky.

He flat out says, flying a fighter plane in combat in World War II, comes down, quite bluntly, to killing or being killed. I've read a lot of books about World War II aerial combat, most of them third-person, and just about all of them often abstract, and "sugar coated", very unlike Gentile's first-person "brick between the eyes" second-by-second detailed descriptions of, basically, killing enemy pilots.

In Chapter 1 (of 8) Gentile talks about aerial combat and dogfighting. Here, (quoted) are his very first sentences:

The theory of fight between fighter planes is very simple. You see the enemy, grab for his coattails, hold on to them, put your guns against his back pocket and press the trigger. [this lasts] *until somebody has grabbed hold for good and the other fellow starts to die. That's the dogfight.*

He then explains the importance of formations and team play, and how a dogfight "goes in a series of wooshes", where "There is no time to think", because "If you take time to think you will not have time to act"!!! Your mind will be very occupied with "...seeing, measuring, guessing, remembering, adding up...worrying...taking...into account...rejecting...accepting...it doesn't feel like thinking."

Once, when he destroyed three enemy aircraft, he estimates he fired his guns "a little more than ten seconds." When clobbering an enemy, "...it seems... he will never die...pieces start coming off him...then bigger things, big, ripped-off looking things...going slowly and endlessly over your shoulder." He explains that enemy pilots, with their oxygen masks on, appear not as men, but as gadgets in their machines.

Two men he once shot down, who each "fought very well", and "were crafty and had courage", at some point in the fight lost it because:

Their brains had dissolved away [from] *fear...They froze to their sticks...and ran into their graves like men stricken blind who run, screaming, off a cliff."*

WHEW!!! No sugar-coating here.................

Chapter 2, "...the air war really started when the Mustangs came." He started flying Spitfires June 22, 1942, but notes that the Spitfire of that day was a defensive weapon. When his group began flying P-47 Thunderbolts, he noted that at the time it "was a plane for limited offensive fighting". Then:

Finally we started flying Mustangs. [A] *plane for unlimited offensive action. It could go in the front door of the enemy's home and blow down the back door and beat up all the furniture in between.*

YES!!!

But...they were still on the defensive. "We had to do more running away than running after." "We couldn't go all out", while flying protective cover for the

B-17's and B-24's. He began flying Thunderbolts on April 2, 1943. But, their limited range allowed them to go only so far. The Luftwaffe waited for the Thunderbolts to turn back, then hit the bombers hard. When the bombers rendezvoused with Thunderbolts on their way home, "...the Luftwaffe strutted back home like dogs which chase a marauder out of the front yard, and are content to let it go at that." But..."With the Mustang there was no place for the Luftwaffe to retreat." **YES!!!**

"[We] could get them...kill them, trample them down." "...when the bell finally rang for the big fight, Colonel [Don] Blakeslee's team became, in seven weeks of the happiest, craziest hayriding ever, the highest-scoring outfit in the whole league."

Chapters 3 and 4: Airplanes, and flying, were always a key part of Gentile's life: "...it's airplanes or nothing for me." "The air to me was what being on the ground was to other people." His parents supported him, and in September 1940 he enlisted in the R.A.F. He soon realized that confidence, and, "offensive spirit", were extremely important for a fighter pilot.

Chapter 5: England, 1942: "I wanted to fight."

I had known from my first flight that I was playing in the big leagues—in a game that is very tough wherever it is played; the toughest, most reckless game, in fact, that any human being ever thought up to play.

On August 19, 1942, over Dieppe he shot down a Ju88: "...I just threw a barn door full of bullets at him." And, an Abbeville Kid FW-190.

Chapter 6: While flying a Thunderbolt, Gentile shoots down two FW-190's but becomes separated from his wingman, and is then attacked by two other FW-190's.

Chapter 7: The entire chapter is an over-four-page detailed blow-by-blow description of the ensuing air battle, where Gentile runs out of ammunition, but ultimately escapes by out-thinking and out-flying the enemy, in a prolonged battle that was "...perhaps, the most critical I had ever fought."

Chapter's 8: "I [picked] the best man I could get to fly on my wing—Johnny Godfrey, of Woonsocket, R.I., who doesn't like Germans. They killed his brother Reggie, at sea, and the name Johnny has painted on his plane is 'Reggie's Reply'. He means it, too"

The book concludes with this:

...I saw a Hun clobbering a Mustang mate of mine. I dropped my easy kills and dove on the Hun to bounce him off that Mustang. I didn't think about it at all; it was just a reflex action...if the feeling for team action had not been developed as a reflex in me...I would have been dead or a prisoner of war a long time ago.

This is one helluva book, and Don Gentile was one helluva United States Army Air Force team-player fighter pilot. Bravo, Captain Don Salvatore Gentile, bravo.

On January 28, 1951, 31-year-old Major Gentile crashed, and died, while testing a Lockheed T-33A Shooting Star trainer.

February 21, 2021
1,233 Words

The *NINE O NINE*

Thursday morning, October 14, 1943 383 8th Air Force heavy bombers—B-17's and B-24's—lifted off from nineteen bases in southeastern England:

destination, the ball-bearing factories in Schweinfurt, in central Germany. Sixteen 305th Bomb Group, 364th Bomb Squadron B-17's lift off the runway in Chelveston, England. My wife Kathy's uncle, Staff Sergeant Russell Joseph Kiggins was a tail gunner on one of the B-17's. Schweinfurt was his sixth mission.

Schweinfurt was very heavily defended. 60 B-17's—600 men—failed to return to England. The mission became known as Black Thursday. Thirteen of the 364th's B-17's never even reached Schweinfurt, lost to machine guns, cannons, and rockets fired by swarms of single- and twin-engined German fighters. Only three actually made bombing runs, and one was destroyed by rockets after releasing its bombs. Two B-17's returned to Chelveston that evening. 130 men didn't; Sergeant Kiggins was one of them.

September 9, 2016, a month short of 73 years after Black Thursday, I clambered into the rear hatch of the Collings Foundation B-17G *NINE O NINE* at Dutchess County Airport, hitting my back and then banging my head in the process. The first thing I did was look back into the very cramped tail gunner's compartment, way back in the very narrow rear of the plane, past the tail-wheel mechanism, pretty much isolated from the rest of the bomber. Even the two waist gunner positions were barely in sight from there. I couldn't imagine what it was like being alone there, in the cold, thin air at 25,000 feet in the flak- and fighter-filled skies over Germany in 1943. A big part of the reason I was here today was to *try* to imagine this...

What lifetime events led me to this moment??? Back in the 60's I'd read Martin Caidin's *Black Thursday* (New York: Dell Publishing Co., Inc., 1960). In the late 80's and early 90's I learned "Uncle Joe's" story from my wife Kathy and her family. In the "Uncle Joe" section of my own 2007 book, *Uncle Ben, Uncle Bob, Uncle Joe, Uncle Pete, P.D., and Pop*—Bataan, Saipan, Schweinfurt, the Bulge, Guadalcanal, and the Philippines 1945—I quoted an excerpt from Martin Caidin's book (his heirs graciously gave me permission to use it).

As related in *A Tale of Two Mustangs* in the 2015 *Boating On The Hudson & Beyond* Holidays issue, the Collings Foundation's *NINE O NINE*, B-24H

Witchcraft, and TP-51C *Betty Jane* visited the Dutchess County Airport in 2009, then returned in 2014 and 2015. I clambered through the very narrow confines of the NINE O NINE and the *Witchcraft*, and wished I could come up with the $2500.00 for an hour's flight in the Mustang. Rides in the bombers were a "mere" $450.00, but in '14 and '15 this seemed like a lot of money. My old Army buddy Tommy Garrison e-mailed me that the Collings planes were coming back September 9-11 2016. My birthday was the 12th: hmmm—I wasn't getting any younger—maybe I should take a shot at a B-17 ride as an early birthday present???

Long story short I called the Collings Foundation and reserved a spot on the NINE O NINE for a flight at 1700 hours on September 9, 2016. They said to get to the airport around 2:00 PM on the Big Day and to let Jamie know I was flying on the NINE O NINE. Here's the long and the short of it:

As in 2014 and 2015, I joined a small group on Route 376 at the end of the airport's long east/west runway to await the arrival of the Collings planes. It was 91 degrees, and muggy... The planes were coming up from Morristown, New Jersey, and were to arrive "around 1:30 or so". At around 2:00 PM I spotted a spec in the sky to the southwest, and, sure 'nuff, it was the NINE O NINE. I stood by the road right in line with the runway, and as it roared over my head, gear and flaps down, I thought "I'll soon be flying in that plane!!!"

Paul Kollor was also at the end of the runway, and he and his son Mark were also going to be on the flight! It took a while for the rest of the planes to show up, and when I spotted three specks in the sky, I knew they were the *Witchcraft*, the B-25N *TONDELAYO*, and the Collin's newest addition, a TF-51D Mustang two-seater *Toulouse Nuts****.

Fast forward to 5:00 PM, and Paul, Mark, and I and seven others gathered, as ordered, next to the rear hatch of the NINE O NINE for a "briefing". Two things stood out: we were told under no circumstances to touch any of the cables running through the fuselage, or "We would be flying the plane........". And, not to step on the bomb bays doors, or we might become a bomb...

When we boarded, two guys—one a real old-timer—got to stand on the flight deck behind the pilots, three people were positioned in the radio room forward of the bomb bay, and five of us, including Paul, Mark, and myself essentially sat on the floor, belted into makeshift "seats", in the waist gunner's area, until the plane reached cruising altitude: about 3000 feet.

The engines fired up, and the plane started vibrating, but us five couldn't see anything! I could see out the rear hatch window, and had some idea what was going on. When I saw cars on 376, I knew we were at the end of the runway, and soon the four big Wright Cyclone R-1820 1200 horsepower engines opened up full throttle, and we were off! I was very impressed by the acceleration: I was actually pushed towards the rear of the plane. The five of us were all grinning like kids on Christmas morning.

We finally leveled off and were given the word we could walk around. Two things: the plane is very cramped: I banged my head about a dozen times, and us ten tourists had to do a lot of dodging and tap-dancing not to knock each other over in our excitement to take it all in, and, take pictures.

First I looked out the waist gunner's windows, then threaded around the ball turret, through the bomb bay on a very narrow catwalk, and into the radio compartment, that had an opening to the sky. We'd been warned the 160 mph slipstream could tear off our hats, glasses, and, our cameras. I took some pictures—carefully—then went up into the top turret, with its 360-degree view above the plane, and then to the flight deck.

We had been told not to talk to the pilots, so I took some pictures, then dropped down into the navigator/bombardier's compartment right in the nose. Whadda view!!! We were heading up the Hudson. I've lived in the Hudson Valley my whole life, but in all the excitement, I couldn't place any landmarks and figure out exactly where we were. We swung majestically around, and headed back to the airport.

All in all, it was an AWESOME—I'd have to say thrilling—experience: LOUD, cramped, lotsa vibration, but, awesome. If you have the inclination, Just Do It.................

***Postscript: As an added bonus, I got to sit in the cockpit of the *Toulouse Nuts*: my THIRD Mustang cockpit.

This first appeared in John Vargo's Boating on the Hudson and Beyond *2016* Holiday *issue.*

The *NINE O NINE* Revisited

Friday, September 9, 2016 was a Big Day for me. I've flown in a lot of commercial airliners: Boeing 747's, 737's, 727's—probably even 707's—Airbus A310's, A320's, even Douglas DC-10's, and, Aeroflot Tupolev's in the Soviet Union. I've flown in small light planes, and twin-engined "puddle jumpers" in the US, the Caribbean, and Central America.

But on September 9th, I flew in a World War II B-17G: the Collings Foundation *NINE 0 NINE,* and detailed this once-in-a-lifetime experience in the Boating on the Hudson & Beyond 2016 Holiday Issue, pages 17-22.

I've been a big fan of the Stow, Massachusetts-based Collings Foundation for quite a while. I admire, and respect, what they're doing: in their own words: to "keep the 'Nine-0-Nine' [and their other World War II planes] flying, as a symbol of American patriotism and as a learning tool for our future generations to learn more about World War II and aviation history". Bravo...

I first became aware of the Collings Foundation when their Wings of Freedom Tour visited the Westchester County Airport in September 2009, and I clambered through the *NINE 0 NINE* and their B-24H *Witchcraft.* I revisited both planes—and their TP-51C *Betty Jane*—at the Dutchess County Airport in 2014 and 2015. In 2016, a light bulb went on in my head—my birthday was coming up on September 12th, so why not wake up and treat myself to a flight in the *NINE 0 NINE*—come on, Ralph, you're not getting any younger; fork over the 450 bucks and Just Do It. I did, and I've very glad I did.

After the flight, I received the Collings Foundation *2016-2017 Newsletter,* with a great in-flight photo of their newest acquisition, the TF-51D two-seater Mustang *Toulouse Nuts.* I devoured the glossy, 34-page magazine. On the back cover was Membership Information. We're now Participating Members of the Foundation.

As part of the membership we received a folder that included, among other things, information sheets on each of their World War II aircraft currently on tour. The *NINE 0 NINE's* information sheet first told the wartime story of the B-17G serial number 44-83575, then how the Foundation acquired it and restored it as the *NINE 0 NINE*, then the "real" *NINE 0 NINE's* wartime history.

B-17G #44-83575 and both the actual *NINE 0 NINE* and the Collings *NINE 0 NINE* had very interesting histories. Here's my summary of their stories, from the Collings information sheet:

B-17G #44-83575 was built at Long Beach, California by the Douglas Aircraft Company and accepted by the Army Air Force on April 7, 1945. Too late for combat, it served in the Air/Sea 1st Rescue Squadron and then in the Military Air Transport Service. Get this: then in 1952 #44-83575 *"was instrumented and subjected to the effects of three different nuclear explosions"*!!! After a thirteen-year "cool down" period it was sold as part of an 800-ton scrap pile...

The new owner, Aircraft Specialties Company began restoration, that included four thousand feet of new control cable, and the replacement of all electrical wiring and instrumentation. The restored *Yucca Lady* eventually took to the skies again, serving twenty years as a fire bomber fighting forest fires, and was sold to the Collings Foundation in January 1986, and "restored back to her original wartime configuration" by Tom Reilly Vintage Aircraft.

In August 1987 things hit the fan: while landing, the now-*NINE 0 NINE* was caught by a severe crosswind and crashed through a chain link fence into a 100-foot ravine. The landing gear was sheared off, the chin turret and Plexiglass nose were smashed/shattered, and the engines and propellers were torn from their mounts. There were no fatalities.

Thousands of volunteer hours, and support and donations from individuals and corporations finally got her back in the air, and then to 2800 tour stop visits. Remarkable...

The original 91st Bomb Group, 323rd Squadron *NINE 0 NINE* entered combat on February 25, 1945, eventually making eighteen trips to Berlin and overall dropping 562,000 tons of bombs. Twenty-one engine changes later, and having "suffered from considerable flak damage", she *completed 140 combat missions without an abort or the loss of a single crewman*. Talk about remarkable...

After the war, she was flown back to the United States, and....scrapped....

Now, thanks to the Collings Foundation—and its supporters—tail number 231909 flies again, visiting over 110 cities annually, nationwide. Makes yah proud: Bravo....

This first appeared in John Vargo's Boating on the Hudson and Beyond *May 2017 issue.*

The *NINE-O-NINE*

April 7, 1945-October 2, 2019

On September 9, 2016 I flew in the Collings Foundation beautiful B-17G, the *NINE-O-NINE* (named after the last three digits of it's tail number, 42-31**909**). We flew from Dutchess County Airport up the Hudson past Kingston (or was it Saugerties???) and back. It was a once-in-a-lifetime, remarkable, unforgettable experience. I wrote about the experience in the *Boating on the Hudson and Beyond* 2016 Holiday Issue, and in the May 2017 issue wrote "The NINE O NINE Revisited" explaining how the "real" B-17G, 44-83575, eventually became the Collings NINE-O-NINE. Ever since September 9, 2016 I've smiled every time "**9:09**" pops up on a digital clock, anywhere.

On October 2, 2019 John e-mailed me that the NINE-O-NINE had crashed, at Bradley International Airport in Connecticut. I was shocked, and stunned.

From what I've read, take-off had been delayed because one of the engines (number four, outboard on the right wing???) wouldn't start. The plane eventually took off, and about two minutes into the flight—about eight miles out—the pilots reported a problem to the control tower and requested an emergency landing. Again, from what I've read, there was no real urgency in the exchanges between the pilots and the tower, but eyewitnesses reported the plane "making loud noises" and flying "really low".

News reports say the plane crashed 1,000 feet short of the runway, and then into the airport's de-icer storage tanks, and was then just about totally destroyed in an explosion. Only the vertical rudder and some of the left wing are recognizable in photos.

I know a lot about World War II airplanes, and, the B-17's. From my readings, it was not uncommon for B-17's to return from missions over France, and Germany, on three engines, and, I think, even on two engines. And, these very tough airplanes often landed, or, crash landed, with minimal damage.

Here's a theory—and this is just *my* theory—if a four-engine airplane loses an engine, it will be very difficult—most likely impossible—for the remaining three engines to allow it to maintain a given altitude. Most likely it will slowly (or maybe not-so-slowly???) lose altitude: let's just say, for the sake of round numbers, about 100 feet per mile.

A World War II bomber, 30,000 feet over France, could then—possibly— make it 300 miles: over, and possibly across, the English Channel. The NINE-O-NINE was eight miles from Bradley, 800 feet up. Do the math... It did make it back to airport property: the de-icer tanks are part of the airport.

To me, on that October 2019 day the veteran pilots did everything they could to save this priceless airplane, but, at some point, things became "in the hands of the gods": and, the gods let us down. And, instead of a belly landing where the plane could have been salvaged, with minimum loss of life, it hit those tanks, and exploded. Plowing into them was just plain rotten, lousy bad luck. Why???

From October 2, 2019, every time I see "**9:09**" on a digital clock, it will be with unutterable sadness; every time....

October 16, 2019
517 words

This first appeared in John Vargo's Boating on the Hudson and Beyond *Feb/Mar 2020 issue.*

Let's Talk About B-24 Liberators

In the 2016 *Boating on the Hudson and Beyond* Holiday issue I described my flight in the Collings Foundation B-17G *NINE 0 NINE*. After the flight I joined the Foundation, and in the May 2017 *Boating...and Beyond* I described the World War II stories of both the "real" *NINE 0 NINE* and the B-17G that eventually became the Collings *NINE 0 NINE*.

The B-24J *Witchcraft* is the Collings Foundation's Wings of Freedom Tour sister ship of the *NINE 0 NINE*. 18,188 B-24's were produced during World War II, more than any other American aircraft. The *Witchcraft* is the *only* true B-24 still flying: *the last one...*

I've read a lot of World War II aviation books, and several specifically about the B-24:

B-24 Combat Missions and *Wings of Morning* (more about this one later). In the book (and movie) *Unbroken,* Louis "Louie" Zamperini's B-24 is on a Search and Rescue mission over the Pacific when the two left engines fail, and the plane snaps into an unrecoverable spin into the Pacific. Sometime afterward I read of a similar incident....

I engage World War II (and Korea, Vietnam, and middle East) veterans any chance I get, and, thank them for their service. I've talked to quite a few B-17 and B-24 jockeys: pilots and copilots, even ball turret gunners. Many have stories: Al, an IBM Electronics Apprentice School instructor, was a bombardier on a Liberator and claimed his pilot once flew the plane inverted!!! Overall, the B-17 guys loved their B-17's, and the B-24 guys loved their B-24's.

The B-24—thanks to its high-mounted, skinny, efficient Davis wing—could fly faster and farther, and could carry a bigger bomb load than the B-17. But, B-17's—the "Queen of the Skies"—got all the glory: think the *Memphis Belle*, and *12 O'clock High*. B-17 jockeys had nicknames for the B-24: "The crate the B-17 came in", "the flying brick", etc. The "whistling shithouse" was considered a compliment.

From my (pretty extensive) readings, the B-24 had its foibles, mostly due to the Davis wing. The B-17, with its low, very broad wing "presented no abnormal characteristics to deal with in close formations". On the other hand, I've read that the B-24 was a handful in close formations, requiring constant corrections, particularly at high altitudes. The nose turret cob-jobbed unto B-24H's "seriously impacted its already cumbersome handling characteristics".

Statistically, crippled B-17's were more apt to bring their air crews home, in spite of serious battle damage or the loss of an engine (or two), than crippled B-24's. And, this is a real zinger: "combat squadrons greatly preferred the B-17...to the B-24 because 'when we send the 17's out on a mission, most of them return. But when we send the 24's out, most of them don't'".

A B-17 pilot once told me he had ditched his B-17. I asked how. He said it was pretty much the same as landing it, except you kept the landing gear up. You kept it above stalling speed, then at the last minute flared it and pancaked it in. The B-24's more aerodynamically efficient bomb bay doors, that retracted up the sides of the fuselage, would rip off when ditched. Enough said...

B-17's have entry/exit hatches both front and rear. The '24's have a single hatch, in the rear. If a plane was mortally crippled this was not at all convenient to all five officers aboard—pilot, copilot, bombardier, navigator, radio operator—who were all in the *front* of the plane. In an emergency, the nearest way out was through the nose wheel doors, if you could get them open...

Lets talk about the B-24's strengths. Early in WWII there was a "gap" in the middle of the Atlantic where German submarines could roam freely since existing anti-submarine patrol planes did not have the range to reach this area. B-24's closed this gap. And longer-ranging (thanks to that Davis wing) B-24's, were *the* bomber in the vast Pacific, before the arrival of the B-29's.

As described in Thomas Childer's *WINGS OF MORNING: THE STORY OF THE LAST AMERICAN BOMBER SHOT DOWN OVER GERMANY IN WORLD WAR II*, a B-24, the *Black Cat*, was shot down on April 21, 1945 (VE Day was May 8,1945), "...its left wing fold[ing] and break[ing] away in an enormous, fluttering fireball": the last 8th Air Force bomber shot down in World War II.

B-24H serial number 44-44052, that ultimately became the Collings Foundation *Witchcraft*, was built in August 1944 at the Consolidated Aircraft Company's Fort Worth, Texas plant. In October '44 it was transferred to the Royal Air Force, and saw combat in the Pacific. After the war it was abandoned in a bomber graveyard in Khanpur, India, with the assumption it would not fly again. It was one of 36 B-24's restored by the Indian Air Force and utilized until 1968, then again abandoned.

It was purchased by a collector in 1981, then by Dr. Robert F. Collings in 1984, who intended to restore it for static display only. Persuaded to restore it to flying status, the restoration involved complete disassembly of the plane and work on 80% of its 1.2 million parts, including replacing more than 420,000 rivets!!!

After more than five years of hard work, and over 97,000 hours of labor, it flew on September 10, 1989 as the 15th Air Force *All American*, then in 1998 was repainted as the 5th Air Force *Dragon and His Tail*, and finally in 2005 as the 8th Air Force *Witchcraft*.

The original *Witchcraft* was produced as a B-24H in Ford Motor Company's Willow Run, Michigan plant. This 3,500,000 square feet plant—"thought to be the largest factory under one roof anywhere in the world"—had an assembly line over a mile long, that featured a large turntable two-thirds of the way along the line that allowed it to make a 90° turn before continuing to final assembly. By 1944, Ford was rolling a Liberator off the Willow Run production line every 63 minutes, 24 hours a day, 7 days a week. Ford produced half of the 18,188 total B-24's at Willow Run.

The *Witchcraft* was assigned to the 467th Bomb Group, and arrived in Rackheath, England on March 19, 1944. In the following year it flew *130 combat missions* with various crews, and never once turned back while on a mission, and never had a crewman killed or injured. Remarkable!!! Its final mission—and the 467th's final mission—was April 25, 1945. Returned to the US after the war, the *Witchcraft* was scrapped October 3, 1945 at the surplus depot in Altus, Oklahoma.....

On Friday, August 21, 2015, I stood on the side of Route 376 between Hopewell Junction and Red Oaks Mills, and watched the Collings *Witchcraft*—gear and flaps down—coming in to land on Dutchess County Airport's east/west runway. I'll never forget the sight—and sound—of it, thundering about 20-30 feet over my head. Never...............

March 26, 2017
1155 words

This first appeared in John Vargo's Boating on the Hudson and Beyond *Holiday 2017 issue.*

Tondelayo!!!

"Tondelayo"??? Am I going to write this whole article in Espanol??? Nope: "Tondelayo" is the name of the Collings Foundation World War II North American B-25 Mitchell. Let's talk about World War II airplane names for a bit. I don't recall ever seeing, or hearing of a Spitfire or Hurricane with a name on its fuselage. Same with ME-109's and FW-190's: every once in a while I've seen a picture of one with some kind of dragon or something else scary and/or "fierce" on the tail, but "names" up front are to me, rare if not totally absent. Japanese planes also. Seems like we Americans may have been the only aerial combatants to embellish our airplanes with names (and, drawings): from my experience it was unusual for an aircraft NOT to be named. Good for the U.S.A.!!!

The names were wildly imaginative, and, outrageously original. I have a whole bunch of Mustang books, and one has drawings of Mustangs and info about their pilots and squadrons, so let's use these as examples. We'll start off with Major George "Ratsy" Preddy's P-51's—a P-51B and two P-51D's— all named "CRIPES A' MIGHTY": he had a liking for "English colloquial phrases". My recollection is the "B" had a much-less-colorful name at first... Preddy was the top-scoring Mustang pilot of World War II, with 25.83 confirmed "kills". He was THE stereotypical WWII fighter pilot—a hard-drinking swashbuckling gambler, with a dapper mustache—and flew with the 352nd Fighter Group out of Bodney, England: the "Blue Nosed Bastards of Bodney". He was killed by "friendly fire"—an American kid manning quad-50-caliber antiaircraft guns—while low-level chasing an FW-190 on Christmas Day 1944, near Leige, Belgium. "The fortunes of war": What a rotten, rotten shame.

Another well-known Mustang ace was Captain Don Gentile, and his P-51B "Shangri-La". He never did fly "D's". Let's take a quick tour through some other unique Mustang names: "Big Beautiful Doll", "Moonbeam McSWINE", "ALABAMA RAMMER JAMMER", "JERSEY JERK", "Nooky Booky IV", "Ferocious Franky": Point made???

Back to "Tondelayo": The real B-25 that is now the Collings "Tondelayo" was built at the Kansas City, Kansas North American Aviation factory as serial number 44-28932 and was accepted into the Army Air Corps on August 3, 1944, and served in the AAF Training Command for the rest of the war, and continued in a training capacity until 1959. 44-28932 was purchased by Earl Dodge, of Anchorage, Alaska and flew as a forest-fire fighter in the Pacific Northwest for the next 25 years (Check out the movie *Always*).

44-28932 was acquired by Collings in 1984: the first World War II bomber in the Collings collection. After two years restoration, it became the "Hoosier Honey", a 12th Air Force aircraft that served in Italy and North Africa in 1944. In 2001 it became the "Tondelayo", that flew in the 5th Air Force, 345th Bomb Group, 500th Bomb Squadron "Air Apaches" in the Pacific against targets in New Guinea, attacking shipping and beating off (name-less???) Japanese fighters. The name "Tondelayo" was inspired by Hedy Lamarr's character in the 1942 movie "White Cargo"!

Fast Forward to Wednesday, October 4, 2017: in the last several years, right about this time, a Collings Foundation light bulb goes off in my head. Dutchess County Airport did not appear in an on-line check of the Collings Wings of Freedom Tour dates for 2017. But, a small ad in the previous Sunday's newspaper said they were a'coming October 4th-6th. I called the airport and was informed the planes would be arriving "between Noon and 2:00 PM".

I hustled over to the "unofficial" parking area on Route 376 at the east end of the main east/west runway ("NINE 0 NINE" flight ("Boating on the Hudson and Beyond", 2016 Holiday Issue). So we waited, and waited, straining our eyes for tell-tale specks in the broad blue sky. A few other people eventually showed up, and we all waited, and waited. Close to two o'clock, an "official" Dutchess County vehicle pulled in, and I thought we were going to be told we couldn't park where we were, but the driver asked if we were "waiting for some airplanes", and said he just heard on a scanner that they were "in the landing pattern"!

We all jumped out of our cars, and sneaking up behind us was the B-24 "Witchcraft", soon followed by the "NINE 0 NINE", and, the "Tondelayo". We watched all three roar right over our heads and land, but, where was the Mustang??? We waited, and waited. Finally, I gave up, and, while stuck behind a school bus a short way's down 376, a plane that gave a pretty good imitation of a Mustang flew over the road with its landing gear down. I did a quick U-turn and got back to the airport as soon as I could (I was stuck at the infamous 376/New Hackensack Road traffic light forever), and when I got back to the end of the runway was informed "the second you left the Mustang did a fly-by, and then landed". Shit. Double Shit... One of the whole points of all the waiting was to see, and hear, a Mustang in the sky, one more time. Some days you eat the bear, some days the bear eats you.

So, like a moth to a flame, I went back to the airport Friday, hopefully to see the planes (including the Mustang) take off. When I was inside the gate Jamie announced they needed two more people to sign up for the B-25 to fly. Out of nowhere, two guys signed up. I said, "Room for one more???" She nodded. Believe me, 400 Bucks has never been, and never will be, "pocket change" to me, but I, Mr. Non-Impulsive, handed her my DISCOVER card.

It took forever to get the signal to board the B-25, and only then did I find out three people would be in front: ringside seats on the flight deck and in the plexiglass bombardier's compartment in the nose—The Best Seat in the House—and I and two others would be "in the rear". It got worse: once "in back", there would be no way to get past the bomb bay into the front. In the "NINE 0 NINE" we could roam the entire airplane. Not so with the B-25. Honestly, if I had known this beforehand, I would *not* have handed over the DISCOVER card.

Aboard, they gave us ear protection. My first thought was "I don't need no stinkin' ear protection: I want to experience the whole nine yards!" The Wright Cyclone R-2600-92's finally fired up, barking and mis-firing for quite a while: loud, but not unbearable. When the pilot revved 'em up at the end of the runway, the sound blast was the absolute **LOUDEST** thing I had ever experienced: unbearably, painfully **LOUD**. I slammed on the ear protection, and wore it the entire flight.

Take off was anti-climactic for me—I had The Worst Seat in the House, facing rearward, my back to the bomb bay wall—the two other "rear" guys were seated at the two plexiglass waist gunner's windows. I couldn't see nuthin'... When we reached cruising altitude, as promised we were given the signal we could take off our seat belts and crawl, one at a time, back to the tail gunner's position. I'd be the last, but I moved up to the left waist gunner's window and, Wow!!!, there was the Hudson down there, stretching north, and we were right over Bowdoin Park!

I finally crawled to the tail, and behind us was the Hudson north of the Bear Mountain Bridge, then the Bridge and the "Bear Mountain Road" looping around Anthony's Nose. Wowser! Soon there was Annsville Creek, Peekskill Bay, Con Ed, Buchanan, and The Point! John later e-mailed me he heard us coming, and ran out and took a picture. We eventually turned back north when I could see the Tappan Zee Bridge in the distance. I didn't want to hog the tail, so I crawled back to my lousy seat.

I went back to the tail one more time and saw hiking-trail-infested Mount Taurus and Breakneck Ridge off our right wing: we were about even with the top of Taurus. After we landed, people asked me how the B-25 flight compared to the B-17 flight. There was no comparison: they were entirely two different animals. Basically, the B-17 was like a commercial airliner compared to the obscenely LOUD, raucous, lurching and swaying, cramped B-25.

All in all, I'm glad I did it: it was a Holy Sh*t!!! experience. But, before you hand over your credit card, get it in writing you're going to be In The Front...

October 10, 2017
1,478 Words

Ralph Joseph Ferrusi

This first appeared in John Vargo's Boating on the Hudson and Beyond *Feb/Mar 2018 issue.*

My All-time Favorite Airplanes

North American P-51D Mustang

Lockheed C-130 Hercules

Douglas C-47/DC-3

Boeing 747

Boeing B-17 Flying Fortress

Consolidated B-24 Liberator

Chance-Vought F4U Corsair

Grumman F6F Hellcat

Supermarine Spitfire

North American F-86 Sabre

AND, ME

SUMMATIONS AND RUMINATIONS

Summing It Up At 60

The Appalachian Trail was, indeed, one of those life-changing "Turning Points". It instilled a taste for adventure, excitement, accomplishment, travel. Some years ago I sat down and listed some of the more interesting and unique things I've done "After the Trail". For the life of me I can't find that two-page list, but here are some of the things I remember from it. [I am not "bragging"; these are what I truly consider interesting unique, or important life accomplishments.]

The first thing I wrote down was that I once sat in the cockpit of the *Jackie C*, a North American P-51D Mustang fighter plane—in my opinion *the* most beautiful airplane ever built.

I once drove a Lamborghini Countach, a half-million-dollar car, with an 800-horsepower V-12.

I've danced in the Rainbow Room in Manhattan, with a belly dancer in the Casbah, and in a cavern *inside* the Rock of Gibraltar.

I survived street riots on Election Day in Nairobi, a Black Taxi ride in still-war-torn Belfast, Northern Ireland, and one New Year's Eve in Times Square.

I've spun all 680 prayer wheels at the Great Stupa of Budhnath in Kathmandu, and then had afternoon tea at the Yak and Yeti.

I shot pool at "The World's Highest Pool Hall"—12,757 feet—in Deboche, Nepal, and saw Everest, Lhotse, Nupste, and Ama Dablam—*by moonlight*—from a Sherpa teahouse.

I've never driven a Ferrari, and I haven't been to Timbuktu—yet.

But, I've killed some time in Africa, Australia, Austria, Albany, Bangkok, Bolivia, Bora Bora, Boston, Chitzen Itza, Canberra, Costa Rica, China, Croatia, the Casbah, Cape Cod, the Catskills, France, Finland, Greece, Greenland, Hungary, Helsinki, Houston, Kathmandu, Killarney, Killkenny, Lima, Lisbon, London, Leningrad, La Paz, Moscow, Morocco, Montenegro, Melbourne, Machu Picchu, Montserrat, Mexico, Montreal, Milwaukee, Nicaragua, Nepal, New Zealand, New South Wales, Nevis, Nantucket, Panama, Poland, Peru, Portugal, Paris, Provincetown, Slovenia, Sydney, Spain, Saint Emillion, San Francisco, Tangier, Tahiti, Toronto, and Venice, and, kissed the Blarney Stone on a pouring-down rainy September day in County Cork, Ireland...

"Summin' It Up At 60"

Restored from the original hard copy May/June 2019

I wanted to rent a Ferrari for my 60th birthday. I have never driven a Ferrari. I wanted a red 308, or a GTO. Not a Testa Rosa, or a Mondial. It would cost $700 a day and 50 cents a mile. Doesn't look like I'm going to drive a Ferrari for my birthday this year. Got me thinking about things I've done in the last 60 years, and some things I haven't done:

I've sat in the cockpit of a P-51D Mustang, and driven a Lamborghini Countach.

I've jumped out of an airplane at 2500 feet, and taken a ballet lesson.

I rode a big Kawasaki at over 100 miles per hour on the Mulsanne Straight at Le Mans, and an aluminum racing bicycle at over 50 miles per hour down Stormville Mountain.

I've traveled half way around the world, from Bora Bora in French Polynesia to Tbilisi in the then-Soviet Georgia, and have been to Bolivia, Bali Hai, Big Sur, Chitzen Itza, Montserrat, Machu Pichu, Morocco, and Milwaukee...

I've danced at the Rainbow Room, inside the Rock of Gibraltar, and with a belly dancer in the Casbah.

I've tossed a coin in Trevi Fountain, and painted in Florence.

I've raced cars, motorcycles, bicycles, canoes, kayaks, and on foot.

I've stayed in the Frontenac in Quebec City, and at the Avenida Palace, in Lisbon.

I shook Richard Petty's hand at Bridgehampton, saw him race at Darlington, and saw his last race at Atlanta.

I've been to Saint Tropez, on the French Riviera, and Sochi, on the Russian Riviera.

I've seen _Les Mis_ twice, and went up on the stage when I saw _Hair_ in the 60's.

I've had poetry published.

I've walked from Georgia to Maine, almost twice.

I've meditated in the Notre Dame, in Paris, and in Saint Patrick's, in New York.

I've run a sub 5 minute mile.

I've sampled the Eight Great Bordeaux from the Classification of 1855, arguably the best wines in the world, and own a bottle of each.

I rode my racing bicycle up Alpe de Huez, the most prestigious climb in the Tour de France, and saw _le Tour_ finish on the Champs Elysees.

I've seen whales; and a huge basking shark from a kayak in the middle of Cape Cod Bay.

I've shared a microphone with Rick Danko, and talked to Kevin Bacon, Robert Joffrey, and Phil Liggett.

I've taken the ferry from Dover to Calais.

I've climbed all 35 3500-foot peaks in the Catskills almost 3 times, all 48 New Hampshire 4000-footers, all 47 Adirondack 4000 footers, and all 114 4000 footers in the Northeastern United States.

I've strolled along the Seine, in Paris, and the Moika, in Leningrad.

I rode a bobsled down the Olympic Bobsled Run at Mount Von Hoevenberg near Lake Placid, and cross country skied UP Whiteface Mountain.

I've seen Paul Simon and Carly Simon on the streets of Manhattan.

I took a Moscow subway to Red Square and back to the hotel at one o'clock in the morning.

I shook hands with Willy Nelson, Harry Chapin, Kris Christopherson, Steve Bauer, Joe Kennedy, and Gorgeous George...

I've flown an airplane.

I've run in the Luxembourg Gardens in Paris, and ran across Paris from the Place de la Bastille to the Arc de Triomphe.

I met Alexis Lichine at his chateau in Bordeaux.

I've hang glided, para-sailed, took a ride in a sailplane, and flown in Aeroflot Tupelovs.

I saw *The Last Tango in Paris* in Rome, and *The Last Waltz* in Paris.

I've skied on a shoulder of the Matterhorn, and climbed on a shoulder of the Eiger.

I've had lunch at the Cafe des Artistes, on a rainy Valentine's Day.

I've rafted 230 miles in the Grand Canyon, and about 30 miles on the Urabamba, in Peru.

I've had an omelet at the Mont Saint Michelle...

All in all, not too shabby for a small-town kid the New Yorkers called "the Buchanan Hillbilly" when I went to an aviation tech school in Queens after I graduated high school.

On the flip side, I've been sued, divorced, robbed, and have had Lyme disease, back problems, and more root canals than any one man should ever have to endure in a lifetime.

And, I haven't:

Driven a Ferrari.

Been to Asia, Australia, or Antarctica.

Had a window office at work in over 12 years.

This could be called "Summing It Up At 70..."

Me, Then

Vision: no glasses, no reading glasses, no eye drops.
Teeth: lousy, but still had most of them, not crowns, bridges, root canals, partials.
Hair: thick, brown.
Hearing: much better than it is now.
Fitness, strength: invincible.
Digestive system: much better.
No blood pressure/cholesterol worries.
Urinary tract/bladder: slept all night, every night; no getting up one to several times a night.
Pills: didn't need any.

Scourges, Etc That Didn't Exist Then

Taxes, bills; never ending.
No deer ticks/Lyme disease.
No terrorists, muslims.
No graffiti.
Downtown Peekskill, Poughkeepsie, Newburgh, Brewster safe to walk in, anytime day or night.
Parent, uncles, aunts, many cousins still alive.
Gas about 30 cents a gallon—about $3.00 filled your tank.
A decent car cost $2000.00, and was made in Detroit.
No TV sickening violence, mind rot.
A few small bags of groceries didn't cost $80.00 at the supermarket.
Things were Made in the USA.
You didn't have to press 1 for English.
The "Super Highway" New Jersey Turnpike was four lanes wide, not 12.

"Turning Points"

There have been some BIG "turning points" in my life, physical and mental—meditation, vegetarianism, fitness—that were mostly lumped in the early to mid-70's. During this same period I walked the Appalachian Trail the first time, bought a Nikon camera, went to Paris for the first time, and oil painted. I'm going to try to "turn back the clock" and trace all this, but, honestly, right now, 40-some years after the facts, some of the exact times/dates are, shall we say, a bit fuzzy.

Let's start with an easy one: fitness. I was a skinny kid, and staying skinny was "natural" to me; I didn't have to work at it. But sometime in the 60's, my first father-in-law, Rene Biourd—he was Physical Director of the Grand Central YMCA in Manhattan, and was extremely fit, running, etc, way before James Fixx—accompanied us on a pretty serious hike in the Catskills. It was a warm, early spring day, and he took a picture of me with my shirt off. I was stunned when I saw what appeared to be a big white inner tube around my waist: winter fat...a Great White Whale. I vowed never to look like that again, and thus began a commitment to "fitness" that has lasted to this day.

One of my "mottoes" became "Why ride when you can walk???", and since then I have been hiking, biking, swimming, canoeing, cross-country skiing, snowshoeing, mowing the lawn, raking leaves, shoveling snow...you get the picture. And, it's pretty much worked: I'm fond of saying that I wear the same size Levis—32 X 32—that I (think!) I wore in high school.

Recently, I've begun to recognize a flip side to my "fitness obsession". Back in the Catskill Tales and Trails heydays, when Kath and Ralph were both pursuing their "regular" and Winter 3500-footers, we'd be out there just about year-round, banging out BIG peaks, sometimes five in a day; in the winter. There's a real satisfaction after a day like this: not just the "endorphin fix"/"runner's high." Nowadays we go to the Catskills a couple of times a year, and since I've stopped riding my bike on the local roads—too many "distracted drivers" out there, texting and blabbing on the phone, while going 60 MPH—the occasional jaunts on the AT over to 52 or Hosner Mountain Road, and the mind-numbing back-and-forth bike rides on the Dutchess and Putnam rail trails that I've ridden 10,000 times just don't cut it.

What is happening more and more is, if I ride the bike, or go for a decent cross-country ski, I'm "happy"; satisfied, whatever. The flip side is if I don't, I'm not necessarily unhappy, but there is a distinct difference how I feel about the day. Factor in that I ski about 30 times a winter (every ski season, I note the number of times I ski in my engagement calendar), and I bike just about the same amount of days spring-fall, and this shakes out to about 1/6 of the year I'm, well, happy with my daily fitness routine.

And, I *am* slowing though: Kath said she noticed it about the time I turned 70. When Kath, Ralph and I climb Catskill peaks, they both just cruise along on the steeps, and I inexorably fall back, and they wait for me, acting as if they'd just decided to stop and to talk about something, but I know otherwise. And, lately, I just don't like to walk, as odd as that may seem to someone else; but, it's true. How 'bout those Mets............

OK, let's tackle vegetarianism and meditation. Being "fit" in our society, is, perhaps, associated with youth, and, I'd venture, might go a ways to make someone appear "younger". I've been, not "ultra" fit, but much more fit than average, and many people typically assume I'm 10, even 20 years younger than I am. I can often carry this off, though the bathroom mirror in the morning always says otherwise. Back a while, when people asked how old I was, my attitude used to be "I'm this age, so I'll tell them." But when I worked as a tour guide, I realized this was detrimental, and "put me in a box" to some clients, so I stopped doing it, and am more tight-lipped about my age now. But there are times when I have to tell people how old I am, or, honestly, decide to, for "shock value", and some of them are indeed shocked, even stunned, when they find out I'm "pushing 80". I must admit I do enjoy watching their reactions: their jaws dropping, and the look in their eyes.

Here are the three things that I feel have helped me—for lack of a better term—"stay young": meditation, and the "extra rest" it gives me every day; vegetarianism, because the single daily biggest use of energy in the human body is *digestion* (more about this later); and a life-long commitment to physical fitness.

Back in those 70's I met someone who "meditated": practiced Transcendental Meditation, with a mantra and all. I must admit I thought it kind of wacko/ weird, but eventually I went over to an apartment in New Paltz to meet a TM instructor and a one-day $250.00 (to me a *huge* sum at the time) TM lesson. As required, I brought some flowers and some fruit. Here's what I remember the guy told me: a good example of how TM works is to picture the surface of a stormy sea, with big waves churning and breaking. But, down below the surface, everything is calm... That's where TM brings you. He also said TM'ing 20-minutes-twice-a-day was equivalent to another whole night's sleep. Wowzer...

He gave me my mantra—basically, a "nonsense word"—and had me say it out loud, for the one and only time, ever. You get comfortable, and think the mantra in your head, over and over. If other thoughts intervene, you gently bring the mantra back. You do this for 20 minutes, twice a day, and, hopefully, sometimes you will "transcend", though this isn't a "goal" you should stress about.

So, I've been doing this, 20 minutes, twice a day, since the 70's. Here's a few reasons why I don't think it's bullshit:

Way back I attended a TM seminar at a Texaco auditorium jam-packed with engineers, scientists, and technicians: a tough audience for something as "mystical" as this. The presenter gave us a "universal mantra", that went something like "Ohm Nah Mah Shiv Eye Ah" (at the time I wished mine was as *cool*), and asked everyone to close their eyes, relax and repeat it in their heads, over and over. The auditorium had had kind of a "hum" to it; people whispering and shuffling around, but pretty soon, the whole damned place went dead quiet, and stayed that way until he brought us all back. It was an unbelievable experience/demonstration...

And, way back, there was a local community of TM meditators, and on rare occasions I participated in group meditations. Word up was the group effect enhanced the meditation, and, for me when I meditated with other meditators it always did.

When I'm doing something rhythmic—climbing a steep mountain on my bike, or paddling a canoe on a long, flat stretch of water—my mantra often pops into my head; a good thing.

My daily meditations are important to me; I've only missed a handful in all these years. I've meditated in the Notre Dame in Paris, Saint Patrick's in Manhattan, on 747's, in Appalachian Trail shelters, in the back seat of a 70's-vintage Chevy Nova with rock music blaring out of the speakers. But, I prefer a nice, quiet, comfortable spot, to just let it flow. My rhythm now is first thing in the morning, shortly after I wake up, and around 6:00 PM. Funny, but I prefer to begin on the hour, the half hour, or at 10-after, 20-after, 20-of, or 10-of; I just about never start a meditation at, say 6:07...

OK, how did I become a vegetarian, after wolfing down hamburgers and cheeseburgers for 30-some years of my life??? Simply put, when this occurred, I had absolutely no concept, or had ever given a single thought about vegetarianism. But I was (albeit a late-blooming) "hippy": hair down to my shoulders, full beard, red bandana, cut-off jeans; and, ready to give things a try (but not drugs; some *very* brief experimentation completely turned me off).

I was going to Dutchess Community College nights, heading for a Liberal Arts Degree/Humanities, and a woman in one of my classes was a vegetarian. Honestly, at the time, as "cool" as I was, I had never even heard of this!!! She did seem at peace with the world, but at the time I didn't attach much significance to this one-semester encounter.

I did, at the time (and I guess I still do) feel that if something whacked me in the side of the head three times, I should pay attention to it. Later, between marriages, two women I dated were vegetarians. One, two, three...

As I recall, my last meat-eating meals were Thanksgiving and Christmas at 195 Centre Street. And, I recall Mom and Pop being very supportive of my new diet. I eventually read *Fit For Life*, that pointed out the biggest daily use of energy for the human body was digestion. A chunk of meat takes 24-48 hours—a full day or two—to digest. A piece of broccoli, for example, takes about 15 minutes. And, while your digestive system is struggling with that chunk of meat, more meat is being dumped into it every day; it would seem to me that this makes it impossible for these digestive systems to ever "catch up". 'Nough said; explains why I have had so much energy to spare for so many years. *Fit For Life* also pointed out that the milk humans consume is *baby cow food*; cows have about eight stomachs, and can digest it. The human digestive system is not set up, by nature, to digest cow's milk... I used to drink big, cold glasses of milk. I stopped. Yuppers, I do like cheese, and ice cream, but for a while I put water on cereal. Now I put ½ and ½ on my cereal; yeah, it's milk, but, fuck it, I like the taste.....................

Life Changers

Vegetarianism: 1975.

Transcendental Meditation: sometime in the 70's.

Commitment to physical fitness: probably also in the 70's. The AT contributed mightily to fitness, that I've maintained pretty well up until this day. I still wear the same size Levi's—32X32—that I did in high school.

"Magic"

As of June 29, 2015 I've lived about 28,500 days, or 684,000 hours. Here's some "magic moments" I've lived in all that time, probably amounting, grand total, to a few days. A bit sad to think of it that way...

Non Travel

Hearing the snarl/growl/whine/whistle/roar of a Rolls Royce Merlin V1650 V-12 in the nose of a North American P-51D Mustang. Gets me every time, in person, or on a U-Tube video. One of the best-ever videos I've seen is the 7:27 minute video of the Bremont Horsemen flying three P-51's in close formation; the sound is tripled.

Kath making a perfectly-timed, perfectly-executed move in the bow of the Penobscot in Class III Zoar Gap allowing us to grease the biggest drop and miss that Big Rock on the left shore by inches.

Turning the key and firing up a Ferrari F430, then slipping it into first gear.

Getting my first ISBN number.

As a kid, hearing Pop speak Italian.

Watching James Cameron's *Titanic* end-to-end, the only person in a big, empty theater.

Having my feet, and toes, expertly massaged by a Licensed Massage Therapist.

Being in a National Geographic film.

Going through the quarter-mile traps at 110 miles per hours in second gear in a 300-horsepower dual quad carburated Plymouth Fury.

Les Mis. Gets me every time............

Travel Related

My first sight of the Eiffel Tower.

The sights, sounds, and smells of Kathmandu.

Seeing Everest, Lhotse, Nupste, and Ama Dablam by *moonlight* from a Sherpa tea house in Pangboche, Nepal.

Along a similar line, waking up in a tent in Zermatt and opening the flap and there's the Matterhorn...

Riding a big four-cylinder four-stroke Kawasaki down the Mulsanne Straight in Le Mans at 100 mph. Then doing a return run.

Venice.

Swimming three laps in an outdoor heated Olympic-sized pool in Reykjavik when the big digital thermometer at the end of the pool says **0** degrees Celsius.

Ever spelling Reykjavik right the first time...

Lake Bled, Slovenia

Running across Paris, from the Place de la Bastille to the Arc de Triomphe, with two people I had met, an American guy (I've forgotten his name) and Anne Charlotte, a Parisian.

Ahhh, yes, dancing with Kath *inside* the Rock of Gibraltar, and with that (kinda plump) belly dancer in the Casbah...

Seeing Moscow from above in early-morning light from the window of an Aeroflot Tupelov circling to land.

The hubbub of the Grand Bazaar, and the swirling currents of the Bosporus, in Istanbul.

Bora Bora.

Standing on our hotel balcony in Tahiti watching a Concorde take off.

The first time I stepped out of the door of an airplane on Antigua, and experienced the blast of heat from a Caribbean island.

Zooming down the 21 switchbacks of Alpe de Huez on my fat-tube aluminum Klein Quantum.

Standing with Kath in the bow of that launch taking us back to Tortola from dinner on Peter Island.

Standing on the rim of the no-doubt-*very*-active Arenal volcano in La Fortuna, Costa Rica.

Watching BIG boats go through the Panama Canal lock from our hotel window.

Dancing with Kath to Otis Redding's *Stand By Me* played by a one-man-band(!) on the promenade overlooking the Saint Lawrence in Quebec City.

I Took Another Pass At This In December 2015, and Here's What Came Up

Moments...

These are pretty much in the order they occurred to me, and, note that some of them may have already appeared above in "Magic" (or someplace else).

When Mom made peas and eggs for me and we sat in the kitchen at 195 Centre Street and talked while Pop sat in the living room and read the paper.

The rare times I heard Pop speak Italian.

My first glimpse of the Tour Eiffel, Paris, 1971.

My first glimpse of Everest, on the Base Camp Trail above Namche Bazaar, Nepal, 2001.

Clean runs through both Chimney and the Stairway to Heaven rapids on the Scantic River in Connecticut while we were racing in the New England Downriver Championship Series (NEDCS).

Going through the traps at the Dover drag strip at 110 miles-per-hour in second gear with the Fury.

The first glimpse of the sign atop Baxter Peak, Katahdin that marks the northern terminus of the Appalachian Trail on July 19, 1975 from Katahdin's Tableland.

Stepping out of the airplane door on Antigua and feeling the blast of heat on my first trip to the Caribbean.

Holding a copy of my first published book in my hands, and having my very own ISBN number.

Turning the ignition key on in a Ferrari.

The sights, smells, and sounds of Kathmandu.

Waking up in the middle of the night in a Sherpa tea house on the Everest Base Camp Trail to go pee.

Seeing myself in a National Geographic film, at the World Premiere of the film in Grosvenor Hall, National Geographic Headquarters, Washington, D.C.

Things I've Let Go Of

That were once very important to me, or that I enjoyed doing very much, or were once part of my life, or....

Downhill skiing
Running/competitive running
Motor boating
Water skiing
Canoe racing
Whitewater canoeing
Bike racing
Bicycle road riding
Motorcycle racing
Drag racing
The Appalachian Trail Conference and the New York-New Jersey Trail Conference
The *Catskill Canister* and the Peripatetic Porcupine
The Northern Forest Canoe Trail
Walkway Over the Hudson Ambassadorship
My award-winning newspaper column

Things I Hate

I just discovered the handwritten "Things I hate:" document I wrote on Christmas Eve, 2000. I'm transcribing it now, February 12, 2016, verbatim.

16 years later I agree with pretty much all of them. "Ally McBeal" was a real surprise...

The New Jersey Turnpike
People who flash their lights at me for me to get out of their way
"Developers"
Arrogance
"Ally McBeal"/Calista Flockhart/anything to do with Ally McBeal
Deer Ticks
Poison Ivy/Mosquitoes/Black Flies
"Pressure"
Most Cops
Most attorneys
IBM
The holidays
Vacuuming
Malls/people who go to Malls
Getting old
Grey hair
Being late
Fat
Bullies—Human and Canine
Being sick

Things I love

Being outdoors
trees
being outdoors on warm, sunny days
Mountains
being fit
traveling
Paris
The Cape/P-town
Quebec
The Caribbean

2015 additions, written *before* I found the 2000 document

Black flies and other buzzing, biting insects might just make the top of the list.
Black-legged ticks: I fucking hate them...
Wooly Adelgid, that's killing hemlocks.
School bus #754.....................

"The Golden Years"

As I write this, my 78th birthday is rapidly approaching: it's stunning to me that I'm "pushing 80". The biggest percentage of my life is behind me, and it doesn't take an Einstein to realize the last 15-years-or-so years (I am not taking these for granted; I realize it could be 15 months, 15 days, 15 hours, 15 minutes, 15 seconds (gawd, I'd better hit Save right now...)) (I did...) of my life are not going to be as big a barrel of laughs as the first 15, when we are growing, and learning: how to talk, walk, read, write, discover. Around the corner: Alzheimer's, a stroke, a walker, a wheelchair, more *&%$#@*& pills: the Golden Years my ass..........

Ralph J. Ferrusi Author Profile

Ralph J. Ferrusi, author of *Uncle Ben, Uncle Bob, Uncle Joe, Uncle Pete, P.D., and Pop: Bataan, Saipan, Schweinfurt, The Bulge, Guadalcanal, the Philippines 1945* and *Catskill Tales and Trails: In Search of the Peripatetic Porcupine* and Award-Winning newspaper columnist is a long-time resident of New York's Hudson Valley. He has walked the 2,189-mile Maine to Georgia Appalachian Trail—twice—and has traveled to 58 countries in 23 time zones on six continents. He is an avid cyclist, a long-time vegetarian, and enjoys fine (and some not-so-fine) wines. He has danced inside the Rock of Gibraltar, and once sat in the cockpit of the *Big Beautiful Doll,* a North American P-51D Mustang.

His works have been rejected by, amongst others, *The New Yorker* and *Playgirl*, and totally ignored by *The Appalachian Trailway News*, nee *AT Journeys*.

He resides on Stormville Mountain, New York, with his wife Kathy and a picture of Luna, their adopted coyote.

50 Years: Written for my 50th Hendrick Hudson High School reunion: 2005

There's one thing I'm pretty sure we'll all agree on: the fifty years went by shockingly fast. So what did I do in those fifty years??? Here's a "Reader's Digest" summary:

Late 50's: Buy my first new car: a 1958 Plymouth Fury. Start working at IBM.

1960's: Get married. Son and daughter born. Buy a mobile home. Buy a 1963 Corvette Sting Ray coupe. Become a "hippy": full beard, shoulder length hair. Buy a small house.

1970's: Buy a 1972 Pinto. Go to Paris. Walk the Appalachian Trail. Divorced. Start going to France regularly. Start re-walking the Appalachian Trail.

1980's: Buy Honda #1, a red 1985 CRX, then #2, a red 1986 CRX Si. Shave beard, trim hair. Start traveling the world with Kathy. We marry August 26, 1989. Honeymoon in Tahiti, Bora Bora. Buy a 19-pound aluminum [Klein Quantum] racing bike. Cycling becomes a passion: race bikes for several years.

1990's: Buy beautiful A-frame ¼ mile from Appalachian Trail on Stormville Mountain. Buy Honda #3: red 1991 Si Hatchback. Travel to Caribbean, Mexico, South America, Australia.

2000's: Finish Appalachian Trail second time: total of 4,217 miles of Maine to Georgia walking. Go to Africa to climb Kilimanjaro, Asia to trek towards Everest Base Camp. Visit Poland, Venice, Slovenia, Croatia. Have been to 41 countries, on six continents, in 23 Time Zones—want to get to at least 50 countries. Buy a red BMW 328i Convertible. IBM sticks it to me: November 12, 2003. That's the thanks I got for 34 years of hard work, in a place I hated... Get a job on a farm: working HARD, feeding cows, pitching hay. Love it... Start writing. Write a book. Start several others, fiction and non-fiction. Write a weekly newspaper column. Delighted to be getting paid to write.

50 years—a half-dozen cars, two houses, two marriages, two kids, two really long walks, a lot of really long airplane trips. Doesn't seem like a lot for 50 years. To be continued, the Good Lord willing and if the creek don't rise...

A Friend Jim's 50ᵗʰ birthday

was on November 18, 1994. I reminisced about the year I turned fifty:

Let's see what I can remember about 1987, the year I turned 50.

This was only the third year that Kath and I were seeing each other, so we were still lovey dovey and all full of hopes and promise.

Went to the Soviet Union, and this is still the best trip I've ever gone on. We'd gone to Montserrat the year before, and I love the islands now. Mexico, Tahiti, Le Tour, The Canyon??? Later....

I don't remember where the AT hike was that year: New Hampshire???

I was living at Hopewell Road, Kath still had her house in Milan, so we were probably still commuting a lot to see each other. The body shop was a big presence. The A-frame in Stormville was beyond my wildest dreams.

Guess dog was still the fastest runner around, and Wailin' was going to live forever, yapping her way through life.

We were still learning a lot about wines, and Saint Emilion's were a big deal. We really enjoyed wine lists, and checking out the Bordeaux racks in the stores. We didn't know about Rioja's, Concho, etc. Boucheron was our jug wine. We saved labels, and Kath rated the wines.

Marcels (or is it Chez Marcel) was a place I can think of that we went to for a fancy meal. Osborne, Cutillo's, were 'way in the future. So was Troutbeck, Old Drover's.

Cross-country skiing wasn't important yet, and kayak's were still a few years in the future.

Where was I working??? At Saint Francis, because I showed the USSR slides to the DP people. AGS, Keane, and IBM Fishkill and Southbury were things I never would have thought would have happened. Grenier Corporation, too. Where was Kath: Hyde Park????

I didn't have a lot of grey hair. Kath had long, long hair, pulled back from her forehead.

My teeth were just as lousy as they are now.

Bicycle??? I probably had the orange Lotus, with the triple crank and the big 32 on the back, and those silver panniers. Wow... Klein Quantum, road-races and crits???? Hah! Commuting, the MHBC Century were big deals. Mountain bikes were yet to come.

We had not met Kathy and Blair, or been to Block Island. We kept our lawns mowed, but never raked leaves.

November 24, 2020

Writers/Authors/Books

This will be a "stream of consciousness".

The first writer that comes to mind is Bill Bryson. I've always admired what I call his "self-deprecating humor", intelligence, and attention to research and details. His *Notes From A Small Island* first caught my attention, and I've read much of his works ever since. I wrote to him once and invited him along on one of my AT hikes, and received a *hand-written* response, thanking me but saying he couldn't go as he'd be in Australia, working on what became *In A Sunburned Country*.

Way, way back in the Fifties I read a lot of science fiction—Arthur C. Clark, Issac Asimov—but I kind of outgrew it.

During my bicycling heyday, I recall being very impressed by Maynard Hershon, who was a regular at the very back of *Velo News*. I've never forgotten his describing Volvos as being "stupefyingly boring"...

Outside magazine was once a fixture in our lives, and Tim Cahill, David Quammen, and Randy Wayne Wright—I guess they were pretty much "travel writers"—were favorites.

Moving on to columnists, Dave Barry is/was superb, and I currently admire Amy Alkon, *The Advice Goddess*: she "gets it", brilliantly.

Let's name a few names/books:

Mary Carr's *The Liars' Club*,
Alexandra Fuller's *Don't Let's Go To The Dogs Tonight*,
Anne Lamott: *Bird by Bird*,
Mark Helprin's *Winter's Tale*,
and very recently, Bibi Gaston's *The Loveliest Woman in America*

And, in the last couple of years, thanks to Kath's brother Dan, I've read, and enjoyed, all 17 (???) of Lee Child's *Jack Reacher* series.

I've also read a lot, and have accumulated quite a collection of "World War II" books. These have expanded to Korea, Vietnam, and, the Gulf Wars. Hal Moore's *We Were Soldiers Once...And Young*, Stephen Ambrose's *D-Day*, Martin Caidin's *Black Thursday* stand out. More recently, Tim O'Brien's *The Things They Carried* was outstanding. I sometimes wonder what is going to happen to this "collection", when The Day Comes.

Oh, almost forgot I was a huge Tom Robbins fan back in the day, though his latest left me cold; as if he had, finally, lost his touch. This seems to be happening to Lee Child, also. How long can you keep writing, essentially, the same tune????

June 3, 2016: I just came across Donald Wetzels *1983 Joel's Journal and Fact-Filled Fart Book*, GREETING BOOKS, Bayside, New York. It had to be included here...

February 3, 2017: I just finished reading James D. Hornfischer's *The Last Stand of the Tin Can Sailors*, for the second time. Basically, an American Destroyer, DD-557, the USS *JOHNSTON*, **ATTACKS** a huge Japanese fleet consisting of four battleships, six heavy cruisers, two light cruisers, and eleven destroyers. He's joined in the attack by two other destroyers, the *HOEL*, DD-533, and the destroyer escort, DE-413, the *SAMUEL B. ROBERTS*. Here's a quote from Herman Wouk's *War and Remembrance*, on Page 406: "The vision of Sprague's three destroyers—the *Johnston*, the *Hoel*, and the *Heermann****—charging out of the smoke and rain straight toward the main batteries of Kurita's battleships and cruisers, can endure as a picture of the way Americans fight when they don't have superiority. Our schoolchildren should know about that incident, and our enemies should ponder it."

***I just noticed this: Wouk got it wrong: the third ship wasn't the *Heermann*, it was the DE *Samuel B. Roberts*..........

A Bill Bryson Funny Story

...a friend of Catherine's moved with her young family into a house next door to a vacant lot. One day a construction crew turned up to build a house on the lot. Catherine's friend had a four-year-old daughter who naturally took an interest in all the activity going on next door. She hung around on the margins and eventually the construction workers adopted her as a kind of mascot.

They chatted to her and gave her little jobs to do and at the end of the week presented her with a little pay packet containing a shiny new half crown.

She took this home to her mother, who made all the appropriate cooings of admiration and suggested they take it to the bank the next morning to deposit it in her account. When they went to the bank, the teller was equally impressed and asked the little girl how she had come by her own pay packet.

"I've been building a house this week," she replied proudly.

"Goodness!" said the teller. "And will you be building a house next week, too?"

"I will if we ever get the fucking bricks," answered the little girl.

WRITING/ESSAYS/"PROFOUND THOUGHTS"

"Writing", From Sometime In 2007???:

I feel that I am a successful writer.

I've written a weekly newspaper column for almost four years.

I just published my second book, *Uncle Ben, Uncle Bob, Uncle Joe, Uncle Pete, P.D., and Pop.*

I'm a free-lance columnist, and an author. The struggle was long, hard, and at times very very discouraging, but I am now very happy and very contented. I could aspire to write for the *Washington Post,* or the *New York Times,* or author ten more books, but this would only be *degrees* of writing success. I may never write another book.

Here's some information, advice, thoughts and opinions about "how I got from there to here".

A Few Words About "Writing"

A former co-worker once said something to me about writing that really opened my eyes. She said "Ralph, I can't write—it is an effort for me to write, and I have to force myself to do it. And that's the way it is with a lot of people. You have a gift— it comes easily and naturally to you. You express yourself easily verbally, and you write the same way."

Though sometimes it seems that about half of the ten billion people on this planet are competing with you to sell their writings, I think that people who are compelled to create "art"—people who draw, paint, write, write poetry—are relatively rare in our society. The vast majority seem more compelled to consume, shop, eat, and... read. We few *must* write...

One of my college art teachers once said, "An artist needs an audience." Though we are writing for ourselves, many of us would really love to have other people read our writings—family, friends or relatives—but there are probably quite a few of us that would like The World as our audience. Otherwise, our "art" is just landfill in waiting. And, we need reassurance about and acceptance of our work. We are much too close to it to see or hear it objectively.

A few words about editors, publishers, and rejections. Imagine that no matter what kind of work you do, you were told every day that every single bit of work you did was no good—it was rejected. How would that make you feel, over the long run, for years and years. It would be pretty hard to face day after day after day, wouldn't it? But this is what the writing business is all about—rejection after rejection after rejection, or, no response whatsoever.

I have been rejected, or totally ignored, by Random House, Simon and Schuster, W.W. Norton & Company, University of Illinois Press, Columbia University Press, Da Capo Press, Purple Mountain Press, Blackdome Press, the Appalachian Mountain Club, *Playboy, Playgirl, The New Yorker, The Washington Post, Outside* magazine, *Cycle Sport* magazine, *Reader's Digest,* Arthur Frommer's *Budget Travel.* You get the picture…

Many people told me to keep plugging away, and some, in an effort to comfort and inspire me, mentioned that about 43 editors rejected the Harry Potter stories—for years and years and years. I wasn't inspired, or comforted. Weren't all 43 of those editors incompetent??? NOT doing their jobs. If all of us were as incompetent at our work, we would deserve to be fired.

Another though about editors/editing: when a painter paints a painting, does someone else come along and say "that eye isn't right—I'll move it over, and make it bluer…", or something to that effect. But an editor can totally change the style and meaning of our written work. Nope, not mine…

But I did plug away, and now I'm a columnist and an author. Here's the story:

"My Story"

I've led an interesting life. I grew up in a small town: Buchanan, New York. When I went to college in Queens, they called me "The Buchanan Hillbilly". My parents were first generation from immigrants: Polish, and Italian. They never ventured out of the USA, and rarely left New York State. I've been to 46 countries, in 23 time zones, on 6 continents.

I've roamed the peace parks and squares of Moscow; been in the thick of political street demonstrations in Nairobi; walked the alleys of Kathmandu during a Nepalese National State of Emergency; peed in the Serengeti when a bus broke down in Tanzania; arrived in Lima just after the terrorists released the embassy and left just before the earthquake; and rode in a black taxi in Belfast past the still-smoking ruins of what had just been a building...

I've always been "artistic", compelled to draw, sketch, doodle, paint, or photograph. I haven't always been compelled to write, but in the 70's I kept fairly detailed journals on my two Appalachian Trail end-to-end hikes, and then kept journals when I began traveling the world. In the 90's, I was required to write weekly status reports for my computer job. I began making them into short stories. My manager, and the administrative staff at the home office, began anticipating my weekly FAX's !!!

In the mid-90's I started writing detailed accounts of my travels: Peru, Bolivia, Ireland, Nepal, Tanzania. I was inspired by Tim Cahill's travel writings in *Outside* magazine, and by Bill Bryson, Dave Barry, and Maynard Hershon, a bicycle magazine writer. My travel writings mimicked their low keyed, self-deprecating, humorous styles. Several bits and pieces, long and short, prose and poetry were published in magazines and newsletters, and I began to feel that I was a fairly successful writer.

On November 12, 2003, I was quite abruptly blown out of a 14-year 3-month job. November 13, 2003 I began to write...books. To heck with magazines and newsletters and newspapers: I had bigger fish to fry... A comment here about "writer's block": this has never been a problem for me—I only hope that I live long enough to write about everything I want to write about.

"Success"

I've been writing the Journal column for almost four years now. I've been getting paid for it for over two years, and just got my second raise, from the Editor of the Sports Section. How did all this come about??? Did I relentlessly hound the Journal for years and years, send them manuscript after manuscript??? Nope. Jim Haggett, an old friend that hiked about a thousand miles of the Appalachian Trail with me called one night and said that the New York/New Jersey Trail Conference was looking for someone local to write a hiking column for the Journal. He knew that I knew a lot about hiking, and that I wanted to write. I went to a meeting at the Journal, and met Pete Colaizzo, the best Editor you could ever want...

February 2006, I self-published *Catskill Tales and Trails* with print-on-demand iUniverse.com. This 10-year work-in-progress, evolved from personal journals, was rejected over the years by about a half-dozen publishers who had already published similar books. I was dead set against self-publishing. Just a few years ago, this was a $10,000–$14,000 proposition, and you had to buy a huge inventory of books because they had to be printed in large lots. Recent technology has changed all this and it cost me $399.00 to have my book published in about a month's time by iUniverse. They were absolutely wonderful to work with, produced a fine product in a very timely manner, and I love them and recommend them to anyone who will listen.

I returned to iUniverse in January 2007 with *Uncle Ben, Uncle Bob, Uncle Joe, Uncle Pete, P.D., and Pop*. I thought at the time it was a ready-to-go product. Silly me... It was published in late December 2007.

Some Advice

If you are compelled to write, WRITE!!!

iUniverse can make a book out of those journals and memoirs: <u>www. iUniverse.com</u>

To tighten up your writing: Long Ridge Writers Group, West Redding, Connecticut. 1-800-624-1476.

*   *   *

Meet The Author

East Fishkill Community Library
7:00 PM, Thursday, February 21, 2008

No one came. No one. I can't describe how bad, how awful this was. I'd spent the better part of two days getting ready. I knew what I was going to say, and practiced how I was going to say it. I knew what I was going to bring, and how I was going to display the carefully-chosen excerpts and artifacts. I knew what I was going to wear. I shined my shoes, and just before I left the house I caught myself fussing with my hair.

I waited in that room with 25 empty chairs 'til 7:30, then put all the stuff away, then stopped at Danny's Pizza and had three slices and a root beer. If anybody had come to pick up a pizza, and bothered to glance over, they would have thought the guy with the brass-buttoned Navy blazer and dark turtleneck with the faraway look in his eyes had had a bad day at the office. Nah, had a "meet the author" and nobody showed.

*   *   *

If Anybody *Had* Come

Thank you [both] for coming.

Five years in the writing: I started January 2003.

80,456 words, 264 pages.

Published December 2007: it's still a thrill to hold it in my hands.

After two months of proof rounds, it still has (as of now) nineteen errors in it. I've been told by people in the business that even the *Harry Potter* books have errors in them.

The last Harry Potter book sold ten million copies in 24 hours.

I'm still eagerly anticipating my eighth sale after two months...

Luna

In August, 2016 friends and relatives were shocked—nay, stunned—when I e-mailed them that my wife Kathy and I, after 25 years of marriage, had adopted an 11-year-old daughter, Luna, who had been left to die alongside a road in Tennessee *with a gunshot wound in her neck.*

They were even more surprised the next day when I e-mailed them a photograph of Luna, the *coyote...* Here's Luna's story:

While walking on the Appalachian Trail through New York's Bear Mountain State Park Zoo we passed a cage where a zoo-keeper in a small cage was— astonishingly—practically hand-feeding a porcupine.

There were two coyotes in the next cage, and one of them was *extremely* agitated, pacing back and forth, making dog-like yipping/barking sounds. The zoo-keeper told us that she, the coyote, was jealous because she, the zoo-keeper, was paying attention to the porcupine next door. I asked if *she* the coyote had a name. The zoo-keeper replied, "Luna."

I stood right in front of the cage, looked directly at Luna, and said, in my best low, soothing, talking-to-a-coyote voice, "Luna, it's OK. It's OK." Astonishingly, she immediately calmed down and stopped pacing and barking. *I had just had a "conversation" with a wild creature. A coyote named Luna...*

Returning to the zoo a month later, I eagerly anticipated Luna's reaction when I again stood in front of her cage. She totally ignored me...Such is Life. We discovered we could "adopt" one of the zoo animals. We discussed it, and soon officially adopted Luna. We received a certificate, and a handsome 8X10 color photo of our adopted daughter.

We learned Loki, Luna's cage mate was a younger male, and "our" Luna was an Alpha female. Later, we received the wonderful news that they had been moved from the much-too-small cage they shared to a new, *half-acre*, fenced-in open-woods enclosure.

We eventually visited the new enclosure. There was a spacious viewing platform, manned by a uniformed zoo-keeper. Try as we might, we could not spot "our daughter" in the half-acre. I asked the zoo-keeper where Luna was, and she pointed to two small greyish-brown "lumps" curled up in balls on the ground, blending in with the leaves, in the far northeast corner of the spacious enclosure. We never would have spotted them if they hadn't been pointed out.

A while later we returned to the zoo, and easily spotted Loki, friskily ranging about along with two newly arrived young coyotes, and, "our" Luna was clearly visible across the way, majestically surveying the scene. She looked fine, and healthy; I was pleased to see her again, and, very proud of our adopted Alpha daughter.

Updated July 10, 2021

Small Pleasures

A cold beer on a hot day.
A steaming hot bathtub on a cold day.
EZPass
Heated car seats in the winter.

Synchronized traffic lights.
Seeing a hummingbird.

Heroes/Persons I Admire

Greta Thunberg, 2019 Time magazine PERSON of the YEAR
Pop
P.D. Reed
Rene "Bud" Biourd
Harry S. Truman
Lance Armstrong
Paul Scrodin, a Computer Operator when I worked as a Computer
Programmer at Saint Francis Hospital

Men That Changed My Life

Bob Turner, a high school classmate who convinced me, then helped me to
"bull-nose" my 1950 Plymouth, leading to a lifetime love of cars.

Ray Orton, an IBM technician/coworker who invited me to go for a hike on
Breakneck Ridge, where I became a "hiker".

Howie Roth, an IBM manager who invited me to hike Slide, Wittenberg, and
Cornell in the Catskills, where I achieved one of my first difficult long-term
goals that I can remember, Catskill 3500 Club member #122 (and, Winter
Member #34W...), that led to the AT, and a love of World Travel.

Benton MacKaye, and the Appalachian Trail. I wrote to Benton MacKaye
back in the Seventies, thanking him for "One Great Idea".

The Cruelest Word in the English Language...

"But" is a very common word, and is uttered daily in conversations, movies,
on TV and radio, etc, etc, but I think because of this many people have never

realized what a cruel word it is. The biggest example I can think of is "I Love You, *but.........*"

"Your X-rays and Cat Scans are all fine, but...."

"Your car passed inspection, but..."

Once you start listening for them, the "buts" go on, and on, and on.

Speaking of "listening for words" the (very, very, very common) phrase "*You know...*" makes my **crazy**... I've done my damnedest to exorcise it from my vocabulary, but once I became tuned in to it, it goes on, and on, and on...

And, speaking of words, I often can't resist using the "word" "irregardless". People's knee-jerk reaction is often "'Irregardless' is *not* a word!" I say it to jerk their chain, and to see the expression in their eyes....

Thoughts on "Winning"

Kath and I raced white water canoes for years, mostly in the New England Downriver Championship Series (NEDCS). We raced in the Mixed Class— one woman, one man—and got pretty damned good at it. We'd trophy most weekends—I hated Fourth Place—but we very rarely "won" our class. First Place was very elusive: there were several veteran Mixed teams that were better than us, and when they showed up at a race, "winning" was out of the question; we knew we'd be racing, at best, for Second or Third.

The local Wappingers Water Derby eventually became part of NEDCS, and by the time it rolled around every year in late April, Kath and I had been racing hard for a month, and had half a dozen long, tough races under our belts.

We massacred all the local Mixed wannabees, year after year. I also observed, over the years, that several other teams "came out of the woodwork" and dominated a class—or several classes—year after year after year, crushing their opposition, adding to their piles of First Place medals.

There was a young local couple who were regulars in the Mixed for several years during this period, and one year, when they saw us pre-race, they said something like, "Oh no, you're here...." They'd think they died and went to heaven if they ever got a First Place medal, happily showing it to family, and friends. Wappingers First Place medals had, sadly, become just about meaningless to us: we pretty much just tossed them on the pile. Thinking about it, we asked ourselves, "What was the point????"

From that "Oh no" day onward, something changed for Kath and I. The next year we did not enter Mixed, instead entering the Competition Cruiser Class (for out-and-out racing boats, hardly any of which entered the Wappingers at that time), to let some of the local up-and-coming Mixed teams duke it out without our interference, one of them eventually feeling the glow of First Place: "winning".

After this decision, I personally felt I had "grown"—reached a Higher Plane—as a human being, first to have recognized a Grander Scheme of Things, then to have had the wherewithal to actually do something about it, to "step down", and allow other worthy competitors to "step up".

We still enter the Wappingers every year, to support it, but we don't "race" anymore: we simply enjoy the river, and the day, using all the skills and experience we'd picked up as long-time racers (Racing does, indeed, "improve the breed").

It's been very satisfying, and, liberating.

Happy/Not So Happy

This may sound ridiculous, but my Summer of 2015 days sometimes come down to "Should I/could I/can I go for a bike ride." Whadda Life, hey??? Among other things, my rides are weather dependent, so there are times—actually quite a few times, Northeastern USA weather being, shall we say fickle—that I don't go, and later wish I had. I've come to realize this somewhat simple thing—a bike ride—effects me more than I ever realized it did in the past.

If I go for a bike ride, or a decent cross-country ski in the winter, I'm "happy"; satisfied, whatever. My bike rides, or Baird Park skis, are not strenuous: I don't push myself hard anymore, so this is not some kind of "endorphin fix". But, the flip side of this is if I don't ride the bike, or ski on a nice winter's day, I'm not necessarily "unhappy", but there is a distinct difference in my personality. And, considering I ski about thirty times per winter, and bike about the same amount of days Spring-Fall, this means about 5/6ths of the year I'm, well, not happy.......

That Picture, right over there...

There's a picture on the wall to the left of my desk; I just glanced at it. It was taken high on a shoulder of Whiteface Mountain in the Adirondacks, about forty years ago. I have a day pack on, my high, tan/green REI gaiters (I still have them), all-leather hiking boots, and I'm leaning on a bamboo hiking stick. The sky is blue, with one small puffy white cloud. I'm young and lean, and as strong as an ox. Stashed away here and there, there are many pictures/slides of me on the Appalachian Trail in the '70's, strong and lean, able to heft 50-pound backpacks up and down gigantic mountains, mile after mile after mile, all day long, day after day after day.

That was then; Glory Days. Reality is, nowadays, most of the time I'm like a beaten dog on the way back to the house after walking over to Hosner Mountain Road, a mere mile away on the Appalachian Trail. I look at that picture, and....................

US Presidential Qualifications

There's an election year coming up and many potential candidates have already been "campaigning" for quite a while. A lying, conniving woman that I feel is eminently unqualified is making a lot of noise, and the starry-eyed media rhetoric concerning her inspired me to list these thoughts concerning characteristics/traits/skills I felt a potential US President should have:

Proven abilities to lead/govern.

Years of experience leading/governing.

Integrity.

A deep-seated patriotism/love of country.

Military service: this person is going to be Commander in Chief of our armed forces. A solid idea of what the common American foot soldier experiences on a daily basis (as I did) should be a requisite.

Christmas "update" Note Goof

Some people regularly include a "This year we..." update note with their Christmas card. Here's a parody I wrote:

We've decided this year to voluntarily limit ourselves to the National Average of $840.00/Christmas gift/person, primarily so we can buy each other "His and Her's" 2014 Escalades—we're both bored with our 2013's. And, the 2014's get *four miles per gallon*!!!

We're also a bit torn whether to expand our three-car garage to a more fitting six—we're tired of alternating the Avalanche and the Hummer in the third bay—or to purchase the 80,000-square-foot home (that we both *adore*), in a gated community, that *already* has a six-car garage. Decisions, decisions...

Daphne just LOVES her new six-figure job (and promotion!). The four-hour door-to-door commute and the 87-hour work week aren't' really all that bad, and they make us appreciate even more the three hours a week we actually spend together, and, our new 50' X 30' flat screen TV: Survivor and Dancing With the Stars have never looked better.

Twin (From Catskill Tales and Trails)

Talkin' the Talk

The east peak of Twin was a pretty easy climb from the Jimmy Dolan Notch col, and it is a great mountain up top – nice trail through the evergreens, then a great open ledge with great 180 degree views. I was impressed – since this peak "doesn't count", I hadn't been on it for many many years. It's a nice walk over to the west summit, and we tagged it and headed back because a strong west wind was blasting the open ledge just beyond it. We ambled back to east Twin, and sat down and had lunch and enjoyed the sun and the magnificent view. We bombed back to the car in an hour...

I enjoyed the heck out of that warm, sunny, relaxed, January lunch break on the east peak of Twin, kicking back and "talkin' the Catskill talk" with R3 – one of those very memorable father and son Catskill mountain experiences. It doesn't get much better than this.

February 2, 2004

"Other News"

Garth Henning Discovers Time Travel.
Can Stay 29 Forever, If He Wants To.

Returns Uncle To 1963 To Buy 500
Brand New Corvette Sting Rays.
Uncle Becomes Multi-Millionaire,
Shares Wealth With Entire Family.
Pop Drives Red Sting Ray Convertible
Around Buchanan At 20 MPH.

Brings Brother Wade Back to 1935 To
Coach Adolf Hitler, Who Shaves Stupid
Mustache, Gets Lance Armstrong Buzz
Cut, and Becomes Mumsy, Successful,
Beloved Artist.
World War II Never Happens.
Korea, Vietnam, Terrorism Never Happen.
Planet Remains Forever At Peace.

Garth Turns 30 When He Damn Well Pleases...

Affluence...

Kath and I have "traveled the world", and have visited many "Third World" areas in Asia, Africa, Central America, and/or Mexico.

Having witnessed the stunningly stark living conditions, and, put simply, *abject* poverty that is prevalent in so much of the world, I am constantly astounded—nay, sometimes stupefied—at the level of affluence that we Americans take for granted: huge, monstrous stores—Walmarts, Home Depots, ShopRites—each containing aisles and shelves stacked high with millions and billions of bright, shiny, brand-spanking-new *things*, at our fingertips, there for the asking.

I'd been doing our grocery shopping at an older, "normal-sized" A&P for decades. Recently, when A&P went belly-up, it closed. The next nearest supermarket to us was a ShopRite, in Carmel. This store, to me about the size of Rhode Island (or, more realistically, a football field) is extremely popular: the big parking lot is just about always jam-packed almost out to the highway, and the aisles between the always-well-stocked shelves are filled with customers bumping into each other who know that—as *everyone* seems to know—ShopRite has "the best prices".

So I walk in, a Stranger in a Strange Land, and am instantly overwhelmed by the aforementioned aisles and aisles and shelves and shelves stacked high with millions and billions of bright, shiny, brand-spanking-new items of all sorts, at my fingertips, there for the asking... One side of a whole seventy-foot-long aisle is stacked with hundreds of different brands and types of... *bread...*

No one else seems to be the least bit astonished or astounded by all this; they're all pretty much grabbing stuff, and tossing it into big, already-piled-high shopping carts, happily, and obliviously taking all this for granted. And, why not??? It's pretty much their "God-given right", and always has been, since the day they were born...

Not for me, not any more. I don't think many, if any, of these grabbing-and-tossing folks could, in their wildest wildest dreams, have the slightest idea of the sights (and sounds and smells) of some of the incomprehensibly *poor* places I've been in this World: from right-around-the-corner Mexico, Nicaragua, or Belize, to far-off Kenya, Tanzania, or Nepal.

In May 2009 we ended up in the tiny village of Hopkins, on the coast of Belize. Neighbors had told us they had a relative living there, and tipped him off that if we happened to be "in the neighborhood", we might visit him. It wasn't easy getting to Hopkins. We traveled in Belize on local "chicken" buses, and eventually ended up in a scary bus terminal in a scary town somewhere north of Hopkins, where a couple of thug-like native guys—who, as many other Belize guys all during the trip who at first were, well, pretty scary, ultimately turned out to indeed be right-there-when-we-needed-them-the-most Guardian Angels—said they would drive us there in their beat-up minivan, for what, at the time, was an astonishing amount of money compared to what everything else had cost us while we were eating-where-the-locals-ate/traveling-like-the-locals-traveled in Belize.

I recall once we left the (paved) "main road" (there were only about two or three in Belize at the time), we traveled about 14 miles or so on a narrow pot-holed dirt road to get to Hopkins. And, it was, well, very basic. "English" was spoken in Belize, but it was not the kind of "English" we understood. We were flummoxed.

Our now-Guardian-Angels asked around, and eventually found the place where the "relative" lived. I, naively, expected "the relative" to greet us with open arms, eager to chat about his relatives in Stormville, then probably inviting us to stay over for a night or two. This last part was pretty important to us, as there weren't really any obvious-to-us places to stay in tiny Hopkins.

We were greeted at the door (and, *not* invited in) by an about-14-year-old Belize girl—his live-in "girl friend"??? I think I now knew why he had elected to be an "ex-pat" there—and were told he "wasn't available", or something like that, and, that he wouldn't be. End of story. See yah later, folks. Thanks a lot, unavailable creepy old fart... Thankfully for us, the two guys asked around and found a very very nice place, with a kitchen, right on the beach run by a very nice Hopkins native that we never would have found on our own. They drove off, and we stayed there for a night or two.

OK, here's what this is all getting around to. We now had a nice place to stay, but we had to eat. At that time, there was only one, very basic, native place to eat out in Hopkins, and we did "rice-and-beans" it there once. But, we also had to figure out the other breakfasts, lunches, and dinners during our stay.

At that time there were (and maybe there still are) only two very small grocery stores in Hopkins. We might have stuck our noses in both— I don't really recall—but at any rate the one we chose to "shop" in was about the size of a one-bay garage in an American home. Inside it was dimly-lit, cramped, dingy, and, dirty. The sparse selection of items on the few shelves looked like they'd been there forever, and, were, dust-covered... Fresh produce??? You gotta be kidding. The two Asians that I supposed were the owners stared, desultorily, at us.

Fast forward to 2015, to a ShopRite in Carmel, New York, and replace it with this Hopkins store and you will have some idea of why I was as befuddled by all the abundance, plenty, and taken-for-granted easy affluence, as I was...

And, still am, every single time I walk into a WalMart, or Macy's or J.C.Pennys, and I flash back to the acres and acres and acres of cardboard/tin dirt-road shacks surrounding downtown Lima, Nairobi, Managua. And the unspeakable, indescribable poverty lining the traffic-/exhaust-fumes-choked road between Kathmandu and Bahktapur in Nepal that I witnessed from a tourist bus window.

And, that "store" somewhere on a dirt road in Tanzania, where the "meat department" was a big bloody fly-infested skinned animal carcass, hanging from a hook outside the left hand corner of the small, shabby wooden building.

ShopRite, indeed....................

1031 Words
February 5, 2016

"Squirrel-Proof" Bird Feeders

I have a suggestion for NASA. You might know who the best person might be to direct it to.

It would involve a slight change to NASA's iconic initials, but the worldwide rejoicing, if the suggested goal—solving one of humankind's most challenging unsolved problems—is accomplished might render this moot.

NOSA's—the National Outsmart Squirrels Administration—mission would be to focus all of its mighty brainpower and resources towards the development of the World's First TRULY Squirrel-proof Bird Feeder.

One caveat: the birds have to still be able to access the bird seed...

Some afterthoughts:

1. It would have to look like a bird feeder—not a lunar landing module or a Mars probe.

2. Cost has to be competitive with the pitifully ineffective bird/squirrel feeders currently on the market.

3. No electricity, snipers, lasers, 24-hour surveillance, automatic weapons.

Pop Music, 1966 To 2009

July 1974

You fill up my senses
Like a night in a forest
Like the mountains in springtime
Like a walk in the rain
Like a storm in the desert
Like a sleepy blue ocean
You fill up my senses
Come fill me again

January 1966

Hello darkness, my old friend
I've come to talk with you again
Because a vision softly creeping
Left its seeds while I was sleeping
And the vision that was planted in my brain
Still remains
Within the sound of silence

January 1970

Sail on silver girl
Sail on by
Your time has come to shine
All your dreams are on their way
See how they shine

June 2009

Tonight's gonna be a good good night
....
Tonight's gonna be a good good night
....
Tonight's gonna be a good good night
....
Tonight's gonna be a good good night
....
Tonight's gonna be a good good night...

Nothing Left to Ooze; My Life as a Leper and Other Career Moves

I now know for certain, indisputably, beyond the shadow of a doubt, that I had chicken pox as a kid. This did not require a trip to The County Medical Department, poring over endless micro fiches in a dingy gray room. Rather, it required a short ride to the local Medical Group, followed in this order by: One: some interminable bickering with a bored, indifferent Receptionist From Hell—who obviously could care less if I collapsed and expired right there in front of her face, and in front of the long line of fellow sufferers extending all the way to the Automatic Doors—concerning my "illegible" Medicare Card. Two: a surprisingly short wait in the overflowing waiting room, packed to the rafters with fellow long-sufferers. Three: a trip through the endless bowels of the Rhode-Island-sized medical building to Examining Room 743, followed by an interminable wait for, finally, a "PA", Physician's

Assistant, who took one look at the red, ugly, blistering, oozing, pus-y mess that the entire right side of my face had become and dropped this bomb, in a so-what-I've-seen-this-a-thousand-times tone, "You Have Shingles."

I sat there like a dope. I had, vaguely, heard of "shingles", but had no idea what it was, or, more to the point, had never thought that I would ever have to deal with it. About a week ago I was Perfectly Normal, happily sawing and splitting firewood, writing my weekly newspaper column, buying water softener salt, getting the Subaru inspected, la de dah. The next morning I had a tingling sensation in my right upper lip, under my mustache. I had never experienced a sensation quite like this before. It was irritating, and felt vaguely "neurological", but I was clueless to why and what it was. I tried to think of anything unusual that had happened recently that might have brought about this strange phenomenon, but could not. I hoped it would go away: we've all Been There Done That. It didn't. Soon, little white blisters began to appear on my right cheek, above my mustache and close to my nose. They also tingled. After several days, the blisters had grown alarmingly, my right upper lip was the size of a watermelon, and the entire right side of my face was swollen, blistered, oozing, and burned. Uh oh, this isn't going to go away...

The PA prescribed Valtrex—some people get paid millions of dollars a year to come up with these silly names... The pharmacist, assuming I, like most other people in the "civilized" world, had prescription coverage, announced that the little bottle of pills was going for $204.50. I stood there like a dope. When I was able to speak, I told her that I didn't have prescription coverage. She asked me what I was going to do. I said, "I have no options", and handed her my Visa. At least the pills are huge—big blue "horse pills".

I've been taking the pills several days. Every day, the swelling, the oozing, the blistering, the pus, the redness has increased. I've become a recluse, a slave to the bathroom mirror, where I stand, staring at the right half of my Middle-Ages-Leper face, hoping for some glimmer of improvement. There hasn't been any. Every day is Worse: the pus and oozing are uglier, the blisters have progressed to the inside of my upper lip and are now shredding. Pieces of my face are falling off. I am a monster from a horror movie. I will not, cannot go out in public. I would scare people. I scare myself.

My wife has been saintly, making me tea, intoning me to drink plenty of fluids, trying to convince me that this all will pass. My sister, once I informed her, has checked in regularly throughout my ordeal (two days now...). She called this afternoon, and we spoke at length. I've been a Pretty Good Soldier in general, but I went on and on and on: the pus, the oozing, the blisters, the pain. I particularly went into a "trapped in the house" pity-party.

At one point, Sis said, quietly, "I'm picturing you standing at a salad bar in a crowded restaurant—one of those without a 'snot shield'..." We both roared.

She then said, "I'll bet you could clear out Shea Stadium." I said, "Get your hot dogs here, folks. Oops, sorry, that's my upper lip on your lap." We roared again.

We couldn't stop. I wondered if there were any places I would *like* to clear out. I thought of going to a mall, and walking up to someone who was obnoxiously yelling, abusing their cell phone, and asking if I could borrow it, to "Check in with my friends at the colony."

It was good to laugh out loud. When the conversation finally wound down, Sis said not to hesitate to give her a call if there was anything she could do, then quietly added, "But *do not* come over".

We laughed...

In two or three days it stopped getting worse—the Valtrex was earning its $204.50—and a week later I was "normal" again, sawing/spltting/writing/spending money.

Recreated from the original paper document, May 9, 2016

873 words

Henry Hudson

Around 2006-2008 I worked as a tour guide for a Pleasant Valley-based company called Cross Country International, run by Karen Lancaster. At the time it was (one of???) the largest equine tour companies on the Planet. They'd decided to branch out to hiking/walking tours. I proposed a Historic Hudson Valley walk: Day 1: the FDR and Vanderbilt mansions. Day 2: Thompson Pond, the Millbrook Vineyard, and Peter Wing's funky "castle". Day 3: Innisfree and Wethersfield Gardens, and Day 4: a 6.6-mile walk on the Appalachian Trail to Cat Rocks, near Pawling. Ultimately I had hikers from 23 states, Canada, and Europe. I wrote this "goof" on the tour, and read it to my hikers at the meet-and-greet the evening before each tour:

"Henry Hudson sailed up the river in 1609, seeking the fabled North-West passage to the riches of India, where he also hoped to pick up some good vegetarian recipes for his sister Harriet. It wasn't the Hudson River then; the peaceful, friendly natives called it "Muhheakunnuk"—the river that flows two ways"—or, more commonly, "the river"; much easier to pronounce, and to spell. Henry briefly considered renaming the river "Harriet", but wisely thought better of this.

He landed at the Rogers Point Marina in Hyde Park on a Monday morning, and walked up the Hyde Park Trail and visited Franklin and Eleanor Roosevelt. They all went to lunch at the Hyde Park Brewing Company, right across Route 9. In the afternoon, he visited the Vanderbilts, and walked back down the Hyde Park Trail to the Half Moon, anchored off Bard Rock.

On Tuesday, he walked around the Audubon Society's Thompson Pond, enjoyed a wine tour and tasting at the Millbrook Vineyards, and then visited Peter Wing at his funky work-in-progress castle, overlooking the vineyards and the valley.

Wednesday he had morning tea with Chauncey Deveraux Stillman in the Inner Garden of his 1200-acre Wethersfield estate, lunched at Uncle Sonny's charming, landmark restaurant, then spent the afternoon strolling with Walter and Marion Beck in the meditative Innisfree Gardens surrounding tranquil Tyrell Lake.

On Thursday, he walked a 6.6-mile section of the Appalachian Trail near Pawling, and took a lunch break at the Cat Rocks viewpoint. He met several thru-hikers, who christened him with the Trail Name "Handsome Henry", because of his quite dashing goatee.

Totally charmed by the area, he purchased the Hilltop House B&B in Amenia, donated the Half Moon to Pete Seeger, who renamed it the Clearwater, and lived happily ever after, never once even thinking of returning to Holland: he hated his job at the Amsterdam WalMart anyway.

He e-mailed Karen Lancaster, and went on and on about his adventures, and now you know where the idea for Cross Country International's Historic Hudson Valley Walk came from.

BTY, Gail, your hostess at Hilltop House, is a seventeenth generation Hudson. She loves to show off her pictures of her great great great great great grandfather Henry.

Just kidding..."

Revised/corrected from the original document, October 4, 2016

It Doesn't Get Much Better'n This

Friday morning, June 16, 2016: sitting at a sidewalk table at *2 Alices*, a cafe on Broadway in Newburgh, New York, sipping a fluffernutter latte.......

Mort

Mort owns the local pizza place, and stands behind the counter, making pizzas. This is what Mort "does".

Doreen's a waitress in a local diner, and hustles back and forth between the kitchen and the tables and booths, delivering diner-sized portions of food to diner-sized people. This is what she does. That she bears a resemblance to the actress Helen Hunt, and has a sadness—perhaps even a vulnerability about her—probably goes unnoticed by most.

So what, in a nutshell, do I "do"???

About once a week or so I have an idea—a light bulb goes on in my head—about some sort of outdoors experience. I sit down at my computer and elaborate on it, refining it over a period of several days. Eventually I e-mail it to the local newspaper, where some people read it in a few minutes, then, turn the page....

This process has been pretty much repeated, 52 weeks a year, for almost twelve years. I enjoy the writing, and the process—it's my creative outlet— and I've become better and better at it over the years.

I wonder: does Mort *enjoy* making pizzas??? Does Doreen really want to spend the rest of her life waiting tables??? I'd like to think there are other ("better"???) things—hopes, dreams— they'd rather be doing. I'll wonder, but to me it's pretty obvious it would not be appropriate to ever ask them.

Do I really intend to spend the rest of my life writing a "hiking" column in the Sports Section of a dying newspaper??? I wonder, but I'm pretty sure I'll just keep doing it until something comes along to stop my doing it. Probably the same for Mort, and Doreen..............

March 30,2015 Terrifying Moments

Every once in a while we all get, well, "scared". There have been a few moments in my life—all things considered—that "scared" has ratcheted up to "terrifying". Here goes:

Being caught in a cyclone in our camper van on the very tip of New Zealand's North Island.

Seeing the huge black dorsal fin of a basking shark (we didn't know it was a basking shark at the time; coulda been a Great White...) coming right at us while we were kayaking far, far from shore in the middle of Provincetown Bay on the Cape.

Being caught by four—yes, four—big thunderstorms all at the same time in a high mountain gap somewhere in the huge southern mountains on the Appalachian Trail.

That thunderstorm that caught us in our dome tent 'way out in the open while we were canoeing on the [???] Canal.

Crystal Rapids and Lava Falls in the Grand Canyon; not really terrifying, but close, in water that strong, and dangerous.

And, While We're At It, How's About The Using Up Of Eight Of My Nine Lives???

Really Biggies (1, 2)

High Altitude Cerebral Edema (H.A.C.E), Hans Meyer Cave, 16,900 feet, Kilimanjaro, 2002.

Pulmonary Embolism, Krakow, Poland, 2003.

In the Catskills (3-5)

'Way back, on that Winter's day when I jumped up on the big flat rock at the head of Kaaterskill Falls and it was covered with glare ice. I have *no* idea how I stopped myself from sliding over the edge.

Flying off an ice-covered ledge, hidden by a little bit of snow, coming down the east face of Plateau, heading down to Mink Hollow.

Above Mink Hollow, heading up the very steep west slope of Plateau as it was getting dark and temps were going to be in the 30's after dark, with no chance of making it over Plateau to Route 214 with *no* overnight gear whatsoever.

Cars (6-8):

In the Corvette down in Florida, the kids in the back, passing some kind of beater Chevy (???) that swerved left right across the road in front of us. Locked up the brakes, have no idea how we missed it...

In the red '91 Honda SI, turning right, swinging north on Route 9 out of Annsville Circle. Somehow a car decided to stay in the circle, and was suddenly right there, in front of us. Locked up the brakes, saved the Honda, and us...

In Aunt Stella's Neon, Kath and I heading north on the Taconic, a car pulled across the Parkway from a side road to the left, smack in front of us. I don't recall if I had time to hit the brakes, but I swerved and the ass end of the Neon got sideways, then I reflexively pulled off a perfect Skip Barber Driving School CPR: Correct, *Pause* (if you don't the car will spin the other way...), Recover...

Poems

Looking out the window on Monday, April 4, 2011:

Can a day
be more dreary
than this,
I ask.
Wait'll Tuesday.

The Weather, 2011

January

Oh no,
It's four below.
What're we going to do
With all this snow???

March

Oh my,
It's the Fourth of July.
And the God-damned snow
Is still piled high.

May

> When April showers,
> Finally came our way.
> They just kept coming,
> ' Til the end of May.

This was published in the Spring/Summer 1989 edition of the ADK 46'R magazine **ADIRONDACK PEEKS**:

#47, Sat. July 20, 1985

I climbed MacNaughton on Saturday.
I wonder how long 'fore the scars go away.

The weather was perfect, a fine Summer day.
Tho the morning was blustery, cloudy and grey.

The 6.7 miles to Wallface Pond went quickly,
then I started the bushwhack, and things got prickly.

I stuck to the bearing of two forty-five,
battling the cripplebush, which was tearing my hide.

I gained the ridgeline, minus some skin,
wondering which direction the true summit was in.

There's the register, looking shiny and red.
Now it's time for the blackflies to be fed.

Number 47, MacNaughton, you're mine!
Now if only Wallface Pond again I can find.

Sixty-five degrees did it, I'm on my way,
and a long swim at Rocky Falls rounds out the day.

Ralph Ferrusi, #2023

On Being 78....

First things first: it's *impossible* that almost eight decades have slipped by, and I'm less than two years from being 80 years old; I still feel like I'm just outta high school. Mom and Pop both lived to be 94, and this is, kind of, a "benchmark" for me. I could live 16 more years, though it's certainly not a given: at 78 I am more and more aware of my mortality, and it could be 16 months, 16 weeks, 16 days, 16 hours, 16 minutes. Or, 16 seconds; maybe this is why I am so compelled to be doing all this writing???

At any rate, I'm in the last 16 (or so) years of my life, and I think about what the first 16 years were like; learning, growing: to read, to walk and talk, to see, hear, smell, experience new things, people, places... And, take all this for granted: it was going to last forever, then.

Now??? Prostate cancer. Cataract surgery right around the corner. Dental problems all the time; I have very few original teeth left. My hearing has greatly diminished. I've been reading the obituaries for quite awhile, and just about every day there are people my age, plus or minus a few years, who woke up for the last time, and are little piles of ashes somewhere, or, a memorial bench on the rail trail.

I don't morbidly dwell on this, but the other day I wondered, pretty seriously, for the first time, what was going to happen to my bicycle, my little car, my books, my tools, my Levi's???

This all sounds pretty silly and trite now. Maybe I'll get around to polishing it up a bit. But, the clock is ticking, isn't it?????

Wednesday Morning, December 9, 2015

5:25 AM: Awakened by Kath's go-to-work alarm. Get up and pee, then go back to bed and roll over.

6:15 AM: Ask Kath to put ear drops in both ears, hopefully to soften up excessive wax buildup.

6:30 AM: Put Refresh eye drops in both eyes, to help eye dryness.

6:30 AM: Do a series of six stretches while the eye drops settle. I do these daily to try to keep my back supple.

7:00 AM: Wash my hair with a CVS coal tar concoction to try to get rid of a persistent itchy/scaly/dry scalp.

7:30 AM: Breakfast. With six pills: two prescription blood pressure pills, a full-sized aspirin, B-12, Gingko, and C/D.

8:00 AM: Prescription eye drops in right eye for November 23 cataract operation.

9:30 AM: Appointment with optometrist to check my right eye: it's been badly blurred for about two weeks.

Monday: Dentist @ 8:00 AM
             Audiologist @ 2:00 PM

10 or 20 years ago this would have read: "Alarm...Breakfast"..............

2016

2016 outdid itself as a generally shitty year. Here's a walk through my 2016 *Downton Abbey* engagement calendar:

New Year's Day 2016: I came down with a *horrible* sore throat that persisted for the first 20 days of the year. January 2nd we went to the Putnam Hospital ER. This highly selective disease affected some people extremely, but the majority were immune to it. I had an awful cough, and I couldn't sleep. I began thinking of it as "The Misery", and despaired that it would never go away. Finally, on January 19th, my "miserable days count" in the 2016 engagement calendar ended. But, the first three weeks of 2016—5.77% of the precious days of this year—were, to put it mildly, awful, and, an awful waste of life.

February 10th: the furnace died; twice. It would die again on February 22nd, at 12:22 AM.

February 15th: Meme died at 3:13 AM, almost exactly a month before her 105th birthday.

April 21st: I fell very hard on my bike on gravel on the Putnam Rail Trail.

May 20th I fell hard again—this time, thankfully on grass—because I was on the big ring and locked in the pedals when I left the parking lot.

April 27th: Smarty's Check Engine light came on. Hopewell Auto turned it off, and told me it had something to do with an emissions valve. June 2nd, then again on June 6th it came back on. I took it to Smart Center Fairfield, where it ultimately cost **$1,067.00**—and two trips to Fairfield—to have it fixed.

May 27th: I had two flat bike tires, on two different bikes. First the rear tire on Tom Best's beautiful brand new white/red/black loner RTB went dead flat while it sat overnight in the garage. Then the Klein's back tire blew *on the way* to the Putnam rail trail. These were the first two of **SEVEN FLAT TIRES** on three different bikes over an approximately three month period. Up to now one flat every year or two was "normal", especially when riding just about exclusively on rail trails.

September 4th the brand new rear tire that I had just put on Kath's Ironman exploded while I was pumping it up. Then, the Klein front tire went inexplicably flat after a WRSDRT ride.

September 12th the Klein's rear tire went flat for no reason at all right after I had lunch in Millerton.

September16th the Klein's rear tire blew after riding only three miles on the WRSDRT.

September 24ᵗʰ the Klein's rear tire inexplicably went flat as Kath and I were doing our first-ever ride on a nice day on the Goshen/Monroe rail trail.

May 28ᵗʰ: the Smart Car key vanished when we canoed down the Fishkill Creek. This would ultimately cost $330.00, and require two round-trips to the Smart Center in Fairfield, Connecticut.

On October 12ᵗʰ: Someone from the Caremount Medical Group informed me over the phone that a Cat Scan that Dr. Gerringer had prescribed had shown that my "thoracic aorta is enlarged", and I have "dense calcification in my coronary arteries"... Thundering Jesus, there's some serious things wrong with my heart!!! No one has talked to me in person about this. 20 mg Lipitor was prescribed; it's a "statin".

October 19ᵗʰ: **MY FUCKING WALLET *DISAPPEARED***, when I stopped for a sandwich at Rennie's Deli in Dover plains after a nice bike ride on the Harlem Valley Rail Trail. It has never reappeared.

* * *

There was only about 13 inches of snow the entire winter of 2015-2016. Previous years there were two-five feet of snow. It was the lousiest cross-country ski winter since I began skiing regularly.

The Summer of '016 was scorching hot much too often, with hardly any rain at all. It's the first summer I ever remember hating the sun...

As usual, I've had teeth problems all year, and right now there's some kind of annoying, lingering abscess in my upper left gum that antibiotics have not fixed. Next year will begin, as usual, with a visit—more likely several [expensive] visits—to Dr. Maiorana. Happy Fucking New Year...

It's December 19ᵗʰ now, and the above is certainly going to sound like a lot of whining. But, yesterday I couldn't find the fucking Smart Car car key, and went crazy looking for it, terrified that it had fucking vanished again....................

December 19, 2016

The Canyon of Heroes, 2009

The Yankees finally won another World Series in 2009, after a nine-year dry spell dating to 2000. On November 6, 2009 I traveled down to the Canyon of Heroes celebration parade.

I was brought up a Yankee fan. With the last name "Ferrusi", and a factory worker Dad in the DiMaggio/Rizzuto/Crosetti/Berra era, how could I not be? But, as time went by, I drifted from the fold. Dave Winfield was playing left field the last time I was at Yankee Stadium. I was reborn in 1996, at least in October 1998, 125 wins—'nough said.

Kath and I went to the Canyon of Heroes in '99, and actually glimpsed Jeter, Brosius, Knoblauch, Tino, Girardi, Bernie Williams, Paul O'Neil, Shane Spencer, Ricky LeDee, Strawberry, David Cone, Roger Clemens, El Duque, Mariano, Andy Pettitte.

After 2000 came the Long Nine Years. We were in Nepal in November 2001, trekking to Namche Bazaar, at 12,600 feet, right around the corner from our first glimpse of Everest, when we encountered an obnoxious Arizona Diamondbacks fan. I got huffed: "Don't bad mouth 26 World Series, jerk..." We were in Northern Ireland when the Yanks were up 3-0 on the Red Sox. I sweated through 2009, and was finally able to sleep after Game 6. Friday, 11/06/09 was a no-brainer.

I left home at 7:00 AM, 27 degrees. I had on my hikin' boots. I never expected to pat Derek Jeter on the back; I just wanted to be "part of it". I enjoyed the crisp walk from the parking lot in Cold Spring, New York, to the Metro North railroad station, the morning sun lighting up Storm King Mountain across the Hudson. I hooked up with Yankee-hatted Cold Springers Wendy, Bill, and Bob and we caught the 7:50 to Grand Central, then hailed a cab downtown—a great $5.00 apiece decision.

There was going to be about three million people in a ten-square block area. We were aware that even arriving at 9:00 AM, the odds were very high that we weren't even going to get close enough to *see*, much less recognize, a single Yankee.

113

We began following the crowd, but hardly anyone actually knew where they were going: *they* were following the crowd. On the plus side, millions just shuffled along, accepting their fate. On the minus side, there were a lot of Really Pushy People. Some people—mostly women about five feet tall—PUSHED.

We inched our way along the few side streets that weren't blocked off, but were inevitably turned back by police or security, then waded our way against the tide, to the next non-barriered street. I eventually became separated from my three companions, and ended up by a barrier a couple of hundred feet from Broadway, where I could at least see the buildings across the street.

A Wall-streeter told me people were lined up three-deep at the barriers at 7:00 AM, when I was just leaving home. At some point, someone jumped a barrier, setting off a mob-mentality stampede. I bailed: it wasn't worth getting trampled. I never got within a football-field length of the parade, or saw a Yankee, but just being there, and seeing a dark blue "**DiMaggio, 5**" t-shirt, was priceless.

Rewritten 07/30/2021

"Local Boy Makes Good"

Saturday night, January 28, 2017, at the New York B.A.S.S. Chapter Annual Awards Banquet at the Hilton Garden Inn in beautiful downtown Auburn, New York, Ralph Joseph Ferrusi III proudly accepted the Non-Boater Lunker*** of the Year award.

Some years (decades...) earlier, Ralph went fishin' on Oscawanna Lake with his grandfather, Ralph Joseph Ferrusi I (Pops), and caught his first-ever fish, a White Perch. Here's how Ralph III tells it:

> "...man was Pops proud !!...we put it in a bucket to take home and I was so happy and I just couldn't leave it alone.... well...the bucket spilled in the backseat and the fish slipped down behind the seat and I started howlin and Pops wasn't

quite as happy/proud as he was just seconds earlier....we
got home and got the Perch out from behind the seat...
unfortunately...Mr. Perch had expired, but we showed him
off to Grams, then he got buried in Pop's tomato garden..."

Ralph III's been a fisherman his entire life.

Around the same time, Pops took his son, Ralph Joseph Ferrusi II ("Junior")
fishin' out on the Hudson in a small, leaky, borrowed wooden rowboat.
Ralph II wasn't lucky at fishin', but boating caught on, and he has been a
"boater" his entire life, once upon a time zooming all up and down the
Hudson in his 14' fiberglass runabout, currently canoeing all up and down
the Hudson (and Beyond) in Kevlar or Royalex racing canoes.

Back to Ralph III:

> "I joined Ulster County Bassmasters in 1997, won my first
> Angler of the Year award in 2000, then went on to win the
> Angler of the Year award 12 more times in a row from 2005
> up to 2016 for my "lucky 13th" time..... I've been fishing in
> the New York Bass Federation on and off since 1998 when
> I found out about it through my Club.... Bass fishing has
> totally changed my entire life....."

Saturday morning, January 28, we picked up Ralph III and Ruby the Wonder
Dog in Saugerties and headed for the Thruway to Albany. We unanimously
agreed not to take the Thruway west from Albany: we'd take "the path less
traveled", and experience a slower-paced, quieter Americana on Route 20.
(A word to the wise here: we jumped off Exit 23 into Albany to pick up 20. It
seemed pretty innocent on the map, but Albany's western suburbs went on
and on and on, with endless traffic lights about every block or so). It seemed
to take forever for Route 20 to become a country road, but finally, we were
cruising through 1950's Americana: farms and small villages; hardly any
traffic at all. Amazin'...

Then, between Duanesburg and Esperance, traffic was stopped, dead, for
a long distance ahead: flashing red and blue lights all over the place, on

both sides of the road. We crept along, stop and go, at about two miles per hour, and finally could see something enormous up ahead, creeping along, pretty much taking up both sides of the road. What the heck??? Long story short, a small Friday, February 3rd newspaper article revealed it was a 350,000-pound (175 tons...) General Electric-built steam turbine on a 20-foot-wide 350-foot-long truck, on it's way to Pennsylvania.

It stopped dead in Esperance, and while we were stopped Ralph figured out a back-roads route that might allow us to get ahead of it, and we finally popped out on now-four-lanes Route 20, cruising up and down long rolling hills, often, amazingly in this day and age, the only car on the road, past big farms and through small towns and villages—Richfield Springs, Sangerfield, Cazenovia, Pompey—and finally into ultra-charming Skaneateles. By the way, somewhere along the way it started snowing: steady but light "lake effect" snow. Halfway between Skaneateles and Auburn we reached our night's lodging, Sue Dove's quiet, clean, comfortable Skaneateles Inn on 20.

A few words about Auburn and Cayuga County: Auburn—a great decent-sized upstate city, a place I might like to live—is perched right above, but not directly on Owasco Lake, the third (from the east) of eleven Finger Lakes. A quick geography lesson: The Finger Lakes, east to west: Otisco (small), Skaneateles, Owasco, Cayuga (the longest—40 miles), Seneca, Keuka, Canandaigua, then the much smaller, Honeoye, Canadice, Hemlock, and Conesus. All the lakes flow north into Lake Ontario.

Cayuga County is named for the Cayuga—"people of the wetlands"—Indian tribe, part of the Iroquois Federation. It has more freshwater coastline than any other New York State County.

Some name-dropping: Auburn was once the home of William H. Seward, co-founder of the Republican Party. Abner Doubleday, baseball's founder, spent much of his life in Auburn. Harriet Tubman settled in Auburn after the Civil War. Millard Fillmore, 13th US President, was born near the village of Moravia, just south of Owasco Lake. Henry Wells, founder of Wells Fargo and American Express, began his career in Port Byron, just north of Auburn.

Back to the Skaneateles Inn on 20: we checked in, cleaned up—there was plenty of nice *hot* water and nice thick white towels— relaxed a bit, then around 5:00 our Garmin led us to the Hilton Garden Inn. As we walked in, we ran into Chris, a fellow N.Y. B.A.S.S. Federation angler, that Ralph knew from the tournaments: good start. The banquet room was nicely set up, with a big table full of cheese, crackers, and veggies.

There were three speakers, all with different Bass-fishing slants: the first speaker provided all kinds of interesting facts and figures on how big fishing was in New York State, and how many billions of dollars it brought into the State's economy. Next, Joseph Sancho, from New Windsor, a Pro whose career Ralph had followed, elaborated on the pros—and cons—of becoming a fishing "pro". Finally there was a taped video of a Skeeter Boats sales rep, describing thousands of dollars in incentives if you placed in a tournament and used one of their boats.

Then, after a nice, filling buffet dinner, awards were handed out, and Kath and I beamed with pride as Ralph accepted the nifty Non-Boater Lunker of the Year plaque and check from Federation president Peter Knight. Pops woulda been sooo proud.

There were raffle tables full of fishin' "stuff" on both sides of the hall. Kath had bought some tickets, and the next thing we hear is "46026": that's us! 46026 popped up several more times, and we left the hall with about $300.00 worth of "swag"; Kath gave most of it to RIII.

The 24 Hours of Daytona was on TV back at the cozy motel. Later, I slept like a brick. We had a nice breakfast at the eat-where-the-locals-eat Hunter's Dinerant perched over the Owasco River on Genesee Street in Auburn, then headed over to the gigantic Bass Pro Shop on the other side of town. Finally, we headed east on Route 20, but jumped on the Thruway before the endless west Albany suburbs.

***A **BIG** fish: a VERY big fish...

"Grown Up"

Years ago I made a short list of things that I thought make a man "grown up". Here it is, in the order originally written, and pretty much as written:

> Owns a tux.
> Knows how to use chop sticks.
> Knows what to do with a wine cork that a waiter places on the table in front of you.
> Navigates a wine list with style.
> *Never* calls any woman over 20 a girl.
> Knows some basic phrases in French, Spanish, Italian (Polish, Russian, Japanese???)
> Knows how to cook/make salads/set a table.
> Is a good dancer.
> Doesn't wear white Jockey or BVD shorts.
> Knows that a Corvette isn't the end-all-be-all car...
> Doesn't call State Troopers "Sir"...
> Has *at least* been to Europe.
> Wears good shoes.
> Knows how to set a place setting...
> Owns a black Cashmere coat.

Lucy Jordan

I once took a correspondence writing course. It was the only formal writing course I've ever taken, and, I didn't finish it. I did learn a lot, especially about tightening up my writing. *2 North* and *Pop*—both included in the beginning of this book—were assignments.

Lucy Jordan, one of my rare works of fiction, was also an assignment. It was inspired by Marianne Faithful's haunting *Lucy Jordan,* that's part of the *Thelma and Louise* sound track.

My instructors felt it was evocative of Guy du Maupassant and Victor Hugo: High Praise!

It has never been published anywhere. Here it is:

Lucy Jordan

*"At the age of thirty-seven, she realized she'd never
Ride through Paris, in a sports car, with the warm wind in her hair..."*

She had watched *Thelma and Louise* last night, and couldn't get Marianne Faithful's words out of her head. She had 9 years to go to 37, and it was slowly dawning on her that her husband John really wasn't ever going to amount to much. He had been smart enough to seduce her when she was barely 18, but dumb enough to get her pregnant a few months later. After 10 years of marriage he had become dull and boring, sporting quite a pot belly at 30, dressing sloppily, spending much too much time drinking beer and watching sports on the TV. They never went anywhere or did anything. She would love to travel: Paris, London, Rome? John could care less. They had been to Disney World once.

He tinkered with his beater Chevy pickup, mowed the lawn, and steadily chopped down more and more trees on their once nicely wooded ¾ acre corner lot. He had decided to use the tall, mature maples and oaks for firewood, as if the small lot was a 3000-acre woodlot in Maine. She pleaded with him not to cut down any more trees; he ignored her. They had tacky Christmas lights attached to the front of their house year-round and a tacky above ground pool perched in the side of their ever-more-treeless yard.

Her prized possession was a maroon Dodge Caravan; yup, riding through Paris in a mini-van. The Chevy was up on jack stands for the third time this month, and he was underneath it, banging away at the rear brakes, trying to finally get them to work right. She didn't think he ever would.

She was standing on the street with the rest of the housewives, as they did 4:15 PM every school day, waiting for the bus to bring their kids home. She stood out from the band of bland, chubby, complacent housewives: lean and fit, long brown hair, cool shades and jeans. It was a warm mid-October day, and a runner went jogging by out on the main road about 30 feet away. He was tall, lean, and very fit: great legs, great not-yet-faded-from-the-Summer tan, fairly long hair, cool pair of shades. She had never seen him before. He ran past several times in the 15 or 20 minutes it took the school bus to arrive, obviously doing laps, looping through the non-dead end streets of the neighborhood. Her street was a dead end. Wasn't *that* just so symbolic. She continued prattling with the housewives, but watched him, trying not to be too obvious about it.

Several days later he ran by again, and she began to look forward to seeing him. One day she caught his eye, and nodded to him. He waved to her. Oh My... This became a regular event, and the other housewives teased her about it, and talked about how attractive "The Runner" was. She was careful not to acknowledge him if John was around; she wondered why. She occasionally saw him when she was out in the mini- van, and would catch his eye and wave, and he would smile and wave back. Damn, he was an attractive man. She saw him several times before winter came, and often wished that he would stop and talk to her, but he never did. The snows came, the roads got lousy, and he stopped coming by. She hoped he would show up again in the spring. She wondered who he was; what his name was, what his story was.

Spring finally came, and the housewives gathered back out on the streets to await the arrival of the school bus. *She* was awaiting the arrival of The Runner. Weeks went by; no runner. Finally, there he was. She waved. He waved. She wished he would stop. He didn't: Business as Usual. Months went by. One day she was out in the street talking to a neighbor, gesturing with her hands, and he went by several times. Then, he actually spoke to her! He exclaimed, "You talk with your hands!" She responded, "I can't help it, I'm Italian." They had actually *spoken* to each other!

She thought, "This is it, he just has to come over and talk to me. Please, please come over and let me see what you look like close up." He didn't, and the moment was lost. She continued the aimless conversation, resenting the woman. If *she* had left, *he* might have come over. For years he ran back and forth, and he never stopped. Finally, he disappeared. She thought that he had probably moved to Paris. She kept looking for him. She never saw him again, but she often thought about him, long, lean, wonderfully fit. She'd never forget him.

> *"So she let the phone keep ringing, as she sat there, softly singing*
> *Little nursery rhymes, she'd memorized, in her daddy's easy chair..."*

——— ——— ———

The woman at the school bus stop was one of the most beautiful, intriguing women he had ever seen, standing there in her boots, snug faded jeans, leather jacket, and sunglasses, a beacon amidst the bland tubbies and fatties. He always thought of her as "The Beautiful Housewife", and had yearned to sweep her away to Paris, to live happily ever after. It would never be: she was a wife, and the mother of two sons: he honored this status quo. His company had transferred him to Nowhere, Arkansas. He often thought about her. He would never see her again. He would never forget her.

> He would never share a bottle of wine with her.
> He would never dance with her.
> He would never make a salad for her.
> He would never wake up beside her in the morning.

So he let the phone keep ringing, as he sat there softly singing
A nursery rhyme, he'd memorized, on his momma's kitchen chair...

Kath's Retirement

Next Wednesday, December 21, 2016, Kath will retire from the Hudson Valley Federal Credit Union on the exact day she started, 35 years ago. Last night, Thursday, December 15th, there was a "retirement party" at the Poughkeepsie Grand Hotel.

It was a very warm occasion, and very well-attended. Sue spoke first, then Maureen Cairl—now retired, but one of Kath's closest fellow employees. I was next:

Kath and I met at the IBM Federal Credit Union trailers behind IBM's South Road Lab in 1984. Kath was a teller, and I was a computer programmer at Saint Francis Hospital, in Poughkeepsie.

I would stop in every two weeks to cash my paycheck, and soon became a regular in Kath's teller line. There were often times when other teller's lines were empty, and they would beckon me to come over, but I always politely declined and stayed in Kath's line. I was smitten (to put it mildly). We talked about travel: Europe, and Caribbean islands. I should note that I wasn't a "typical" white shirt/tie/ grey three-piece suit IBMer: I had hair down to my shoulders and a full beard, and arrived, winter or summer, rain or shine, on my bicycle.

I wanted to ask Kath out, but did not feel it was appropriate to do this at her place of work (or, maybe I simply didn't have the nerve). I tried to find her phone number, in phone books, and called information, without any luck (later she told me her phone number was under her maiden name; her "name tag" at her teller's station was her (former) married name).

Unable to call her, my recollection is I finally wrote a letter to her c/o the Credit Union branch. After this, we were able to talk on the phone. I asked her out, but she said she was seeing someone else. I persevered, and, finally, late in 1984, we met for lunch at the Ground Round, a steak house that had vegetarian options.

Long story short, we were married at the Oldstone Inn, overlooking the Hudson River, at high noon on Saturday, August 26, 1989. We honeymooned in Tahiti and Bora Bora.

Over the years we have visited 58 countries, in 23 (of the 24) Time Zones, on six (of the seven) continents.

On our 25th wedding anniversary in 2014 we returned to an island, treating ourselves to a week at the fancy Bay Gardens Beach Resort on Rodney Bay, in Saint Lucia.

As of today, we have been married 27 years, 3 months, 2 weeks, 5 days, and about 8 hours.

Next Thursday, December 22, 2016 the clock radio alarm will not go off at 5:55 AM. A new era, a new "life" will begin.

December 9, 2016

The Unicorn of Assateague Island

Six-year-old Wendy loved Unicorns. She was enormously excited when her dad told her they were going to camp for a week at the National Seashore Park on Assateague Island, home of the world-famous Assateague wild ponies.

When the Big Day finally came, they saw several ponies as they crept along the long 25-mph road to the park. As always, the ponies beside the road were often surrounded by picture-popping tourists, many of them ignoring the clearly posted warnings to stay 40 feet away, as the ponies could, and sometimes would, bite and kick.

Wendy thought, "What a perfect place for a unicorn to live." She had brought along the small stuffed unicorn that her beloved aunt and uncle had given her for Christmas.

She loved water, and their tent site at the Oceanside Campground was just over the dunes from the long, long beach, extending north and south for miles and miles along the Atlantic Ocean shoreline.

She loved the ocean, the waves, and the water, and they walked the beach and she frolicked in the gentle surf. In the evenings they cooked hot dogs on their camp stove, and toasted marshmallows, and at night they were lulled to sleep by the sound of the surf, just over the dunes.

Late one night, Wendy was wakened by a soft light outside the tent door. Her dad was sleeping soundly, and she quietly slipped out of her pink sleeping bag and quietly unzipped the door of their tent.

Standing right outside the nylon door was...softly glowing, a small white unicorn, surrounded by several Assateague ponies!!! She was stunned: she'd been correct: this *was* the perfect place for a unicorn to live, a very long barrier island, with miles and miles of untracked, unexplored wilderness.

Her father woke up, and was astonished by the group of ponies right outside their tent; amazingly, he did not comment on...the unicorn. How could he not see her??? Then, she realized he was a "grown up". She always knew unicorns existed, and that one day she would see one; but, not many grownups shared this belief.

Her dad warned her not to get close to the ponies, and when they soon wandered away, as if by some unspoken word, went back to his sleeping bag. Wendy said she wanted some air, and remained by the door. When she was sure he was asleep, she reached out and touched the unicorn, her small hand glowing softly as they made contact: this was *magic*.

Then the unicorn—Dora—spoke; very softly: "I came to you because you brought your own unicorn with you, so I knew where to find you, and that it was OK to show myself to you. The ponies take care of me, and make sure no one ever sees me. YOU can see me because you believe in unicorns. I have never seen another unicorn; when we have a chance, I would like to see yours. Oh, by the way, this is Misty, of Chincoteague."

Misty nodded...

Dora, along with Misty and their small entourage visited Wendy and her dad often in the evenings during their stay. Her father was quite surprised by the herd's interest in their campsite, and went along with Wendy's apparent conversation with her *stuffed* unicorn, now a regular attendee at their nightly dinners and marshmallow roasts. One evening, they even saw a Snowy Owl fly by.

Dora told Wendy that she lived in the mostly untracked part of the island between the south end of the paved Assateague road and the north end of the Chincoteague road that headed north from Virginia. She rarely ventured into the heavily-touristed areas of the island in daylight: being spotted by a "believer" would be a catastrophe. She also would not—could not???— venture onto the mainland, across the Verrazano bridge.

All too soon, their vacation was over. Wendy could not bear to leave Dora, who assured her she would know when she returned, and would seek her out.

As they drove along Route 611 leaving the island, her father, and dozens of tourists were astounded by the small herd of ponies keeping pace alongside his Prius. Just before the Verrazano Bridge across Sinepuxent Bay Wendy asked him to pull over and stop. She got out of the car, and walked over and hugged...a unicorn...that her dad then saw, with his very own eyes............ Dora walked over to him and said, "Great kid you have there, Roger. Come back soon..." Misty said, "I double that. Welcome to The Club..."

762 Words
February 28, 2020

Then And Now: April 1, 2013

Vision: no glasses, no reading glasses, no eye drops.
Teeth: lousy, but still had most of them, not crowns, bridges, root canals, partials.
Hair: thick, brown.
Hearing: much better than it is now.
Fitness, strength: invincible.
Digestive system: much better.
No blood pressure/cholesterol worries.
Urinary tract/bladder: slept all night, every night; no getting up one to several times a night.
Pills: didn't need any.

Scourges, etc

Taxes, bills; never ending.
No deer ticks/Lyme disease.
No terrorists, muslims.
No graffiti.

Downtown Peekskill, Brewster safe to walk in, anytime day or night.

Parent, uncles, aunts, many cousins still alive.

Gas about 30 cents a gallon—about $3.00 filled your tank.

A decent car cost $2000.00, and was made in Detroit.

No TV sickening violence, mind rot.

Blacks were in the south, Mexicans were in Mexico, Bolivians were in Bolivia, not Brewster.

A few small bags of groceries didn't cost $80.00 at the supermarket.

Things were Made in the USA.

You didn't have to press 1 for English.

The Jersey Turnpike didn't have to be 10 lanes wide.

The River, and, The City

"Welcome to the Hudson Valley! I'm Ralph, and I'm going to be your tour guide for the next four days."

2006-2008 I led hikers/walkers from 23 states, Canada, and Europe on a four-day Historic Hudson Valley Walk. We toured the FDR and Vanderbilt estates, the Millbrook Vineyards and Peter Wing's "castle", Innisfree and Wethersfield Gardens, hiked up to Cat Rocks on the Appalachian Trail, and had grilled cheese sandwiches and tomato soup at Uncle Sonny's in Standfordville.

I greeted them with a Hudson Valley overview: How the Hudson—"Muhheakunnuk": "the river that flows two ways" to the natives—is truly an estuary, a tidal body of water where salt water and fresh water meet and combine. How the Vanderbilts immigrated to the New World as indentured servants, and eventually owned 16 railroads, and various mansions, yachts, and race horses. How Henry Hudson sailed up the river in 1609, past the Walkway, seeking the fabled Northwest passage to India, where he hoped to pick up some vegetarian recipes for his sister Harriet.

I referred to the Hudson as "The River", and to New York City as "The City", quick to point out that I wasn't being snobby, putting down other rivers and cities—Paris, London, Rome, Des Moines, Saint Louis; the Seine, Thames,

Nile, Mississippi—rather this was simply the way us locals thought of "our" river, and the city at its mouth.

Kathy and I have had our share of "New York City Moments", once dancing to *New York, New York* in Sochi, on the Russian Riviera, the band playing it specifically for us two New Yorkers in the crowd. We've cross-country skied in Central Park, walked along the High Line, and along the East River up to Gracie Mansion. We rode the Five Borough on our mountain bikes, and I raced my fancy street bike in Central Park.

We've seen *Les Mis* several times, danced in the Rainbow Room, and dined at Cafe Des Artistes and The Tavern on the Green, and celebrated special occasions at Windows on the World. We've picked up fresh-baked bagels at Taal's, and dined at Angel's on the East Side. I saw the New York Yankees in the Canyon of Heroes in '09, and once spotted Paul Simon on a Manhattan street on Halloween, and Carly Simon getting out of a cab at Grand Central. You get the picture...

The River... Recently, while walking across the Bear Mountain Bridge, heading to the only zoo the 2,182-mile Appalachian Trail passes through, I stopped half-way across and looked up the Hudson, and was blindsided by an overwhelmingly powerful wave of emotion: how much this body of water has influenced my entire conscious life.

When we were kids, Pop took us fishing on the river in a leaky rowboat: Mom and Sis always caught more fish. As a teenager I swam at White Beach and "Beauty Rock". Grown up, I water-skied in Peekskill Bay. Even more grown up, we've canoed into the 79th Street Boat Basin, as if we owned it.

I've always been keenly aware of the Hudson's tides—high, or low—whether "reporting" them to my Dad at the Montrose VA before our weekly Friday rides, that always included the Steamboat Dock in Verplanck, or, nowadays when Kath and I go canoeing in Constitution Marsh.

"Tide's up, Pop...."

October 3, 2016
549 words

Eulogies

Pure Christine

In a too-short span of 93 days, my little world lost two very significant, very special people: a very extraordinary man, and a very extraordinary woman.

Christine always seemed to connect at a deeper level than most of the rest of us. She always had a strong connection with my Dad. Many years ago, Pop was rushed to the ER, and Chris was at his bedside with the rest of the family. None of us seemed to know what to do. Chris reached over and gently held his hand. Pure Christine.

Chris asked me for her very own copy of my book. I dedicated it to her, and signed off with 19 X's and 19 O's, the way I signed any cards and writings to her. She thanked me for the book in that quiet little voice of hers, smiled, and hugged the book. Later, Kath relayed Chris's review of the book: "Great Book! It put me right to sleep!" Pure Christine...

Chris had nicknames for a lot of people [so did Pop!]—not everyone, but a lot of us: "Pal", "Miss America", "Miss Angel". I joined the club while I was working on The Farm, feedin' cows, pitchin' hay. I had begun to call Christine "Spunky", and when Kath would hand me the phone to talk to Chris, I'd say "How's it going, Spunky Spunky Spunky!!!" She'd respond, "How's it going...Cow Man!" Pure Christine.

Pop was rushed to the ER on April 2, 2006. Six months later, to the day— October 2, 2006—Chris was admitted to Atlantic General. Pop left us July 3, 2006, 3:15 PM, just before the Holiday; Chris, October 4, 2006, 1:15 PM, three months later almost to the day, just before Columbus Day weekend. They were connected. They are together now, in a better place.

When I visit Pop in the cemetery, I always say three things to him. I'll say them now to Chris:

Love you a bunch, Princess.

Gonna miss you.
I'll see you in a bit........
I'll see you in a bit.

Meme Biourd: March 16, 1911-February 15, 2016

On March 16, 1911 a baby girl was born
in the tiny village of Lausaux, in North-Central France.
Her parents named her Madeline.

March 16, 2016

Johnny Rit, Sonny, and Patty

As of Saturday, August 29, 2015, I am the oldest living member—unless there's somebody out there in the wings somewhere that I don't know about, or don't recall—*of an entire Ferrusi/Mrozak/Ritornato generation.* It doesn't seem all that long ago that I was the fourth oldest, Sonny, Patty, and Johnny Rit were ahead of me.

Friday, July 11, 2014, Cousin June, Patty's wife, left a phone message that Patty had died "two days ago". Johnny Rit called us every once in a while, "checking in", and I called Sonny down in Florida every once in a while, but not all that often, but I hadn't contacted Patty in quite a while. I knew he was living in an assisted living place in Montrose, but figured he was OK in general; no health/sickness problems that I was aware of. It was a complete surprise to hear that he had died.

Tuesday morning, February 25, 2014, we were on the Jersey Turnpike coming home from Maryland when we received a (stat-icky) phone call on Kath's cell that, I thought at the time, Sonny had died. Sonny was the oldest, and had been dealing with Parkinson's for years, and he always told me when I called that his quality of life was, in a word, awful. We detoured right over to the Rit's house in Buchanan and offered our condolences to

"Young" Johnny, Mike, and Johnny's (or Mike's) daughter. It didn't register on me at first that "Old" Johnny wasn't there. It finally hit me, like a ton of bricks, that Johnny Rit had died. Johnny was one-of-a-kind, an icon, in the family, the community, and beyond.

I wrote the following, eulogy summing up my feelings. I would have liked to read it at the Catholic church service in Peekskill, but as in all Catholic funeral masses, family speaking time is limited to just about one adult, and, often in my experience, one grandchild. Such is life, and, the strict Catholic church rules. So, the filled-up-church congregation at large never heard this, but I did give a copy to Johnny and Mike:

My Cousin Johnny

JOHNNY RIT WAS ONE OF A KIND; LARGER THAN LIFE.

IT'S HARD FOR ME TO IMAGINE A WORLD WITHOUT JOHNNY RIT.

HE KNEW EVERYBODY, AND EVERYBODY KNEW HIM.

OUTWARDLY, HE WAS MACHO, OFTEN BLUNT, AND, PROFANE. HE WAS ONE OF THE FEW PEOPLE WHO, IN MY ADULT LIFE, CALLED ME "RALPHIE": "HEY RALPHIE, HOW YA DOIN' ???"

BUT, AS MANY OF YOU KNOW, BENEATH THAT ROUGH, TOUGH EXTERIOR WAS A BIG-HEARTED, VERY GENEROUS MAN.

MOM AND POP INSISTED THAT WHEN I WAS A LITTLE KID JOHNNY RIT HIT ME IN THE HEAD WITH A SLEDGEHAMMER. IMAGINE THIS LITTLE KID NOODLING ALONG AND JOHNNY WINDS UP AND SMACKS HIM IN THE SKULL WITH A SLEDGEHAMMER.

A COUPLE OF YEARS AGO I FELT MY FOREHEAD AND, THERE IS A DENT IN IT.

SO, I ASKED JOHNNY: "DID YOU REALLY HIT ME IN THE HEAD WITH A SLEDGEHAMMER???"

HE SAID, "YES I DID, RALPHIE, BUT I DIDN'T MEAN IT."

I'M PRETTY HAPPY WITH WHO I AM TODAY. I SAID, "THANKS JOHNNY: I WOULDN'T BE WHO I AM TODAY IF IT WASN'T FOR YOU."

THERE'S PROBABLY QUITE A FEW OF YOU OUT THERE RIGHT NOW WHO COULD SAY THE SAME THING.

IT'S HARD FOR ME TO IMAGINE A WORLD WITHOUT "OLD" JOHNNY RIT.

THERE'S PROBABLY QUITE A FEW OF YOU OUT THERE RIGHT NOW WHO WOULD SAY THE SAME THING.

Ralph J. Ferrusi Jr., February 28, 2014

Saturday, August 29, 2015, Toni Ann, down in Florida, called to say Sonny had died. When Toni Ann said "Hello", I knew what she was going to say. I immediately made arrangements to fly to Fort Lauderdale, get a room in a motel, and rent a car. At some time I wrote my heart-felt feelings about Sonny: about Indian Point Road and the Clayhole and Sonny, Joey, Patty, Ronald, and Johnny being the older kids and me being the youngest, and about what a gentleman Sonny always was, and about how he and Pop and Ronald had hooked up in Hawaii in 1945 during World War II.

I figured this was on my computer, but I have not been able to find it, and, right now truly don't recall whether I wrote it on a piece of paper, or in an e-mail; point is, I can't find it. I did tell Shelly that I wanted to speak at some time during the wake/funeral. At the wake, Todd tried to talk about his Dad, but broke down, and (the funeral director???) asked if anyone else wanted to speak. Surprisingly to me, there was a long silence. I was sitting in the back of the room, and Shelly, up front, caught my eye with a questioning look.

In my experience, it is not common practice to speak at wakes, so I did not have a copy of my eulogy with me, and felt I could not "wing it": I need a written copy to do it justice and not leave out anything. I shook my head "No." Shelly turned away, disappointed. I felt that I had missed my chance, as I knew I would not be able to speak at the funeral mass.

Todd spoke eloquently at the mass, with Shelly, Marcy, and Toni Ann with him at the podium on the altar, and a young man, one of the grand kids, spoke brilliantly about his grandfather. After the mass, we all went to an Italian restaurant, where the wonderful food kept coming and coming. As it was a public setting—people were getting take-out at the counter—I felt, again, that I had missed my chance, thinking it would not be appropriate, but at some point Shelly asked me to, and I agreed, and Shelly announced, "Cousin Ralphie has a few words to say...".

The place became silent, and I talked about about Indian Point Road and the Clayhole and Sonny, Joey, Patty, Ronald, and Johnny being the older kids and me being the youngest, and about what a gentleman Sonny always was, and about how he and Pop and Ronald had hooked up in Hawaii in 1945 during World War II.............

I'm now the oldest living member of this particular Ferrusi/Mrozak/Ritornato generation: no parents, no aunts and uncles, no older cousins. Kathryn, up in Connecticut, is the next oldest, then Sis. Here are the families, as I remember them:

Mrozak/Ferrusi/Ritornato

Mom and Pop; Aunt Lil and Uncle Pete; Aunt Mary and Uncle John; Uncle Pat and Aunt Mary; Uncle John and Aunt Helen; Uncle Harry and Aunt Ann.

Me and Sis; Katherine and Peter; Nita, Sonny, Johnny Rit; Joey, Henry, Ronald, Patty; [????]; John Mrozak.

A Few Good Words

ON JANUARY 5, 1942, 23-YEAR-OLD PHILIP DUANE REED OF SYRACUSE, NEW YORK ENLISTED IN THE UNITED STATES MARINE CORPS.

ON AUGUST 7, 1942, CORPORAL REED LANDED ON RED BEACH, GUADALCANAL, 3rd, BATTALION, 3rd, PLATOON, FIRST MARINE DIVISION, UNITED STATES MARINE CORPS.

GUADALCANAL IS 8,359 MILES FROM CORPORAL REED'S SYRACUSE, NEW YORK HOMETOWN.

HE MANNED A 30-CALIBRE WATER-COOLED MACHINE GUN ON EDSON'S "BLOODY RIDGE", OVERLOOKING HENDERSON FIELD.

HE WITNESSED THE UNITED STATES NAVY BEING BADLY TROUNCED IN SAVO SOUND, SOON TO BECOME KNOW AS "IRON BOTTOM SOUND", FOR ALL THE SHIPS—ALL TOO MANY OF THEM UNITED STATES NAVY CRUISERS AND DESTROYERS—LYING ON THE BOTTOM.

THINK ABOUT THIS: 23-YEARS-OLD, 8,000 MILES FROM HOME, WATCHING, WITH YOUR OWN EYES, *RIGHT DOWN THERE*, UNITED STATES NAVY WARSHIPS BEING *BLASTED* OUT OF THE WATER. HE VERY RARELY TALKED ABOUT THIS.

ONCE A MARINE, ALWAYS A MARINE: SEMPER FI, CORPORAL REED.

SEMPER FI...

Ralph Joseph Ferrusi
November 18, 2018

SOME WORDS OF TRUE WISDOM, AND, SOME FUNNY THINGS

We are in the beginning of mass extinction, and all you can talk about is money and fairy tales of eternal economic growth. How dare you. (Greta Thunberg, *TIME* magazine PERSON of the YEAR 2019, speaking to the United Nations General Assembly)

"In the past two decades, breast cancer has claimed more lives than the total fatalities of the Korean War, the Vietnam War, World War I, and World War II combined." (*Journal of the American Medical Association*, 1995)

The goal of living is to grow. (e. e. cummings)

There's only one pie; it's how you slice it. (A "hiking buddy")

You can always tell the class of person from the class of dog. (Flannery O'Connor)

Erectile Dysfunction: Like trying to stick a wet noodle up a wildcat's ass! (???!!!)

Another shitty day in Paradise. (A friend)

SSDD: Same Shit, Different Day (yup...)

Meet the new boss; same as the old boss. (The Who)

You don't always get what you want; you get what you need. (The Rolling Stones)

Greed, and stupidity, will prevail.   (Me)

The problem is, we're all essentially large, bratty   (Amy Alkon,
children. We want what we want when we want it.   columnist)

If you put cheese on a brick, it'll [the brick] taste   (A contractor)
good.

Life is seldom fair. War never is.   (Andy Rooney,
                                                        My War)

[Philosophers are] good at asking questions;   (Shannon Moffett
they're usually very bad at giving answers.   quoted, (*The Three-
                                                        Pound Enigma*)

Whether you're white, black, red, yellow, gay, lesbian, (A magazine ad)
straight.....you're either an asshole or you're not.

There's nothing as overrated as a piece of ass, and   (A classmate)
nothing as underrated as a good shit.

Some days you eat the bear, some days the bear   (A fellow canoe racer)
eats you.

Never underestimate the power of ignorance.   (A receptionist)

Men are like snowstorms; you never know how   (A co-worker)
many inches you'll get, or how long they'll last.

Youth is a blunder, manhood is a struggle, and   (Alfred North
old age is regret.   Whitehead)

I wonder what the poor people are doing today??? (A relative, while on
                                                        vacation)

[watching] freakishly large, overpaid men with histories of substance abuse and beating their girlfriends slam violently into each other...

(A magazine, describing American football)

Our doctor's offices, our hospitals, our cemeteries are filled with folks who think (thought) binge-watching football and stuffing their pie holes with, well, pie (pizza and otherwise) is (was) 'living the life'.

(Ditto)

We will remain the Home of the Free, As long as we remain the Home of the Brave.

(?????)

It's just that all that technology stuffed into one place kind of gives me the techno-creeps. I really hate being at the mercy of technology and its everlasting characteristic of stabbing you in the back when you have to depend on it.

(A magazine article)

For a woman the time is often the time. After the time it is sometimes still the time, but before the time, it is never the time.

(*Mirror of Venus*, Wingate Paine, 1968)

I'm sick of the abuse of language and what it says about us...We are indeed a nation of pinheads and ciphers, rats loose in the mall. Perhaps we deserve what we are getting. Rubbish passes for communication. Hype, spin, cant and deception are everywhere. Technological advances are making it ever easier to say nothing of consequence to one another—and to offend and intrude in the process. And civility is out of place in a self-absorbed lifestyle. Whose concept of the good life is this? What moral hack wrote this script?

(An old friend)

...thanks to a...bar association judgement against an attorney who mistook me for an ATM machine...

(The same old friend)

If you're not bleedin' you're not working.

(Someone who does *real* work, outdoors, using his hands and his back)

If our ship appears to be sinking, it's OK to request divine interventions, but don't forget to <u>keep rowing</u>.

(???)

On the day Rick Danko was born, the angels sang. Rick sang harmony.

(In Memory of Rick Danko)

Communion with nature is the most authentic form of spiritual pursuit. All else is elaboration, embroidery.

(*Catskill Rambles*, Kenneth Wapner, 1992, Page 185)

The popular Earth Day cliché...of nature harmoniously balanced (an interwoven, interdependent, symphonic complex euphorically floating in a photosynthetic ambrosia) is simple-minded and regressive.

(*Catskill Rambles*, Kenneth Wapner, 1992, Page 191)

The Bear Mountain Zoo: "Last time I was at the zoo I was really impressed. They were doing a great job with their docent program and just overall I thought the zoo was really spiffed up and lovely. I've been going there since the 1960s (first few times were in a stroller—I can only dimly remember at about age 3 someone complimenting my mom on what a cute little BOY she had, and I cried."

(An e-mail)

I often thought of birding, being up on a branch of a tree in my underwear and interacting with the birds. (A good friend)

All movement ceased and everyone turned to stare. It was as though Sophia Loren, in a bright red cocktail dress, had just walked provocatively through a garden party of English schoolgirls. (A magazine article)

I didn't know whether to shit, go blind, or wind my watch... (???)

Our 10-year-old son masturbates when he goes to bed at night. It keeps him awake for an hour or more and as a result he is not getting enough sleep. (An Advice Column question)

I was talking to my radar detector this morning. Afterwards, I thought, "Is this NORMAL??? Have I been on the road too long???" (Me)

Every day you wake up above ground and your car's check engine light isn't on is a blessing. (Me)

YOU CAN'T FIX STUPID MY OTHER CAR IS A PIECE OF SHIT TOO (Bumper stickers)

Nice people make nice drunks.
Nasty people make nasty drunks. ????, sometime in 2019

We admire Jim, Jack, and Johnny:
Jim Beam, Jack Daniels, and Johnny Walker (At a distillery in Scotland)

And in a mystery to be   (e. e. cummings)
When time from time
Shall set us free
Forgetting me
Remember me

Friends don't let friends hike in white shorts.   (After a group hike in
the Catskills)

"Under a cheddar-colored moon that rose   (*THE HAPPY ISLES*
through black shreds of cloud and glimmered in   *OF OCEANIA,*
shattered light on a rippling tropic sea…"   *PADDLING THE*
PACIFIC, Paul
Theroux, 1992, Page
386) I guess you hadda
be there…

"Generally, the traveler is anonymous, ignorant,   (*THE HAPPY ISLES*
easy to deceive, at the mercy of the people he or   *OF OCEANIA,*
she travels among…A traveler was conspicuous   *PADDLING THE*
for being a stranger, and consequently was   *PACIFIC,* Paul
vulnerable."   Theroux, 1992,
Page 446)

"Metro North: Where happiness goes to die"   (A newspaper column)
and, "The only thing worse than going into a
public restroom is not being able to get into a
public restroom. The 'occupied' sign might as
well say 'Ha ha!' It mocks you as you use every
muscle in your body to stop from doing the wee
wee dance in front of strangers."

"I've heard all kinds of horror stories from friends who had important phone calls interrupted by flu-ridden kids walking into the room and blasting breakfast, lunch and dinner from both ends like some kind of super-charged garbage disposal stuck in reverse." (Another newspaper column)

"...Billy was a hardscrabble country boy, maybe forty years old, lean and furtive, like a fox and a squirrel had a kid..." (Lee Child, *The Midnight Line*)

"Marine: Muscles A Requirement, Intellect Not Essential Army: Aren't Ready for the Marines Yet" (Lee Child, *Blue Moon*)

"...[she] had already gained some celebrity through her travel writing, and a great deal more on account of her vagina." (Ben Macintyre, *Agent Sonya*)

"...writing a daily newspaper column: It's like being married to a nymphomaniac. The first two weeks it's fun." (Lewis Grizzard, *They Tore Out My Heart & Stomped That Sucker Flat*)

"[Like]...an ant farting in a windstorm." (*The Ultimatum*, Dick Wolf, 2015, Page 281)

"If people concentrated on the really important things in life there'd be a shortage of fishing poles." (Don Larson, QUOTEABLE QUOTES, Readers Digest)

"This was a filthy, disgusting piece of perversion and I loved every word."

(Jennifer Weiner, commenting on Fanny Merkin's *Fifty Shames of Earl Grey*)

"...every word [she] wrote was a lie, including 'and' and 'the'."

(From Nora Ephron's *Imaginary Friends*)

Wannabe writers use words like "pelucid" and "cerulean" in the New York Times Travel Section. Stunningly brilliant writers like Nora Ephron create phrases like "This man would have sex with a venetian blind.", and "...screaming and cursing at each other and killing turtles."

(Me, June 28, 2021)

Once upon a time I wrote "two letters to advice columnists" goofs. I am going to break my "no sex rule" for this document by including them, but at this time I feel they are funny, and clever enough, to include:

> *I'm a normal, red-blooded American male. I think about sex every 37 seconds or so, and am often hornier than a three-peckered goat in a forest fire.*

> *Fairly recently I've crossed paths with two bona-fide, card-carrying lesbians.*

> *Dominique and Angelique (not their real names) are both very attractive. Dominique is slender, with a cute little ass and a Kevin Bacon strut. Angelique is tall, with long, tanned legs, and beautiful shoulders.*

> *I consider both D&A good friends, have visited both of them at home, had lunch, hugged them, enjoyed walks, and met both their (blend in with the wallpaper) partners—D&A are definitely the Pick of the Litter(s).*

I must admit to having "prurient thoughts" about both of them. They are, physically, women: they have all the required plumbing and accessories, and could never be mistaken for longshoremen or long-haul truckers, but I find my attraction confusing. Hell (make that "my goodness"....), they shouldn't be the least bit interested in me—a guy—they like women.

Irregardless (love that non-word), I wouldn't mind a roll in the hay with either (or both) of them, however that would shake out.

Whaddaya think, Advice Goddess???

My new girlfriend Svetlana, she's from Yugoslavakia or someplace like that, is a contortionist. She can bend over backwards so her head comes out in front of her belly button and then she can reach down and paint her toenails. Things like that. She has one of those little "Smart" cars, and the other day she said we should "do it" in the car.

Well, she really got into it, and when everything came to The Grand Finale she kicked off the rear view mirror, the glove box door, and kicked out the back window, all at the same time. As I said, she's a contortionist, but she still had a helluva time getting her head out from between the gas and brake pedals, and one of her legs was stuck under the emergency brake.

She said all the damage was my fault and I should pay for it, even though she left her 8-inch high heels on and I was just hanging on for dear life.

My question is, do you think that goofy little car really gets 50 miles per gallon??????

Newspaper column: Kathleen Norton's (Boomer Gal) "March is gone; where's spring?" column:

> Oh sure, there is a crocus or two scattered about in the mud. But you know what they say about the crocus. It struts its stuff, gives you hope and then... nothing.
>
> The little purple tramp.
>
> March, after all, is like the class clown of the calendar. It's fun to be around, but has trouble written all over it.

NPR: "And now, reporting directly from Egypt, Deborah Anus..." Did I hear right: Deborah *Anus*??? Is her husband Harry???	(Me)
Frank Sinatra gave a concert at the Paramount Theater in New York City, and the place was packed with "bobbie soxers" "who would not leave their seats even to go to the lavatory". The next day a newspaper columnist glibly reported "There wasn't a dry seat in the house..."	(???)
"England has finally decided to drive on the right hand side of the road. They're going to start with the trucks and buses first..."	(A British co-worker)
One should never start a fight with someone who has an unlimited supply of ink and newsprint.	(A writer...)
To the interest of our country, all inferior considerations must yield.	(George Washington!!! To me, this is another way of saying "My Country, Right or Wrong")

143

A magazine ad

It doesn't matter if you're male, female, or confused; black, white, brown, red, green, yellow; gay, lesbian; redneck cop, stoned; jibber, racer, weekend warrior, creeker, beginner, expert, ugly; military style, doggy style; fat, rich or poor; vegetarian or cannibal; bum, hippie, virgin; famous or drunk...you're either an asshole or you're not!

From my 70's "Nothing Book"

Back in the 70's I somehow ended up with a "Nothing" book: a 9' X 6" tan hardcover with an inch-worth of empty (nothing on them) pages. The idea was to fill them with your own versions of "nothing". Here's some of the poetry and profound thoughts—both mine and others—that ended up in mine, and, 40 years or so ago, influenced/shaped me; made me who I am/became today:

"o purple finch, please tell me why, this summer world (and you and i who love so much to live) must die" e. e. cummings, *73 poems* (#64)

"simplify..." h. d. thoreau

"all in green went my love riding, on a great horse of gold, into the silver dawn" e. e. cummings, *100 selected poems* (2)

"if a painter wished to see beauty that enraptures him...he has the power to create it...whatever lies in the universe—in essence or imagination—he has first in his mind and then in his hand..." leonardo da vinci

Newspaper clippings:

Liquid Air Corp. to Sell Farts.

PERSONALS: DEAR ANITA: We are switching to prune juice and will send you the results.

[This was in an e-mail, and is along the same line: "I used to kiss her on the lips, but I've left her behind for you."]

"elves have been known to hold a grudge for hundreds of years..."

"NEVER LAUGH AT LIVE DRAGONS"

"THE WORLD IS A COMEDY TO THOSE WHO FEEL AND A TRAGEDY TO THOSE WHO THINK" shakespeare

"there is more to life than increasing it's speed..."

"I HAVE ALL THE CONFIDENCE IN THE WORLD, BUT IT'S A VERY FRAGILE THING..." ferrusi, 1975...

"the BUY centennial..." ferrusi, 1976

"A MAN CAN MAKE THE SAME MISTAKES FOR YEARS, AND CALL IT EXPERIENCE" magazine ad

"he often argued that human intelligence was more trouble than it was worth. it was more destructive than creative, more confusing than revealing, more discouraging than satisfying, more spiteful than charitable." michael crichton, *the andromeda strain*

"what is forbidden...is not something eternal; it can change. that is why each of us has to find out for himself what is permitted and what is forbidden— forbidden for him." hermann hesse, *demian*

"the english language is a form of communication. conversation isn't just a crossfire where you've got to duck for your life and aim to kill. words aren't only bombs and bullets—they're little gifts, containing meanings." philip roth, alexander portnoy, *portnoy's complaint*

"**...that nobody had ever bothered to think deeply for her, neither loving, nor hating, nor in any way caring...**"

"when a man despoils a work of art we call him a vandal, when he despoils a work of nature we call him a developer," joseph wood krutch, quoted in colin fletcher's *the man who walked through time*

got a minute? I'd like you to read my autobiograpy... ferrusi, november 25, 1974

it's the american way

does <u>any</u> car (do you think?)
really <u>need</u> (do you think?)
thirty six taillights???
hell, I saw one (just yesterday)
that was getting along (just fine)
with only twenty two...

ferrusi, december 1, 1974

appalachian haiku

two thousand mile path
four million freedom footsteps
and the birds singing...!

heavy haiku

empty eyes, shuffling
feet...windy dark deserted
street...don't turn around...

humankind 1974:

they grow scared,
they grow scared,
they wear the bottoms of their trousers flared...

ferrusi, november 23, 1974

october u.s.a.:

I
I want
I want to live
I want to live
      in a world
            where people
                   don't
I want to live
      in a world
            where people don't
                 smash

I want to live
      in a world
            where people don't
          smash
                 pumpkins in the street...

                      ferrusi, november 23, 1974

so many things to do.
so much life to live.
god damn it time to go to work again...
                      ferrusi, january 13, 1975

monday morning(aware...):

walking across (that)
big cold foggy early morning empty
parking lot (and)
all that hair (and)
that fancy denim jacket
skinny
      splendid
            grinning
                proud
alive (dying, knowing) and
no boots (on) and
two different color wool socks (and)
only one
(brown
      leather
            $7.00 apiece)
glove
left of the pair....   ferrusi, november 11, 1974!

"I have wrapped my dreams in a silken cloth; and laid them away in a box of gold; and laid them away in a box of gold." (Me, The summer of '76........)

"Each person is his own way of growth...If a way becomes bigger than you, you have either made a wonderful discovery or an enormous mistake." (*A Catalog of the Ways People Grow*, Severin Peterson)

modern man: too much tension, not enough attention... ferrusi, july 29, 1976

"Everyone has inner voices, but it's hard to hear them over the din of normal life." (Joanne Kates, *The New York Times Travel*)

"I never love my fellow creatures better than when I am secure from their (???) and the smell of their cooking." (*At Home in Dordogne*, Frederic Raphael)

"He would have liked to ask her out to dinner or something. But the moment had been lost, and there is no social sin like poor timing."
"Jonathan watched the...jet...turn, and with a majestic conversion of power into pollution..."
"Neither heaven nor reincarnation attracts me. The one seems dull, the other undesirable."

(*The Eiger Sanction*, Trevanian)

"The huge Centrum [Moscow] department store smelled as though the clothes were made from wet dogs."

(*The Berlin Ball*, P. J. O'Rouke, *Rolling Stone*

A visible symbol of pure idiocy.

(???)

The flight attendants in back were saying the Lord's Prayer out loud.

(On a scrap of paper)

Page 47: "I had a crush on him for a while, the kind of crush you get when you get fed up with square dancing at the YWCA. He never knew, and it went away gradually, like athlete's foot."
Page 113: "...the fear that is never far from the hearts of affectionate people." Page 125: "[Laura] whose hair was straight and dull and who danced like the Washington Monument." Page 138: "...late July in New York [City] is the time when the hot days run in packs."

(*A Fine and Private Place*, Peter S. Beagle)

"If you walk down Fifth Avenue smelling of camel shit and talking to yourself you get avoided like the plague."

(*TRACKS*, Robyn Davidson)

Country Music Wisdom

I listened to country music awhile back in 2006-2007, and saved these "gems of wisdom". Following are four lines (max) of each:

I was drunk the day my mom got out of prison.

I Love This Bar

The front door swung wide open
and she flung her diamond ring
She said give it away,
just give it away.

I like my women just a little on the trashy side,
where they wear their clothes too tight,
and their hair is dyed.

She's got her daddy's money
her momma's good looks
more fun than a stack of comic books

And what became of what's her name,
after she spent all your money

I got a brand new girlfriend
flew out to LA for the weekend
spent the whole time on the beach
wearin' nuthin' but a smile

After eighteen years little pony tail girl grows up in the blink of an eye.
She left the suds in the bucket and the clothes hanging out on the line.

I'm not as good as I once was, but I'm as good once as I ever was.

Just you and me with the lights down low.
Nuthin' on but the radio.

The Lord made me hard to handle.
I've got a lot of leavin' left to do.

I want to do it all: see the Yankees play ball, see Paris in the fall.

We'll stick a boot in your ass
It's the American way.

I can't call in sick on Monday,
when the weekend's been too strong.
I work right through the holidays,
sometimes all night long.

I keep a close watch on this heart of mine (Boing Boing)
I keep my eyes wide open all the time (Boing Boing)
I keep the ends up for the ties that bind (Boing Boing)
Because you're mine, I walk the line.

It's five o'clock somewhere.

My give a damn's busted...

JB is a cross-country trucker.
He called last night from South Carolina.
He'd fallen in luv with a waitress,
that he met in a Waffle House diner.

My panty line shows, there's a run in my hose...

Takin' off my makeup.
Don't know why I bothered to even put it on.

You came upon me wave on wave

I took a Louisville Slugger to both headlights...

Ralph Joseph Ferrusi

Who's meetin' who
who's cheatin' who
who don't even care anymore.

From the day I left Milwaukee
...
You've done all the best things
you'll never remember
with me, alcohol…

Here's a quarter, call someone who cares.

My pappy said his pappy said
"In my day son, a man had to answer for the deeds that he done."

'cause I got friends in low places

A man came on the six o'clock news,
said somebody'd been busted,
somebody'd been abused,

somebody'd been arrested,

You gotta know when to hold 'em,
know when to fold 'em,
know when to walk away,
know when to ????

That Georgia rain,
on the Jasper County clay

One of my IBM "Out of the Office" e-mail notifications

"We found a really good deal on the Internet for an adventure trip to a remote Pacific atoll inhabited only by head-hunter pygmy cannibals, where we will swim with great white sharks in the lagoon during their mating season and rappel into active volcanoes. We're still really surprised at the low cost for this great adventure."

Not a single person questioned or commented on this...

And what do YOU do, Ralph???

The instructor at the Defensive Driving Course last night asked each of us to tell the class a little about ourselves: what we "do", how long we have been driving, how many crashes we have been in... I think most people get a bit nervous about these 30 seconds of you-are-on-the-spot/in-the-spotlight "public speaking", and I'm no exception. When my turn finally came, the instructor said, brightly, "and what do YOU do, Ralph???" I hesitated a heartbeat or two, and announced, "I'm a male lap dancer—I get paid to sit on women's laps."

The whole room got kinda quiet.......

Along this same line, I once found myself in a room with a bunch of well-dressed, but "snooty" women. One of them asked me "what I did". I hesitated one or two heartbeats (this has always seemed to me a good ploy to get people's undivided attention) and said, looking down towards my shoes, "I just got out of prison. If only those people in the convenience store had done what I told them..."

The room got very very quiet....

My All-time Favorite Limerick

There was a young man from Madras,
Whose balls were made out of brass,
When he clanged them together,
They played *Stormy Weather*,
And lightning shot out of his ass.

Farts

A newspaper column once reported that human beings fart on the average 17 (maybe it was 14) times a day!!! From a supermodel's gentle pooooof to a drunken biker's blow-out-the-seat-of-the-pants **BRAAAAAAPPPPP**??? Gawd, who did this study??? And, I would presume it was funded by the National Fart Association???

More Fart Facts:

Stick with me, baby, and you'll be farting through silk...   (Unknown)

Never pass up a toilet, never trust a fart, never waste a hard-on.   (From *The Bucket List*)

I once told my hiking buddy Pete that I fart less since I became a vegetarian. His heartfelt reply: "Oh, that's too bad...."

Paper Clips

It's 7:30 Monday morning. It had snowed all day Sunday, and there was a foot-and-a-half on the ground. It was still snowing very hard; six inches an hour. Alyssa was standing at the front door, all bundled up, her Jeep Cherokee keys in her hand.

Roger, her hubby: "What are you doing??? It's dangerous out there! The state has declared a snow emergency!!!"

Alyssa: "Roger, you *know* the first quarter paper clip usage report is due today. I *have* to get to work."

TRAVEL/ADVENTURE

When Kath and I first began seeing each other, one of the (many) things I found very attractive about her was our common interest in travel. She had been to Spain as a teenager, and to Mexico, Saint Kitts and Nevis, and several other Caribbean islands. I had never been to any of these places, but had been to France several times, and to Italy and Switzerland.

We did a three-week wine tour of France in 1985: the Loire, Bordeaux, Burgundy, and Champagne, and every year after that made at least One Big Trip. I realized that as time slipped by, I might not remember where we went and when, so I wrote them down. Here they are, year by year, with islands highlighted in **red**:

Our Vacations, 1985 To 2020

1985: France
1986: Montserrat
1987: Soviet Union
1988: British Virgin Islands
1989: Tahiti, Bora Bora +
1990: Mexico

1991: Nevis, Saint Kitts, Saba, Statia
1992: Tour de France
1993: Canada (Instead of Chile...)
1994: Grand Canyon +
1995: Portugal, Spain, Morocco
1996: Peru, Bolivia
1997: Yampa, Green, Utah, Colorado
1998: Gaspe, Canada
1999: Australia
2000: Ireland
2001: Nepal
2002: Kenya, Tanzania, Kilimanjaro
2003: Poland
2004: Venice, Croatia, Montenegro, Greece
2005: Prague, Czech/Slovak Republics
2006: New Zealand
2007: Costa Rica, Nicaragua
2008: Panama
2009: Belize, Guatemala
2010: Barbados, Dominica
2011: Mount Robson, Canada +
2012: Turkey
2013: Scotland
2014: Iceland, Saint Lucia
2015: Tuscany
2016: None...
2017: The Azores, and, a Baltic cruise: Denmark, Finland, Russia, Sweden, Estonia, Germany, Holland, Belgium, and England.
2018: Bulgaria, Romania, Serbia.
2019: Canaan Valley, West Virginia. Alaskan cruise: CANCELLED. Trans Atlantic cruise: CANCELLED.

A Tale of Two 777's

I first flew to Europe in the early 1970's—JFK to Charles de Gaulle—on Air France 747's: magnificent airplanes. The stewardesses—they were "stewardesses" then, not "flight attendants"—were all young, attractive white women: think of Cher. They were pleasant, courteous, and attentive, and, all nicely dressed, in the same snappy uniforms.

The tourist-class seats were comfortable and reasonably wide, and there was decent space between you and the seat back in front of you. You were given menus, and selected your meals.

All in all, a pretty positive experience, that I repeated several times over the years.

Fast forward to a 2016 (or so) American Airlines 777 tourist-class JFK to Heathrow flight. There was a stunning amount of people crammed 10-across (?) in the the rear of the plane. The seats were about a foot wide, and the seat back in front of you was just about right in your face. If you dropped anything, say your glasses, you would not be able to get to it until you left the plane.

Menus: you gotta be joking. The crappy food was plopped in front of you by a big-assed, overweight woman who could obviously not give a flying shit about you and who banged just about every seat on both sides as she rammed the food cart down the too-narrow aisle.

Her co-attendant—there were only two for the 800 long-suffering people crammed in the rear of the plane—was a young don't-give-a-shit with long dreadlocks. They weren't even dressed alike—some kind of generic sloppy clothes—and their indifference was astounding.

The entire experience can be summed up in one word—shitty—that I have absolutely no desire to repeat.

And, even more so because in 2012 we'd flown tourist class in a Turkish Airlines 777 to Istanbul, and were served by a half-dozen young, attractive, pleasant, courteous, extremely attentive, nicely-uniformed flight attendants. The seats were comfortable and reasonably wide, and there was decent space between you and the seat back in front of you. We were given menus, and selected our meals. They gave each of us little souvenir packets, and warm, moist towels to put on our faces.

All in all, a very very pleasant experience, that I would, and have, recommended to anyone who'll listen..

My New Favorite Place in the World

France was the first "foreign" country I visited, 'way back in the early Seventies, and I was completely smitten by Paris, returning time and time again. France became my first Favorite Country, and Paris my first Favorite Place in the World. I must note I haven't been to either Paris or France since 1992—remarkably, a quarter of a century—and have visited 61 other countries in the meantime, so if and when I return my impressions may change a bit; thinking about it, probably quite a bit.

An oft-told tale is that at dinner Kath and I occasionally talk about the many countries—and specific places—we have visited, and I once asked Kath to name a single country that came to mind of all the countries we had visited. I already had one in mind. She said, "New Zealand", and I agreed. So, New Zealand held my Best Place in the World for a long time.

Over the years, Slovenia jumped on The Country List, and Montecatini Terme (and Alto) in Tuscany and Rodney Bay in Saint Lucia were tops on the "Places" list.

Then we went to Terciera, in the Azores, for ten days or so in February 2017. This is going to sound silly, but my one word description of this place is "perfect". I've been "contributing" to John Vargo's *Boating on the Hudson and Beyond* since 2015. He's never "rejected" anything I've sent him, but he did say he would not publish the "Azores" article I sent him, because "it was too far away", or words to that effect. Anyway, here it is, and hopefully it will somewhat explain the "perfect":

Boating in the Azores: Paradise Found

We have little red stickum dots on the 32" X 50" Rand McNally world map on our dining room wall that indicate places we have set foot in/on. The dot furthest north is on Iceland; south, New Zealand's South Island; west, Kathmandu, Nepal; east, Tbilisi, Soviet Georgia. There are only two of the World's Time Zones—out of 24—without dots: the Middle East, and a chunk of the Pacific Ocean west of Hawaii with very very little landmass: Midway Island or American Samoa look like two of the few places that "normal" people could fly to and set foot on.

In late 2016 Kath e-mailed me "Would you like to go to the Azores in February 2017?" She'd come across a week-long Azores Getaways bargain trip to the Azores: $499.00 apiece included airfare, hotel, airport transfers, all breakfasts, taxes, and fees. I responded, "Let's go!!!" We jumped on it.

I knew approximately where the Azores were—west of Portugal, about ¾ of the way across the Atlantic—because I knew the US Army Air Force had built an air base in the Azores during World War II where US airplanes could land and refuel on their way to Europe. But, I really didn't know much else. Poking around the Internet showed lush, green, inviting landscapes, laced with something like 64 miles of hiking trails.

On our wall map, the Azores are indicated by two tiny dots: identified as Pico and Sao Miguel, about two inches (a thousand miles...) west of Portugal. On our illuminated one-foot-diameter World globe, there are three dots: Faial, Terceira, and Sao Miguel.

From the wall map, it looked as if we could paddle down the Hudson, through New York Harbor, and then (if we were out of our minds) head pretty much due east and run smack into the Azores. I'm glad we didn't try it, for two reasons. One, a closer look, at the globe showed if you went due east from the mouth of the Hudson you'd miss the Azores by a mile (or hundreds, to the north). Next stop would be Portugal, after another thousand miles of ocean. Second, it took our A-310 AirBus, traveling close to 600 mph, four hours and 15 minutes to get from Boston to the Azores. That translates into a really longggg time in a boat....

We told quite a few people we were going to the Azores. Only two people admitted to not knowing where they were—one confused them with the Aleutians—but I'd bet the farm that more than two were truly clueless about their location on the globe.

Here's a quick geography lesson. There are *nine* islands in the Azores Archipelago: from west to east: Flores, Corvo, Faial, Pico, Sao Jorge, Graciosa, Terceira, Sao Miguel, and Santa Maria. An "autonomous region" of Portugal, they're volcanic, and consist of three groups spread over 400 miles. "Remote, weather-beaten" Flores and Corvo are in the west. Grouped in the middle are Faial, Pico, Sao Jorge, Graciosa, and Terceira. East are Sao Miguel—the largest island—and Santa Maria. The regional capital, Ponta Delgada, is on Sao Miguel. Pico Alto, a 7,700-foot extinct volcano on Pico, is the highest point in Portugal. There are airports on five of the islands. We were going to Terceira, and were landing on Aeroporto das Lajes, aka the US air base. There was one "fly in the ointment": we were flying out of Logan, in Boston. Stay tuned...

We started receiving e-mails from Getaways: one of them listed "optional" excursions. I'm a little leery about these, since they're often a bit pricey and can soon bump a trip out of the bargain category. We looked them over, and agreed on three trips: a hike on the northern coast, a full-day bus tour of the island, and a boat trip out to two small "islets" near the town we'd be staying. As it turned out, the $238.40 was money very well spent.

The Big Day finally came. We had fretted for weeks about getting to Boston: we had never flown from Logan, and it had been buried in snow the week before we were to fly out. The weather was fine, and we cruised across I-84/I-90 until we entered a huge underground "parking lot", aka the long, long I-90 tunnels under Boston. Ugh....And, Logan's about the size of Rhode Island; why do I always think international airports are going to be, well, a reasonable size???

Soon, jet-lagged as hell, we were checking into the Angra Garden Hotel, on the main square in ultra-charming, white-washed-buildings/red-tile-roofed/cobblestoned-streets downtown Angra do Heroismo.

The next day we walked all over town. And the next we walked from our room, across town, and up hiking trails to the top of Monte Brasil, in a big beautiful Forest Preserve. We had excellent pizza at Agra Pizza on the way back. Next was a guided hike above the rugged, cliff-lined Bays of Aqualua on the north side of the island, and the following day was a guided full-day island tour in a BIG, modern bus, along the south coast, then up the east coast to the only other city on the island, Praia da Vitoria, then to a walk down *inside* a dormant volcano... Yikes!!! Another great day.

OK, let's head out into the Atlantic. The Ilheus das Cabras, "Islets of Goats", the largest islets in the Azores, are about a half-mile offshore, about four miles east of Angra do Heroismo. We boarded Ocean Emotion's cabin cruiser in Angra's well-protected marina. Our ship was a very fine, strong, sturdy craft: it was spotless, and looked brand new. Skipper Paulo Fernandes told me that it began life as a commercial fishing boat, in Gloucester. I immediately assumed Gloucester, Massachusetts, and was enormously impressed that this boat had come about 4000 miles across the Atlantic! I never did ask, but it probably came from Gloucester, England, a mere thousand miles away: still no slouch of an ocean crossing.

There was a pretty strong southeasterly wind, and we headed out directly into a pretty strong chop, with occasional whitecaps, not enough to bury the bow, but certainly enough to make things interesting. Our on-board marine biologist filled us in on the islet's history, facts and figures. Legend has it that goats were put on the islets "back in the day" before Terceira was inhabited, to see if they would survive. If they did, regular humans would give the main island a whirl (and, I thought, eventually us tourists would also).

The islets top out at 72 feet, but from the boat looked even higher. They are private property, and—if I heard this right—have been owned by six generations of the same family. They are inhabited only by birds—lots of them—and even if you could get permission, it is very very difficult to land on them. We went between them, and around them, and the skipper brought us—to me—surprisingly close to them: I was once even tempted to try to touch the rocks—dumb tourist—but wisely thought better of it. We were out for a couple of hours: all in all, a super trip out into the Atlantic!

Settled in back home, I put a new little red dot three-quarters of the way across the Atlantic on our dining room wall World map.

March 7, 2017
1,222 Words

OK, I wrote this with a slant towards convincing John that it had at least something to do with boating, and, tried to make some kind of connection to the Hudson. He didn't bite... The article ended up as pretty much a description of our trip, but it really didn't spend a lot of time gushing about the perfection of Terciera. Let's see if I can expand on this a bit.

Angra do Heroismo is a small city nestled in a bowl overlooking a picture-perfect small, protected harbor on the south coast of Terciera. In mid-February flowers were blooming, birds were singing, everything was lush and green, and we often wore t-shirts and shorts.

There is only one other "city" on the island, Praia da Vitoria, catty-corner across the island on the east coast. It's smaller than Angra, and has the only other beach on the island (Angra do Heroismo has a small, semi-circular beach at the end of the harbor: it was not very appealing to me in September, but there were a few hardy souls lounging on it and a guy actually swam out into the harbor).

Angra was ultra-charming: classic "old European" red-tile-roofs, cobble-stoned streets, low, pastel-colored or white-washed buildings, cafes and shops. We walked all over town, and never felt unsafe or threatened in any way. Hiking trails in The Forest Reserve and Leisure Area of Monte Brasil to the top of Monte Brasil were within easy walking distance of the main town square.

Right off the square was a big, picture-perfect public garden/park: for it's size one of the best I've ever seen. Half way to the Preserve was Agra Pizza, overlooking the bay, and serving excellent pizza: we stopped there twice for lunch. I don't recall seeing a single mall or fast-food place, any grafitti, or any run-down "slums" anywere in or around Agra (though I was very surprised to see a very small SUBWAY in Praia).

The main road north from Agra was nicely paved, soon heading through vast green pastures and very-lightly-inhabited farm country. And, from what I saw on our travels on the island, there are NO as we know them—e.g. the now-12-lane New Jersey Turnpike—INTERSTATES or expressways (though the beautiful, virtually traffic-less main road slicing across the island between Angra and Praia is (proudly) identified as a *Via Rapida/*

Expressway). The whole place was friendly and peaceful: no gotta-get-there-screw-you urgency/hustle/bustle. We were told *there are more cows than people on Terceira..*

There's plenty of hiking along the cliffs up north, there are eight other (relatively) nearby islands to explore, and, *some folks swim at the Angra beach all year 'round:* Frosting on the Cake...

November 26, 2017
1949 Words

Getting to Scotland, September 2013

From the pages of my "trip journal": Getting There Wasn't Half the Fun.

Page 1: 34 hours from the time we woke up 09/15/13 to the time we finally got to bed 09/16/13. Maybe two hours sleep in between.

American Airlines Triple Seven 300's—AWFUL. First Class/Business Class like kings and queens. The other hundreds and hundreds *crammed* into absurdly narrow spaces, elbows overlapping, knees against the back of the seat in front—AWFUL—6 awful hours. No sensation of flying/flight whatsoever—

Page 2: trapped in an enormously long aluminum tube—like a flying subway tunnel—with countless hapless souls. Turkish Airlines versus AA: AA can learn a lot about how to treat their "steerage" passengers from Turkish Airlines: Four *lovely*—yes lovely—gracious, (nicely) smiling, courteous, uniformed, pleasant, helpful Flight Attendants. AA: three or four dour, indifferent, mostly overweight, dread-locked, aged, dark-uniformed/un-uniformed "Flight Attendants".

Page 3: Warm, moist white face towels. Are you kidding??? First Class/Business Class probably had built-in hot tubs or saunas—us—misery. Food: Turkish Airlines—MENUS, really good, nicely presented decent meals. AA—crappy, tasteless agida-afterward *airline* food. Turkish Airlines: FOUR

STARS. AA: no stars... The mucky mucks who run AA should spend 6 hours in their 777-300 steerage sections...

Page 4: JFK/AA: chaos...mob scene. Self check in is bullshit—everybody clueless, confused—Heathrow: when you leave at approximately 8:00 EST, when you arrive at Heathrow it's 2:00-3:00 *AM* EST—the time of night the Gestapo was infamous for kicking down doors—particularly after 6-10 miserable/anxious/confused/unable to sleep/eat hours. Customs was a NIGHTMARE: I gasped out loud when

Page 5: we entered a football field-sized room jam-packed with tired hopeless/hapless souls, jet-lagged, sleep-deprived souls, trudging through 16—count 'em—16 long, long, long "bank corrals"—stupefying—followed by the "take off your shoes/belt/treated like criminals" British Security before boarding for Glasgow—horrible/degrading.

Page 6: The British Airways 767 was almost a delight. Window/aisle seats, *normal* personal space, elbow room/knee room, courteous Flight Attendants, normal-sized. You actually felt the sensations of *flying*—the power and rumble of the takeoff, getting to altitude, clouds...

Scotland—first glimpse through openings in the clouds—WOW! The sensation I just

Page 7: about universally feel when I first lay my eyes on a country I have never seen before (and this was about the 57th time I've experienced the feeling...).

Glasgow:
        Airport "normal" sized.
        Taxis "normal".
        Cabby: "No Problemo".
        Room: big, spacious, clean, big cozy comfy beds.
        Breakfast: filling.
        Weather: SHIT..

Rediscovered 01/19/2019
390 words

Alitalia

My wife Kathy and I have been traveling the world together since 1985. We've visited 58 countries, and have flown many airlines, but somehow had never flown Alitalia. Last November we booked a package trip to Tuscany that included round-trip JFK to Milan via Alitalia.

I'm of Italian heritage, and eagerly looked forward to my first flight on an Italian airline. After researching Alitalia's guidelines, we bought brand-new carry-ons for the flight that met Alitalia's specifications, and spent a great deal of time carefully packing them, making many compromises, as these were the only luggage we were bringing.

We checked in early at JFK—there was no one else in line—and my wife told the check-in woman TWICE that we wanted to carry on our tiny luggage. The woman told us to put them on the scale, then tagged them and quickly put them on the checked luggage conveyor, and they were whisked away. We were shocked, and told her (for the third time) we had wanted to carry them on. She said, "Too late…" and made no effort at all to stop the conveyor.

This was a TERRIBLE first impression of your airline. We were picking up a rental car at Malpensa, and had hoped to save a significant amount of time by not having to wait for checked luggage. As it turned out, it was TWO FULL HOURS from the time we exited the aircraft until we were finally on the road in the rental car. This was an extremely frustrating waste of time, and a terrible start to our long drive down to Montecatini Terme.

We are seasoned travelers and, as I said, I had really high hopes for Alitalia. I am not a chronic complainer, but I am very sorry to say that just about everything about our flights were, in a word, mediocre. *Every single one* of the flight attendants seemed distant and harried: surprisingly to me, *none* of them were in any way cordial, or personal. It's almost a cliche to complain about "airline food", but we've had some very decent meals over the years, but all the meals, on both of these flights, were, in a word, disappointing, both in packaging, presentation, and overall quality. Again, sorry to say, this was a huge surprise to me.

We loved Montecatini Terme; it really would have been nice if getting there and back had been a bit more pleasant.

Ten Guardian Angels; in *Belize!??*

Kath and I have "traveled the world", and have visited many "Third World" countries in Asia, Africa, Central America, and/or Mexico.

We'd been to Costa Rica and Nicaragua with a tour company in 2007 and to Panama in 2008 on a bargain package tour. In May 2009, having somewhat "learned the Central America ropes", we were ready to tackle Belize and Guatemala on our own. The Plan was to fly to Belize City, then head west across the country to the Guatemala border, traveling, as the locals did, on local buses, staying in modest local places, and eating where the locals ate.

As usual, we did our homework beforehand. The guidebooks weren't all that encouraging, particularly about areas in Belize City were we were advised to "Avoid deserted streets, even in daylight....Don't walk alone at night." Some sections were described as "...a favorite area for muggers..." On the bright side they did steer us to the "Toucan Trail": small hotels and guest houses all across Belize aimed at the "budget traveler".

In Belize City we checked in at the Hotel Mopan, a clean, inviting Toucan Trail hotel on Regent Street, a block east of Albert Street, the main north-south drag. We explored the small city—there was not really that much to write home about in general—then had dinner at Macy's Cafe on Bishop Street, a tiny five-table rice-and-beans local eatery. While we were there, two really tough-looking black guy local everyday citizens walked in with *handguns* strapped to their waists!!!

That night we made plans to get the first bus outta Dodge the next morning, and ride west 70 miles, just about across the entire country (about the same size as Massachusetts) to San Ignacio, a jumping-off point to Tikal, across the border in Guatemala.

The bus terminal was 15 blocks west across town from the guest house, and we asked at the Tourist Board if they thought it would be OK for us to walk there. They said it would be, but I was a bit uneasy about us two very obvious gringos ambling away from the more touristy coastal part of town with all our "worldly" goods in a couple of fair-sized backpacks: we "might, ummm, stand out" a bit. I'm always the "mother hen" when we hike, or travel. Even though this was an "adventure trip" (and, a "budget trip"), I felt, to be on the safe side, we should take a cab. Kath: "It'd be silly to take a cab 15 blocks, let's go."

So, we bit the bullet and walked. Once off main-drag Regent Street the neighborhoods began to look more like the DMZ than, say, Woodbury Commons. We walked down the center of the street, past boarded-up, burned-down, garbaged-up, falling-down building after building, and I truly began to doubt this walk was such a good idea.

Then, a tall scary-looking black man appeared out of nowhere and stopped right in front of us, blocking our way. We were, quite literally, about half-way between "normal" Regent Street and the crowded, busy, bustling bus station. If this guy intended to rob us—and/or kill us—we were pretty much isolated and vulnerable; burdened with fair-sized backpacks, we truly had no place to run, no place to hide.

He looked us over, then said, in a very polite voice, "Are you looking for the bus station???" He pointed: "It's straight ahead, right over there." He stepped aside, and we thanked him. We didn't know it at the time, but we had just encountered our first Belizian Guardian Angel....

The bus station, like most bus stations, Third World or not, was creepy, scary, chaotic, and confusing. We just kind of stood there, confused and uncertain. A black man approached us and asked us where we were going. "San Ignacio." "That's your bus, sir, right over there. You'd better hop on, it's leaving pretty soon."

We thanked him—Guardian Angel number two—and hustled over to the bus, and off we went, two gringos, heading across Belize on a "chicken bus" full of locals. (A quick word here about my impressions of Central American local buses: they are pretty much old worn-out American grammar school buses, with seats designed for 10-year-olds, and worn out springs and shock absorbers. Bathrooms??? Air conditioning??? Get Real....).

I really enjoyed the ride across Belize, fascinated by the locals using the bus (it stopped, it seemed, about every 30 feet)—ordinary people going to work, well-dressed business people, students, nuns, priests. I smiled and waved out the open windows at the locals along the road: they smiled and waved back. I don't recall talking to any of the other people on the bus (one guy really *did* bring a chicken aboard with him....), but as we were getting off the bus in San Ignacio, Franco —an older American ex-pat white guy—asked us if we had any plans.

We didn't. He told us to stay at Wally's—cottages owned by a former British paratrooper—to have breakfast at Pop's, told us where we could rent canoes, and to book a day trip to Guatemala at PACZ Tours, around the corner from Wally's. We thanked him very much, and headed down San Ignacio's main street. I immediately liked this town: small, pleasant, touristy, Colorado-like. We rented a wonderful little cottage at Wally's, thanks to Guardian Angel number three....

The 7.4 earthquake at 2:30 am that almost shook the cottage off its foundation is a whole other story, but the next day we walked around the corner to PACZ Tours, where co-owner Jamaal, a huge, black "dude" arranged a day trip to Tikal. 7:30 the next morning (after breakfast at Pops) we met Hugo, our guide for the day, who eased us across the Belize/Guatemala border as if we were crossing into Connecticut, or New Jersey.

In Guatemala, we all hooked up with Edgar, our local driver, and were welcomed aboard a shiny red air-conditioned Toyota van that looked as if it had just come off the showroom floor. Tikal, and Hugo and Edgar, were awesome. A super day. And, Guardian Angels number four, five, and six....

I really enjoyed our time in San Ignacio. When it became time to move on, we boarded a local bus headed east, our destination, Hopkins, a tiny town on the Caribbean coast. Kath's parents had told us their neighbor's son's wife's brother lived there, and he had been tipped off that if we happened to be "in the neighborhood", we might visit him.

About half-way back across Belize, the bus stopped in a big busy bus terminal in Belmopan, the country's capitol. Somehow I had figured the bus would take us straight to Hopkins. A guy in the terminal pretty much out of nowhere told us it didn't. He told us we would have to take the bus all the way to Dangriga, a small city on the coast, and then find our way down to Hopkins. Guardian Angel number seven. At this point I first became aware that something was going on: every time we needed a bit of help, a nudge, some important information or advice, someone—a stranger—somehow appeared, to help us, guide us, inform us.

We eventually ended up in a scary bus terminal in a seedy part of non-touristy Dangriga, pretty far north of Hopkins. What to do??? How to get to Hopkins??? Somehow we arranged for a couple of local guys with a pretty beat-up minivan to take us there, for what, at the time, was an astonishing amount of money compared to what everything else had cost us while we were eating-where-the-locals-ate/traveling-like-the-locals-traveled in Belize. And, at this point in the trip we were going 'way off the "beaten path", and this was, gulp, a real "leap of faith".

Once we left the (paved) "main road" (there were only about two or three in Belize at the time), we traveled about 14 miles or so on a narrow pot-holed dirt road east to Hopkins. And, at the end of the road, the "town" was, well, very basic: pretty much just a small scattering of dilapidated buildings. We were flummoxed.

The two guys in the minivan asked around—"English" was spoken in Belize, but it was not the kind of "English" we understood—and eventually found the place where the "relative" lived. I, naively, expected "the relative" to greet us with open arms, eager to chat about his relatives in Maryland, then probably cordially inviting us to stay over for a night or two. This last part was pretty important to us, as there weren't really any obvious-to-us places to stay in tiny Hopkins.

We were greeted at the door (and, *not* invited in) by an about-14-year-old Belize girl—his live-in "girl friend"??? I think I now knew why he had elected to be an "ex-pat" there—and were told he "wasn't available", or something like that, and, that he wouldn't be. End of story. See yah later, folks. Thanks a lot, unavailable creepy old fart... We were, pretty much, screwed.

But...the two guys with the minivan again asked around and found a very very nice place, with a kitchen, right on the beach run by a very nice Hopkins native that we never would have found on our own. Guardian Angels number eight and nine then drove off, and we had a very enjoyable stay for a couple of nights.

We local-bused back to Belize City, then water-taxied out to blissfully car-less—imagine, NO CARS—Cay Caulker, somehow, all without the help of a Guardian Angel (or two). As soon as we stepped off the dock at Caye Caulker, a local approached us offering to take us to a place to stay. My knee-jerk reaction to these guys is usually "No way, Jose,", but there was something about Sam that made us trust him. He led us to the aptly-named Tropical Paradise, a small collection of clean, spiffy, orange/yellow cabins, 150 feet from the Caribbean, with a porch, refrigerator, and A/C. Perfecto. A super way to wrap up a super trip. Thank you very much, Sam, aka Guardian Angel number ten............

Looking back, somehow, on this particular trip, we were "watched over", and very kind, helpful strangers just about always appeared when we needed them, or needed help. It has never happened, to this extent, before, or since. I'm not going to try to speculate how, or why, it happened. I am just aware that it *did* happen—these occurrences were more than mere coincidence—and I am very grateful they did.

March 14, 2016

An Extraordinary Day

Most of the days of our lives are pretty ordinary, filled with the "gotta's" of our daily routines. Every once in a while an <u>extra</u>ordinary day sneaks up on you. Friday, July 30, 2004 was one of these. Here's the story:

A couple of years ago Kathy decided that she wanted to paddle the whole length of the Hudson River, from its source at Lake Tear of the Clouds, at about 4200' elevation on the west slope of 5344' Mount Marcy in the Adirondacks, all the way to The Battery at the tip of Manhattan.

We would not do this all in one marathon shot; we would do it in sections, on day trips and maybe some overnight adventures, camping along the river. By July 30, 2004, we had paddled from the Troy Lock, just north of Albany, all the way to the public boat ramp at JFK Park in Yonkers, a distance of about 145 river miles. We had had a lot of good days on the river, but on days when the Hudson kicked up it got very exciting, and sometimes downright dangerous, dealing with big daunting waves and nasty whitecaps.

Today the plan was to catch an outgoing tide at Yonkers around 10–10:30 AM and to paddle to the George Washington Bridge, then turn back north to the Metro North train station at Spuyten Duyvil (the Dutch explored the Hudson, and this is one of many Dutch names along the river), where one of us would wait with the boat while the other took a train back to Yonkers to get the Subaru (if it hadn't been stolen...).

Kath and I would be paddling our 17' Sundowner: it has been our boat of choice for about 90% of our trips. It had proven itself to be the best boat during the Hudson's "uh-oh, here comes the wind and the whitecaps" moods. Tim Lewis agreed to join us, and would solo paddle his red 16' Penobscot. It took quite a while for all of us to get our acts together, but we somehow managed to arrive at the ramp at 10:30 AM, after picking up sandwiches at a Spanish deli in northern Yonkers.

The day was cloudy and grey, with a thick haze over the river. The wind was calm and so was the Hudson – very rare at 10:30 AM. The river typically calms down at night, and is calm early in the morning, but then kicks up more and more as the day progresses. We put in and headed out. The ramp faces north, and as we turned the corner and headed south, the George Washington Bridge, about 8 miles downriver, and the famous Manhattan skyline below it were invisible, obscured by the thick haze.

We settled into a strong, smooth rhythm, and quickly reached our first checkpoint, the Philipse Manor railroad station, a mile below the launch. Railroad tracks parallel the Hudson all the way to Spuyten Duyvil, and the stations make good, easy to spot checkpoints. Our next checkpoint was the Riverdale station, 4 miles from the ramp, and surprise, surprise, we were there in an hour. The outgoing tide was enhanced by a full moon, and was *very* strong. At this pace we could reach the GW Bridge in another hour.

The currents at Spuyten Duyvil—it translates to "Spirit of the Devil"—are some of the most treacherous on the whole Hudson. When the tide changes, all of Long Island Sound rushes in or out of the East River at Hell's Gate, and then meets the Atlantic Ocean water surging up the Hudson at Spuyten Duyvil.

I was very concerned about this notorious stretch of water, and very wary as we approached it. There were some very odd currents, swirls and bubbles, but in general the river remained as calm and placid as it had been all the way down from Yonkers, and we passed through the area uneventfully and started down the west shore of Manhattan Island, heading for the bridge 2 ½ miles to the south.

There is a park along the whole upper west side of Manhattan, with a bike path running along it. It is green and wooded, and from the low vantage point of a canoe seat, it looks as if Manhattan is a wonderful, green wooded paradise! We saw runners, and cyclists, and before we knew it, we were passing under the George Washington Bridge.

OK, it was Decision Time now. We had made really good time, and the 79th street boat basin, about ½ to 2/3 down the side of Manhattan, was now only about another hour or so south of us. It would be a real coup to reach it. But the river is Big Water down here; we're talking New York Harbor, and it <u>looks</u> big and intimidating. If the wind and the weather held, we would be fine; if not, not so fine…

Kath had a good idea; there was a wooded point a little ways ahead, and she suggested that we paddle around it and pull into the cove below it and discuss our options. We did, and, Holy Cow, there was a beach in the cove: a *beach*, on the Manhattan shore of the Hudson River!!! This was by no means a white-sand Caribbean beach, but it was a nice typical Hudson River beach. We pulled in and Kath spotted a picnic table a hundred feet north, with a dramatic view downriver of the Manhattan and Jersey shores, and a dramatic view upriver of the George Washington Bridge. There aren't many days you have a picnic in a spot like this!

We broke out the food and the highway map I had brought along, and discussed our options. We estimated that the boat basin was about another 4 miles below us, and that we could get there in around an hour, if nature continued to smile on us. After much deliberation and hemming and hawing, Kath suggested that we make a run for a prominent landmark about a mile downriver, where we could see how things were going and then make another decision. Good Plan.

We got to the landmark quickly, and nature was still smiling on us, so we decided to Go For It – the 79th Street Boat Basin – the only boat basin on the Hudson in downtown Manhattan. We all paddled well, and strongly, and waved to bicyclists, runners, tourists, and drug dealers on the bike path all the way to the boat basin.

The boat basin sports a lot of big fancy yachts and ships, but we paddled our canoes into it as if we owned the place. We pulled right up to the best mooring spot all the way inside the basin and tied the boats up. Yowzah, we had made it!!!

We had come up with a revised end plan: Kath and Tim would hob-knob with the rich and famous at the boat basin, and I would walk into Manhattan and get a cab down to Grand Central Station on 42nd Street, where I would take a train as per our original plan. So, I set off in my river clothes: wet trail running shoes, wet socks, wet hiking shorts, and wet "Hudson River White Water Derby" t-shirt, walking cross-town towards Broadway. Just before I left Kath and Tim, I had the presence of mind to get the Subaru key from Kath: GOOD THINKING!

Walking east across Manhattan, I felt a little oddly dressed for The City, but it didn't take long for me to realize that no one cared: this *was* New York City. I hailed a cab and hopped in and said "Grand Central Station", in my best Big City Manner, and off we went. The cabbie was really nice. I told him my river story and he said that he thought that I looked a little "different". We chatted all the way to Grand Central: he used to be a waiter, but liked driving a cab better. He lived in Queens. It took quite a while to get to Grand Central in the traffic, and across the long, long crosstown blocks. The ride cost $14.00, and I gave the cabbie a two-dollar tip.

I went into Grand Central and couldn't figure out the Big Board in my just-canoed-from-Yonkers addled state of mind. I went to the information booth, found out the 3:16 local was leaving from track 41, and bought a one-way ticket for $5.50. It was about 3 PM. I scooted over to track 41. The train ride went fairly quickly, even though it was a local and stopped at every station there was. It took about a half hour to get to Yonkers.

When I got off, there were no cabs in sight, but there was a big white Ford Crown Victoria parked there, with a big woman behind the wheel and two other people in it. I asked the driver if she could take me up to the boat ramp.

174

She knew where it was, and said to get in. I got in the back, and the other two people in the car acted as if I was a Martian.

I babbled my story to them all, and they thawed out a little... We got to the boat ramp and the Subaru was still there, and the driver said "Six dollars". I gave her seven. It had cost about 27 bucks to get back to the car; a little steep, but a lot better than jackassing *two* vehicles all the way down to the city and back.

Now I had to navigate, solo, through the Yonkers ghettoes to the Saw Mill River Parkway. I had looked at maps before we left home, and knew that the Saw Mill should dump me into the Henry Hudson Parkway, down the west side of Manhattan. It took a lonnnng time to find the Saw Mill, bobbing and weaving through the mostly street-sign-less ghettoes of Yonkers. I relied a lot on instinct, and with a bit of luck finally, miraculously, found the parkway.

I wasn't Out Of The Woods yet – I had to navigate some wickedly confusing interchanges with a lot of big, confusing signs, and crazed Westchester County drivers swerving all over the place all around me at high speed. I finally reached the Henry Hudson, got off at the 79th street ramp, and drove into a dark, ominous looking tunnel that looked like part of a sewage system, with garbage strewn inside of it.

It led to an eerie underground parking garage, that looked more like a cave than anything civilized, and I found some signs that said "PARKING FOR BOAT OWNERS ONLY". I parked–we were boat owners... I found Kath and Tim, we racked the boats, and Got Outta There. It took *forever* to get out of Manhattan: it was Friday afternoon, around 5 PM, and *everybody* was doing their best to escape the city. We finally arrived home in Stormville around 7:30 PM, and Tim put his Penobscot on his truck and wearily pointed it towards Rocky Hill, Connecticut, an hour and a half to the east.

Us??? We quickly showered and changed and got back in the Subaru and headed for a yacht club on the Hudson, where a couple of friends played guitar in a local band. We later danced right alongside the Hudson, with the lights of Poughkeepsie's Mid Hudson Bridge to the north, and the Beacon-Newburgh Bridge to the south. It was a good feeling to know that we had now canoed all of this beautiful historic river, from Troy to the 79th Street Boat Basin. When the band finished up around 10, it started to rain like hell. We walked over to the Subaru in the rain, got in, drove back to Stormville, and collapsed, with the good feeling that a really extraordinary, memorable day had indeed snuck up on us.

Ralph Ferrusi
34 Kim Lane
Stormville, New York 12582-5305
(845) 227-6217

August 17, 2004
1992 words

Saranac May 2015

I grew up in Buchanan, not a true "river town", but The River was, and still is, "in my blood". In the Buchanan/Montrose/Verplanck area owning a boat was pretty much a rite-of-passage. My Dad would borrow somebody's rowboat every once in a while and strap his dinky half-horsepower outboard motor to the stern and Mom and Sis and I would pile in and we'd set out from Lent's Cove and eventually stop in the middle of the Hudson, off Peekskill Bay, and "fish". Four people in a leaky ten-foot wooden boat, no PFD's, sitting in the Hudson's main channel... By today's standards it would be suicidal. It probably wasn't a helluva good idea back then either, but they were much simpler times.

Eventually, as a "grown-up", I bought a boat: a used light blue/white 14-foot fiberglass Crestliner, from Zoeller's down in Croton. A red (yes, *red*) 40 horsepower manual start Johnson was on the stern. I was *so* proud of it; I owned a boat, and a speedboat, no less. I had *arrived*. Pretty soon I put **THUMPER III** down both sides with 10" black Instant Letters. We'd put in at the now-long-defunct boat ramp at the river end of Broadway in Verplanck, and I'd chase the big Hudson River Dayliners—the Alexander Hamilton, and the huge three-stack Robert Fulton—and play, full throttle, in their enormous wakes, catching and sailing over the waves, burying the bow, surfing them. Thinking back, probably not a helluva good idea; actually maybe bordering a bit on suicidal.

I used to water ski in the sheltered water behind the "ghost fleet" across from White Beach. Hmmmm, that was quite a while back, wasn't it??? One day I had the bright idea to top off the two six-gallon tanks (probably cost less than four bucks) and head south to go around Manhattan Island, diving into Spuyten Duyvil, down the East River through Hell Gate, around the Battery, and back north up the Hudson. With four adults in a 14-footer... Ahhh, youth; I miraculously pulled it off.

Well, the times they eventually changed—last I heard Thumper III was somewhere up in Rhode Island—and I bought a dark green 17' polypropylene Old Town canoe. I put THUMPER III down both sides with 10" white Instant Letters, and we soon discovered the thrills of Class II/III white water. My wife Kathy and I now own four canoes, and, after a long, successful career, have pretty much retired from whitewater racing, instead applying the many skills we developed over the years to exploring calm, peaceful, flat-water creeks, ponds, and marshes, and, of course the Hudson. Over the years we've paddled the whole Hudson—excepting a few miles up north between Riparius and The Glen—from the Indian River rafting put-in to the 79th Street Boat Basin in Manhattan.

In early May we headed up to our beloved 'daks—the Adirondacks—the plan being to camp out a couple of days along some waterway, do some hiking while we were up there. We'd bought Dave Cilley's *Adirondack Paddler's Guide* a while back, and checked out several options: the Saint Regis area, the Saranacs. We didn't want to deal with shuttles, or rapids, or long "carry's", and finally came up with A Plan: we'd stay in a motel in Saranac village, then head south through Lake Flower (Interesting Thought: Saranac Village is on Lake Flower. Tupper Lake village is on [Raquette] Pond. Lake Placid village is on Mirror Lake. Go figure...) down to and across Lake Oseetah to the Upper Locks, then along the Saranac River to the Two Ponds leanto, where we'd camp for a couple of nights, then canoe-explore during the day. We'd already canoed these waterways while doing a section of the 750-mile Old

Forge, New York to Fort Kent, Maine Northern Forest Canoe Trail, and had camped at the leanto. Two concerns were the early May weather—it could be very cold—and bugs: they could be unbearable.

After all kinds of planning, and digging out all kinds of gear—water/ camping/rain gear/cold weather clothing—and food and water, the Big Day finally came. We put our Best Canoe—a dark green 17' WeNoNah Sundowner—I'd replaced the stock cane seats with low-mounted fiberglass "tractor seats" (front slider) and the heavy stock ash thwarts with lightweight aluminum, and installed front and rear foot braces—on the roof, we packed the back of the Subaru almost to the inside roofline (It'd hit 90 degrees in Stormville before we left: very un-May-like temps, so we piled on some shorts/t-shirts "just in case"). I thought the Subaru's front wheels might leave the ground.

717 Words

Hello, Goodbye, Please, and Thank You

I pride myself that I can say "Hello", "Goodbye", "Please", and "Thank You" in "about 20" different languages.

Here's the current "Hello's":

Swahili	Jambo
Nepalese:	Namaste
Polish:	phonetically: "Jhen doe bray"
Russian:	phonetically: "Doe bray oot trah"
Italian:	Buongiorno
French:	Bonjour
German:	Gutten tag
Spanish:	Buenos dias
Australian:	G'day, mite!
Japanese:	phonetically: "Koe knee she wah"

03/22/17: sign language!!!

Auschwitz, Birkenau

Wednesday, October 19, 2016. Last night we watched a movie from the local library system about a group of old, well-dressed, well-healed Jews who were staying at some cabins in the "borscht belt" in the southern Catskills.

The film had a home movie quality about it: lot of bouncy hand-held camera sequences. This technique can be effective, but it also can be very annoying if overdone. In this film, it was annoying... The film seemed pointless: to me, directed by a very minor-order talent.

Eventually you find out the people, as they ramble on and reminisce, are all Auschwitz survivors. OK, now I get it... I had just finished a novel that centered around a Holocaust survivor; it was extremely powerful, extremely disturbing, and very fresh in my mind. To me, the person who made this film wanted to say something about this horrific event, but really didn't have the talent or wherewithal to pull it off. I went upstairs and went to bed. But, I got up, got a pen and a piece of paper, and began writing this:

Mom's roots were in Krakow, Poland. We went there in 2003, on vacation. Auschwitz and Birkenau were nearby, and we went. We walked through the ARBEIT MACHT FREI gate, and saw the railroad tracks that ended by the big brick buildings with the tall smokestacks. We walked into the showers. We saw the piles of eyeglasses, and shoes. We saw the bullet-pocked cement wall. We went to Birkenau and went into one of the huge, stark, dingy barracks: the living conditions were still inhumane, deplorable.

I wept then; I have tears in my eyes as I write this. I'm proud of us for going: we didn't have to, but we did. It changed me, forever. Don't anyone *ever* tell me the Holocaust didn't happen...don't..........................

A Single Drop of Water??? Or Rum???

Snow is melting on a balsam fir branch extending out over Lake Tear of the Clouds. Lake Tear, at 4,293 (or 4,322) feet elevation on the southwest slope of 5,534-foot Mount Marcy, New York State's highest point, is the generally-acknowledged highest source of the Hudson River,

A single drop of water falls—*SPLAT*—into the lake. The drop becomes part of this small lake, and at the lake's outlet becomes part of westward-flowing Feldspar Brook, that dumps into the Opalescent River. The Opalescent flows into Flowed Land, just below Lake Colden, where it heads pretty much due south, and Calamity Brook heads southwest towards Henderson Lake, where the Hudson "officially" begins its 315-mile journey to New York Harbor.

The Hudson eventually picks up speed, and strength, roaring through the 17-mile white-water rafting Hudson River Gorge, then down to intimidating Rockwell Falls just above Lake Luzerne, to the dam-dest part of the whole river, a thirty-mile stretch between Lake Luzerne and Champlain Canal Lock 7 in Fort Edward, blocked by seven massive dams: Curtis, Palmer, Spier Falls, Sherman Island, Feeder, Glens Falls, and Baker Falls (*River Once-Wild: Not Your Father's Hudson*, **Boating On The Hudson & Beyond**, October 2008, Volume 16, Number 9).

And, it ain't over yet: looming south is the Federal Dam in Troy. Below it the Hudson, *Muhheakantuc*, "The River That Flows Both Ways" is tidal. It's said that a twig tossed in the water here will take approximately 126 days, going back and forth on the tides, to travel the 150 miles to New York Harbor. On its way it will pass, many times, all the classic Hudson River river towns: Coxsackie, Hudson, Catskill, Saugerties, New Hamburg, Chelsea, Cold Spring, Garrison, Verplanck, Croton, Ossining, Haverstraw.

Finally passing the Palisades, the George Washington and Verazano Narrows bridges, and the Statue of Liberty, the mighty river enters New York Harbor, and, the Atlantic Ocean, 315 miles from where it began its journey in Lake Tear of the Clouds, and joins the Gulf Stream, scooting northeast up towards Newfoundland.

Seven Atlantic currents split up in the Newfoundland Basin: three head up to Greenland, Iceland, and the Arctic Circle. Four swing south. Our little drop of water, tired of being ice or snow, heads down the Canary Current, past the Canary Islands, and Morocco,

Mauritius, and Senegal on Africa's northwest coast, and joins the North Atlantic Current, now hell-bent westward back across the Atlantic towards the distant Caribbean's Windward Islands.

The Windwards extend pretty much north-south from Martinique down to Grenada. The Leewards extend from Puerto Rico in the west pretty much in an arc southeast to Dominica, north of Martinique. Our little drop has a goal, and a destiny: idyllic Rodney Bay, on the northwest corner of Saint Lucia, in the Windwards, south of Martinique and north of Saint Vincent.

Kath and I aren't known for taking "resort" type vacations. We're more apt to be in Nepal heading towards Everest Base Camp, or on Kilimanjaro, or rafting the Urabamba in Peru or the Grand Canyon, or, bungy jumping into active volcanoes on a Pacific island inhabited only by head-hunting pygmy cannibals.

We had a "special" wedding anniversary coming up recently. We've been to several Caribbean islands, but had never been to Saint Lucia with its unique, spectacular Grand and Gros Pitons. And, though we usually stay at modest hotels, inns or guest houses, we decided to treat ourselves and splurged, looking forward to pampering ourselves for a week at the fancy Bay Gardens Beach Resort on Rodney Bay in the northwest corner of Saint Lucia.

Our third-floor room had a private balcony with a view of the bay, Pigeon Island, the super-exotic swimming pool, and half-mile long white sand Reduit Beach, "The long stretch of golden sand that frames Rodney Bay", that "Many feel [is] the island's finest". The lush white bath towels on the bed were shaped like love birds, and there was a complimentary bottle of French Champagne in the refrigerator...

One of my first impressions was "I think I might really like this place!"

It didn't take long to get into the "luxury" swing of things: big fancy breakfast buffets, nice dinners, wine, lounging on the beach in beach chairs, swimming in the warm, clear blue Caribbean waters. We did walk the whole beach, and walked into town and took a boat out to Pigeon Island to explore its fort and trails.

There was an "events" desk at the hotel, and Kath was interested in a day-trip catamaran ride down the west coast to Soufriere, the original capitol of the island, way down at the far southwest corner, just north of the Pitons. Sure, let's go!

A fancy mini-bus picked us up at the hotel and took us over to the the the fancy-schmancy Rodney Bay Marina, where we boarded the slick white catamaran, and headed out through the inlet at the north end of Reduit Beach, past the Bay Gardens Beach Resort, and southward down the coast.

It was a beautiful Caribbean day, and I gravitated as far out as I could on the starboard prow of the right-hand outrigger, enjoying the sun, waves and spray. On board, there was reggae music and all-you-can-drink rum punch and all-you-can-eat mini-bananas. I stuck to non-alcoholic punch and, bananas; a "party pooper", but I wanted to keep my wits about me and absorb as much as I could of this unique trip.

We docked at Soufriere, and though a lot of Caribbean cities and towns we've been to are "tourist friendly", this place, to me, wasn't, and the tour company must have agreed, and as we were quickly whisked through town I didn't spot any touristy cafes, gift shops, etc. We were driven up to Diamond Falls, "one of the natural wonders of St Lucia", where I couldn't resist taking a dip, then to Sulphur Springs, "the world's only drive in volcano", teaming with hissing/steaming/burbling/gurgling lava vents, then to a magnificent old plantation/estate high above the city, and finally to lunch at a nice restaurant north of the city.

Then, it was time to head back north, Mon... On the way south we had had a following wind, but the wind was pretty much in our face on the way back, so the bow was buried every once in a while, and I took much more spray than I did on the way down. At one point, I took off my sunglasses and shook the water off, but a single drop hung on, and—**SPLAT**—hit the white fiberglass deck. I'm not making this up, but for some strange reason I had a very clear vision of the big Federal Dam across the Hudson at Troy.

Hmmm, and, I hadn't even had a single drop of rum,..............

1134 words

This first appeared in John Vargo's Boating on the Hudson and Beyond *February/March 2016 issue.*

A Tale of Ten Cities

We went On A Cruise this September, our first "cruise" in 32 years of World Travel. We'd cruised the Adriatic in 2004 on the 250-passenger Dalmatica, but the homey Dalmatica was a quaint little hamlet on the sea compared to the monstrous 50-story-high 4000 passengers "cities on the seas" that cruise ships have become, so I don't think of the wonderful short jaunt down the Adriatic as a real big-ship cruise experience.

Oceanic's 824 passenger/386 crew Nautica is not a "monster" ship, but when I first caught sight of it berthed in Copenhagen, I was WOW'ed, and impressed, by its size.

We visited ten ports, in nine countries, in style. Here's a quick summary:

We flew JFK to Copenhagen on a Delta Airlines cattle car: as with just about all contemporary American-based airlines everything reeked of "last class" mediocrity.

Copenhagen: we had to take a cab from the airport to the pier, and the cab driver barely said a word to us during the half-hour (or so) ride. A lot of airport cabbies are very talkative and welcoming: not this guy. My first impressions of Denmark: kilometer after kilometer of bland, nondescript buildings. My first impression of the Nautica: WOW, it's BIG!!! And graceful, and beautiful.

We were welcomed aboard, and had some time to explore the quite modern dock area. There was some kind of concrete "park" across from the ship, and we walked over to it, and though it was (I think) Saturday, it was surprisingly empty and lifeless. We walked along the dock a ways until I could step on some grass—Danish soil—and Kath walked further through a water-side park until she—surprise—spotted The Little Mermaid!!! Jet lagged and tired, I missed this sighting.

After "a day at sea"—I was stunned at how VAST the Baltic was—we landed in Helsinki, our first from-the-ship landfall. Impressions: a nice, manageable, normal-sized, not overly busy city, with a nice water front open-air market, and a very nice, big park and nice boulevards and stores and shops along our walk to where we met our kayak guide and fellow kayakers. Our guide was superb, and the kayaking was spectacular.

On to Saint Petersburg (we'd flown into "Leningrad" in 1987: *30 YEARS AGO*). First impression this time around, arriving by sea, was endless, endless, endless industrial docks, cranes, piers, wharves, then finally endless, endless, clean, low, pleasantly warm-colored—yellows, golds, tans—"palace" after palace after palace all the way to all the very distant horizons. And the streets were jam-packed with endless, noisy, silver SUV traffic jams. In '87 there were a few "Ladas"—Russian Fiat 124's—here and there, but things had obviously gotten really ugly—"Westernized"—in the intervening years. Our first excruciating "TMI" (Too Much Information) tours (many were to come) were in Saint Petersburg. And, it took us a while to realize that "Petegof" was Petrodvorets, that we had visited by hydroplane in 1987.

Stockholm: a HUGE bicycle event colored just about our entire visit: zillions and zillions of bike nerds of all ages, shapes, and sizes, having the time of their lives. Big Fun when you are a part of it, a pain in the ass when you are an outsider on your first visit to the city. "The Old Town" consisted of surprisingly drab, boring streets, then, finally, two colorful buildings in the drab "town square": San Gimignano it wasn't. The canal trip we had booked before we left the USA was, truthfully, pretty boring...

Visby, Sweden: a long long walk from the ship to the town. Woulda/coulda/shoulda been charming except it rained steadily: the only full rainy day we had while ashore. Nice walk up to and along the city walls, saw a SUBWAY, didn't bother to go into The Big Church.

Tallin, Estonia: another TMI over-zealous young woman local tour guide—"that's the ex-mayor's step-cousin's former orphanage", etc, etc—who mumbled and didn't project, pissing off a lot of the old farts on our tour. We finally told her we had decided to go on our own 'way up in the upper Old

Town, then got hopelessly lost in the narrow, maze-like, tourist-jam-packed, coulda-been-charming streets of the lower Old Town. Tired and near-crazed, we finally stumbled onto a bus with "Nautica" written on it and escaped!

Warnemunde, (former) East Germany: the most charming stop of the trip. Ultra-charming streets, buildings, shops. Long, long beautiful Baltic beach. Old fashioned narrow-guage train ride to another charming town with another long, long beach, and, a long boardwalk/promenade. Wunderbar!!!

Amsterdam: I was looking forward to Amsterdam: for decades people have been going on and on about Amsterdam and its zillions of bikes and cyclists. Here's the dark side: 99.999% of the folks riding the heavy, crappy, black "commuter" bikes are as joyless as the endless daily commuters on the Taconic State Parkway and I-84/-684. And, they'll bulldoze over you as soon as look at you: getting across the heavily trafficked bike lanes was worth your life: it's up to *you* to dodge THEM!!!

The Dutch were the only rude people I encountered on the trip. On the street, a tall young man came up behind me and slammed into my left shoulder, hard enough to almost knock me over, and just kept walking, not turning around or saying a word. Believe me, I've been in a *lot* of cities all around the world, and this was the rudest thing that ever happened to me. It got worse. While riding my heavy, evil-handling rental bike our "guide" suddenly stopped, and it was all I could do to stop my shitty rental bike without crashing. A local cyclist loudly yelled (and probably cursed) at me for "being in his way". We had to take a bike/pedestrian ferry on our bike tour, and a whole bunch of locals angrily yelled at us because we tourists didn't get out of their way quickly enough when the ferry docked. The charming, scenic canals were overrun/jam-packed with tourists and loud, raucous drunks. I have no desire to ever return to Amsterdam.

Bruges: it was raining, and, surprise surprise, Bruges was about 30 miles from where we docked (this was the first, and only time that a city/town that was on our "itinerary" was so far from where we docked) and it would cost each of us about a hundred bucks to get into town!!! Bullshit!!! Throw in my very negative experience at our last port of call, Amsterdam, and I was ready to pass on Bruges. But, a woman from the ship organized a "car pool" into the main downtown square (and we took a train/bus back). It was ultra-charming, and under crowded: finally, the Good Old "Real Deal" Europe. It put me back on track. A fellow tourist recommended a canal trip, and it was superb. Fuck Amsterdam.

Finally, to Southampton: the place we docked overlooked trillions and trillions and acres and acres of brand-new cars: very weird. We were tied up and waiting to go ashore, and I was selecting my final breakfast aboard in my favorite on-board eatery, the Terrace Cafe, when I heard the unmistakable sound of the theme song from James Cameron's *Titanic* piped over the ship's PA system. WHAT!!!??? "My Heart Must Go On" from *Titanic* being played on a modern cruise ship??? I was astonished: stunned. And, looking around, everyone else in sight mooching down their last breakfast on board appeared oblivious to it. Thinking about it, I figured since we were safely moored, this just might be some kind of Last Port "tradition".

At home months later I mentioned this to Kath, and she said "Didn't Titanic set sail from Southampton?" My knee-jerk reaction was no, Titanic sailed from Belfast. Well, it was built in Belfast, and entered the water in Belfast, but, it did indeed "set sail" from Southampton on April 10, 1912, and never reached another port.......

Somebody on the Nautica purposely played this song on the PA system after WE had safely arrived at Southampton. This was very very moving to me. But, I couldn't help but wonder: Do all ships that end their voyage in Southampton play this music??? Or, just Oceania??? Or, just the Nautica??? Or, just someone on the Nautica???

In Defense of "Real" B&B's

When I worked as a Cross Country International (CCI) Historic Hudson Valley tour guide I was based at two B&B's, first in Millbrook then in Amenia.

Porterhouse, in Millbrook, was an imposing old stone building one block off Millbrook's main drag, Franklin Avenue. I recall it was a "special place", and had "history": it looked it. I recall the living room was pretty grand, and the guest bedrooms were large and "special".

Hilltop House in Amenia made the Porterhouse, and just about any other house, look pretty common. An imposing yellow Victorian with a big yard and wrap-around porch, it was just about on the top of a steep hill above town. There was a spiffy formal dining room, and a big stone fireplace in the high-ceiling living room. There was a pretty grand wooden staircase leading upstairs to several big, unique, distinctive, welcoming, cozy, plush, comfortable bedrooms; my recollection is they had names: The Green Room, The Blue Room, the Pink Room. The furnishings, drapes, and bedspreads were cushy, posh. Any guest had to feel special, and, a bit pampered. That was what it was all about.

Gail and Lou were superb inn-keepers, and welcomed all my clients and made them feel at home. There was a large selection of books, and wine and cheese was served the first night of a tour. The porch was also a perfect "wine and cheese" setting.

Every morning low, soft classical music would be heard coming from the kitchen, where breakfast was being prepared (the night before the guests had been asked what they preferred for breakfast: Lou's (the cook!!!) specialty was "coddled eggs". The big dining room table setting was a knockout, and Gail and Lou were the perfect inn-keeper/servers. During and after breakfast they engaged the guests, and told stories and tales. The experience was very "family". I helped in the kitchen a bit, and helped clear the table.

Fast forward to 2017, and "Airbnb's". "B&B" is short for "Bed &Breakfast". Getting a bit ahead of my story, I found out the "bnb" after the "Air" (whatever the hell that means) means "bed *no* breakfast"...

Scotland

Jim, Jack, and Johnny

We went to Scotland in 2013 to walk all—or as much as we could—of the 96-mile Milngavie to Fort William West Highland Way, Scotland's most reknowned long-distance hiking trail. We landed in Glasgow (via London...) and spent some time there. I had expected the Scots to be reserved—maybe even aloof—but was very pleasantly surprised at how open, and *friendly*, they were. And, by the Scottish vegetarian pub food.

We took a train to the small village of Milngavie and began our walk: in the rain. Over the next several days the rain was so insistent that we bailed out: it always bothered me that we had "failed", and for a long time I had hoped we could go back and finish what we had begun.

We caught a cab and rented a car (near Glasgow???) and headed north, taking a boat ride on Loch Ness, driving to Fort William, and exploring the Isle of Skye. We went as far north as Inverness, where I recall we took a very nice walk. On the way back south, we stayed in the charming little village of Pitlochry, and visited Edradour, Scotland's oldest distillery, established 1825. During our tour, they told us that they greatly admired "Jim, Jack, and Johnny": Jim Beam, Jack Daniels, and Johnny Waker!!!

At the time I was enormously impressed that they so admired these three American distillers/distilleries, and I think of this to this day just about anytime I sip Irish Cream from my "Official Tour Glass" from our Edradour tour.

Thus, I am writing about Jim, Jack, and Johnny on this rainy December 14, 2020 day........

December 14, 2020

Mike and Victoria, our neighbors down the block, run very successful trips to Ireland, and knowing I was a writer, they asked me to write something about Scotland that they would present at a conference in Scotland concerning tourism and their potential role in increasing it. Kath also took a shot at it, and below is what we came up with, Kath first and then me:

Goal: More American Tourists To Scotland

Mike and Victoria have valuable assets and experience, and well-healed clients asking about Scotland after they have been on their Ireland trips.

What are some of the reasons why they might like to go to Ireland???
> Scenery
> Culture
> Religion (Saint Patrick cathedral)
> History
> Recommended
> Bucket List
> Family Connections
> Common (but a bit foreign) written and spoken language
> Price
> Movies/books
> Well-known cities:
>> Dublin
>> Belfast
>> Waterford
>> Cork
>> Kilarney
>> Kilkenny
> Well-known regions/attractions:
>> Ring of Kerry
>> Dingle Peninsula
>> Cliffs of Moher
>> Aran Islands

Scotland/Ireland Similarities

Geographic location, in the British Isles right across the Atlantic
Language: English spoken with sexy(???)/down-home/lyrical accents
SAFE
Economically secure

Ease of transportation
History
Proud self-reliant people
Connection to the sea
Christian religion(s)
Writers/Poets
Scenery
Architecture
Castles/churches/cathedrals
British rule/influences
Great Pubs!!!

Differences

Ireland	Scotland
IS an island	Has many islands
Sweaters	Kilts
People are more "down to earth"	People are more "direct"
Roads: more narrow, less signage	Better roads/pavement/signage
Whiskey	Scotch
Corned beef and cabbage	Haggis...
Closer to America	Closer to Scandinavia/Europe
Penninsulas	The Highlands
Crystal and lace	Scotch and kilts

So.........Let's Talk About Scotland:

In the 30,981 square miles of Scotland *there's only one natural lake!!!*

And, with 10,250 miles of coastline and 790 islands there isn't a single beach that most anyone else in the world would recognize by name.

BUT.......................

Besides the "natural" Lake of Menteith, there are 31,469 Lochs, including The Most Famous Loch in the World, and, its elusive "Monster".

And, the glorious beaches at Camusdarach, Udrigle, Bhatasaigh Bay, Traigh, and, Mellor.

And, over 3,000 castles, and somewhere between 4,000 and 7,000 plaids/tartans.

Saint Andrews (and 549 other golf courses).
Glenfiddich and, THE Glenlivet.
Bagpipes, and kilts.
And...Haggis.

Alexander Graham Bell, and Robert Louis Stevenson were born there.

And, James Watt, Kirkpatrick MacMillan, Sir Alexander Fleming, and John Chalmers: inventors, respectively, of the steam engine, the bicycle, Penicillin, and adhesive postage stamps.

And, the inventors of raincoats (I wonder why???), chloroform, tarmac, and pneumatic tyres.

Not to forget a certain Mrs. Keller, of Dundee, who "invented"....marmalade.

And...the *unicorn* is the National Animal...!!!

And then there's Outlander!!!

So..............................What's not to love???? What's not to love???

I rest my case.

Thank you................

372 Words
Combined, and updated January 10, 2020

CARS: MY RECOLLECTIONS OF EACH ONE

Let's list them first, to get an idea what we're dealing with, then visit them one by one.

Light green 1950 Plymouth fastback, dark green interior (used).
Light grey 1936 Ford coupe, tan interior (used).
Black 1958 Plymouth Belvedere two-door hardtop, red interior (new).
Black (???) 1934 Ford convertible (junkyard).
Silver 1963 Chevrolet Corvette Sting Ray split window coupe. Red interior (used).
Red Fiat 600 (used).
White Fiat 600 (for parts) (used).
White/red stripe 1974 (???) Dodge Dart two-door hardtop, ??? interior (used).
"Butterscotch" 1972 Ford Pinto fastback, tan interior (new).
Red 1974? Fiat X 1/9, black interior (used).
White/red stripe 1962 Chevy Impala two-door hardtop (used).
Red 1985 Honda CRX, black interior (new).
Red 1986 Honda CRX Si, black interior (new).
Red 1991 Honda Civic Si hatchback, black interior (new).
Purple Dodge Neon four-door, ??? interior (used).
Red 1996 BMW 328i convertible, black interior (used).
White 2006 Chevy Aveo hatchback, ??? interior (used).
Red 2009 Smart FourTwo Passion Coupe, red interior (new).

18 (that I remember as of now) cars, six new, 12 used.

Four Chrysler products,
Three Fords,
Three GM,
Five European,
Three Asian...

My First Car: a 1950 Plymouth fastback

It was a Big Day (I had most likely recently turned 18) when Pop took me to a used car lot somewhere on the north side of Peekskill to buy a car. My recollection is that the choice, in my price range, came down to two cars: a 1950 (or so) Ford coupe, and a light green 1950 Plymouth fastback. All the local hotrodders (the "Road Knights") had souped-up V-8 Fords or Mercuries. Don't know why I picked the flathead straight-six Plymouth... $450.00—of my own money (earned at the local Food Center supermarket)—sealed the deal.

At some point my best high school friend Bob ("Do Do": pronounced "Dew Dew" not "Dough Dough") Turner suggested we "bull nose" my car: the local hotrodder's cars were all "bull-nosed" the factory hood ornament that all cars had was removed, and the holes welded shut and filled in with lead. Bob and I, having no knowledge of welding, etc, used fiberglass. I didn't realize this at the time, but this would be a life-changing experience for me. From then on, cars would not be just "transportation:; they would all become personalized—special—in some way or the other.

The bull-nosing eventually led to the car being "decked": the handle to open the deck lid was removed and the license plate recess on the rear deck lid was filled in. The trunk was now opened by a cable (that ran up to the dashboard???), and the plate was moved down to the middle of the back bumper.

Along the way, the engine now sported a dual carburetor manifold, and the exhaust manifold was split, with two exhaust pipes running through two glass-packed mufflers. All the local hotrod V-8's had "duals", and a nice, throaty V-8 sound. The Plymouth sounded "different": not like the V-8's. At the time, this was not a good thing to me...

A lot of other changes were going on. The door handles, inside and out, were removed, and the doors could only be opened by solenoids inside the doors controlled by buttons. The outside buttons were up inside the now "frenched" (all the hotrod Fords had their grilles "frenched": the chrome around the "mouth" of the grille was removed, and the grille area was rounded off like the 49-51 Mercury grille areas) front grille area, and the inside buttons were both under the dash on the driver's side only!!! I can't imagine something like this passing inspection nowadays!!!!!!!!

The chrome grille was now "floating" inside the mouth of the grille area, and the chrome headlamp rings were now the same color as the car, quasi "frenched". The square-ish stock taillights were filled in, and replaced by 1939 Chevy bullet-shaped taillights on the lower outside of the rear fenders. I will mention here that these were found at Sellick's junkyard, on Route 9 in Buchanan, just north of the "iron bridge" railroad bridge. This is where I found a lot of parts to customize both the Plymouth and, later on the '36 Ford. Mr. Sellick wasn't the most cordial guy in the world, but he let me roam his junkyard to find parts.

Chrome "half moons" covered the top of the headlights, and chrome "spinner" hubcaps were on the front wheels. The rear end was lowered several inches with "lowering blocks" between the rear springs and the back axle. 1955 Oldsmobile-like chrome ran back to the sides of the doors, and I painted the front of the car above the chrome dark green (with a vacuum cleaner attached to a paint sprayer) so it was now "two-toned". I eventually repainted the whole car: black in front, the rest gold!!! I sent a picture of it to one of the hotrodding magazines and they published it: "Black/Gold Custom in a Summer Setting"!

We used to street race in those days: if you ended up lined up with another hot rod at a traffic light, you would pretty much glance over at each other, and when the light changed you would drag race the other car. The Plymouth, being a "mere" six-cylinder, was never expected to stand up to any of the V-8's, but I proudly—and to the other drivers quite unexpectedly—"blew the doors off" a '49 Mercury flathead V-8, and '53 Mercury and '53 Cadillac overhead valved V-8's!!!

Oddly enough, I now have no recollection of what happened to this car years later when I bought my brand-new 1958 Plymouth.

1936 Ford coupe

30's-vintage Fords were the classic hot rods of the 50's, and the '32 Ford coupes and roadsters were the most coveted of all. The Peekskill-based Road Knights built a '32 roadster as a club project. They "channeled" it, lowering the body 'way down over the frame, and installed a souped-up Ford flathead V-8: aluminum high-compression heads, dual (maybe triple) carb intake manifold, probably steel-tubing headers. It was a beauty, painted refrigerator white with a red grille.

Somehow I found out about a 1936 Ford five-window coupe for sale in Croton. It only had something like 30-40 thousand original miles on it, and I bought it from the original owner's cousin for (astonishingly!) $45.00, and drove it home, unlicensed, uninsured, un-whatever.

I recall driving Mom to work at the shop at the Buchanan Circle with it, and driving it down to the Point and around the big quarry. In all the time I owned it, I don't recall it ever being licensed, much less insured.

I eventually took the hood side panels off, installed hydraulic brakes (from a '48-or-so Ford in Sellick's junk yard) with a '53 Ford swing pedal (again, from Sellick's) mounted on the firewall, de-arched the front transverse leaf spring to lower the front end, and replaced the original spoked wheels with late-model rims: 15" on the front, 16" on the back. I put white-wall "rings" on the tires. I painted it white, with an orange grille with flames on the top of the hood and along the side of the doors. This car was our answer to the Road Knight's deuce. Bob (he had a mildly-customized '48 Ford flathead V-8 coupe) and I had become the Buchanan-based "Night Knights", and I hand-painted small plaques to put on our cars. I had put a chrome air cleaner on the old '36 flathead V-8's single-barreled carb, but this did not hold a candle to the Road Knight's tricked up V-8 with twin, maybe triple carbs.

At some point I repainted the whole car (except the hood) with dark-gray primer, and painted the wheels red. Then, at some point the car was stashed away in the shed behind the two-car garage at 195 Centre Street. The shed roof began to leak, and rodents got inside the car and chewed up all the upholstery. The now-sad car was flat-bedded up to 34 Kim Lane, where I put it up on cinder blocks and put a tarp over it, where it sat for years, ignored, while we hiked, biked, canoed, and traveled the world.

Finally, one day I took the tarp off, and was shocked at how badly the car had deteriorated: I should have bought one of those "mobile garage" tents years ago. At this point in life I knew that I was never going to restore it—at one time I had visions of it totally restored, painted a gleaming lemon yellow—and did *not* want this beautiful car to deteriorate any further. I called a friend who had restored several '30's-vintage Fords with his brother—and he came over to look at it. Eventually he called me and offered me $4500.00 for it—a very fair price—and I sold it.

Time went by, and I sometimes thought about my '36 and wondered what was going on with it: the second car I had ever bought, and had owned for something like 50 years. I finally called the friend who had bought it and he said he had sold the car to "somebody in Connecticut". I said if he was ever in contact with this person to let me know, so maybe I could see the car. I don't think I ever will.

1958 Plymouth Belvedere two-door hardtop

A beautiful black 1958 Plymouth Belvedere two-door hardtop with a red interior and a 350 cubic-inch 305 horsepower dual-quad "Golden

Commando" engine was my first brand new car. The car was striking; low and lean, with big tail fins. The Gurran brothers—Jim and Joe, leaders of the Road Knights—were both mechanics at the Plymouth dealership in Peekskill where I bought it. I recall that I paid $2650.00 for it. I think Jim, the older brother, had a 1957 Plymouth Fury, with a dual-quad 318 cubic-inch "A block": the 350 cubic-inch Golden Commando was the first year of the "B block". This engine would ultimately be punched out to 361, 383, and 426 cubic-inches.

I soon began customizing the Belvedere. I had the hood and trunk dechromed (the '58 hood ornament, along with the hood ornament from my '50 Plymouth, are currently on my bureau in our bedroom...), and had six (???) rows of louvers stamped into the hood. I painted the stock aluminum grille flat black, and added '57 Chevy taillight "bullets" to the stock taillights. I had functional chrome "Lake's pipes" welded to the exhaust pipes, coming out just behind the front wheels. I installed glass-packed mufflers, and removed the tail pipes, replacing them with short chrome extensions. I began entering the car in hot rod/custom car shows as "The Black Fury", and "Little Al" pinstriped it.

I drag raced it at the Bridgehampton, Long Island and Dover drag strips in the Super Stock class, once turning 14.9 seconds in the quarter mile, going through the traps at 110 miles-per-hour in *second* gear (the car was a three-speed manual). My nemesis's, and biggest competition, were 1958 348 cubic-inch Chevys: the 250 horsepower version with a single big quad, and the higher horsepower versions with triple carbs. I could beat the 250's, and recall once beating a triple-carb.

I could not compete with tricked up '57 327 Chevy's: there were legal things you could do to cars and they would still be considered stock: "lower" (numerically higher) rear axle ratios made the cars accelerate much, much quicker, and "stickier" tires gave a much better grip off the line: speed was not wasted as you "burned rubber". The hot '57 Chevys had 4.11, 4.56, or 5-something rear ends (compared to my 3.70, that I was never going to go through the bother, and expense, to change), and would hit top gear about a hundred yards down the strip and wind up all the way through the traps, whereas I never got into high, always going through the traps in second. There were several "hot" '57 Chevys in Super Stock at Bridgehampton, but I recall a guy named Mike Quindazzi and his '57 Chevy Ruled the Roost.

I eventually replaced the stock grille with something like 21 '57 (???) Chevy chrome bumper guards: a real "toothy", but outrageously different look. Keeping up with the times, I lowered the front end by adjusting the torsion bars, and put oversized tires on the rear, thus having the first "California rake" in the area.

I slid on ice at the entrance to Little Falls Trailer Park where we lived in Wappingers Falls and hit the brick wall, banging up the left front fender and bumper. I primed the fender and somehow straightened out the bumper, but the car was never the same after this.

A '63 Corvette split-window coupe was in the wings, and I sold the Fury to a friend's younger brother, who was, essentially, a "car beater". I always have been "easy" on cars, even rentals. It's not in me to abuse anything. Sadly, he beat the living hell out of that beautiful car—everybody knew it—but nobody, myself included, could do anything about it.

1934 Ford convertible

The '36 coupe was a real find, but I guess I still desired a roadster, like the Road Knight's '32. It would also seem I spent a fair amount of time in junkyards—mostly nearby Sellick's—back then, scrounging parts to customize the Plymouth and the '36. Somehow I found the '34 Ford convertible (roadsters had a windshield secured by post to the cowling: convertibles had an integral windshield frame that was part of the car's body) in a junkyard in Garrison, just north of the school and across the road from the stone church. It was undamaged, but I don't recall it having the convertible top. I paid (astonishingly) $75.00 for it.

Now here comes the most astonishing part. Sis and I drove up to the junkyard in the '58 Plymouth, and I tied the front bumper of the '34 to the back bumper of the Plymouth with a not-all-that-long length of rope!!!

Sis got in the '34: no seat belts, no top, no idea how the brakes and/or tires and/or steering were going to hold up, and off we went down the road!!! Nowadays we both would have ended up in jail.

I told Sis to keep tension on the rope as best she could. It must have been terrifying, and, it was extremely dangerous, but we got the car back to 195 Centre Street. I don't recall Mom ever really yelling at us, or getting really upset, but when we pulled into the yard, she yelled "***GET THAT THING THE HELL OUT OF HERE!!!***"

Mom was, well, furious. I'm sure I hadn't said something like "Hey Mom, we're going to go up to Garrison to buy a 1934 Ford from a junk yard and tow it home with a rope tied to the back bumper of the Plymouth." The car was a treasure to me, but to Mom it was just a rusty piece of junk. Seeing Sis sitting in it must have been a jolt to her, but I'm sure the fact that Sis had, somehow, made it home safe and sound was also a big relief.

The car ended up alongside the garage (in the "boat port???), and there are pictures of a young friend Larry Maurer (???) and I posing with it partially disassembled. I/we removed the fenders, running boards, and hood (I recall it had a rumble seat), and somehow got the original flathead out (to make room for a later model flathead or a Chevy 327...) and somehow got it into the woods at the end of Centre Street, a dead-end at the time, just beyond 195's property line.

I don't recall much happening to the car after this. It was never primed, or painted, or upgraded in any way. I guess it just sat there, as "life got in the way". I eventually sold it to a friend for $400-$500, maybe a thousand, with his promise that he would basically restore it for street use, maybe put a Chevy V-8 in it, hydraulics and late-model wheels.

He lived in Garrison, interestingly just a little ways up 9D from the (now-defunct) junk yard where I had originally bought the car, and I stopped in, unannounced, one day to see how he was doing with it. There was a '34 Ford convertible in the garage, and I assumed it was the selfsame car that I had sold to him (I never really asked or confirmed this, but it was a very good assumption, as '34 Ford convertibles weren't a dime a dozen back then). I was shocked to see that the car had been heavily modified into a Bonneville-style race car.

I got very angry about this. Looking back, I feel bad about this because he was a quiet, gentle, nice guy, and I really wish I had said something like, "Shit, why'd you do this??? I was hoping to see it painted lemon yellow, all set for street use.". But I didn't, and, at any rate, this was the sad ending of my 1934 Ford convertible dream/saga.

Having written the above, the ride from Garrison, from my 2015 perspective, seems like an outrageous, outlandish, patently stupid thing to have done. And, in many ways, it was. I called Sis yesterday and asked her about it, and, for the first time I can remember, we talked about it; I don't recall talking to Sis about it back then. Let's take a look a Then and Now:

Back then, Route 9 was pretty much a quiet country road, particularly when compared to the commuter-rush-hour super-speedway it has become at times today: just about everyone doing 60-70 mph, in a huge rush to get, *someplace*. Sis recalls seeing very few other cars on the whole ride home back then!!! And, she pointed out, we were "just creeping along", not doing 50-55 mph.

And, cars, and the whole car-mentality, were very very different back then. Nowadays, all cars have seat belts (it's hard to remember a time when they didn't), shoulder harnesses, multiple air bags, etc., etc. Seat belts in passenger cars were unheard of back then: my top-of-the-line '58 Plymouth hardtop did not have seat belts. I don't think they were even an option. I eventually installed aircraft seat belts (I have no recollection how or where I found them)—driver's side only—when I began seriously drag racing it.

So, the cars and traffic of those times, and, importantly, the *mindset* of those times were very very different than they are now, over 55 years later. Sure, what I did was dumb, but not quite as dumb as it seemed to me at the beginning of this particular bit of writing.

1963 Chevrolet Corvette Sting Ray Split Window Coupe

I bought the 1963 Split Window at Don Allen Chevrolet in mid-town Manhattan sometime in 1965 for $2,850.00. I was around 28 years old, and recall I was told the original owner was "a 55-year-old pharmacist who only used it on weekends," and that the original price was $5,000.00. In 1965 that was a *lot* of money for a car.

Getting the car out of Manhattan: my younger sister drove me into mid-town Manhattan in her Volkswagen "Beetle" to buy the car. This was a very, very daunting thing at the time for her (and, me). Getting us both out of Manhattan, me driving a two-year-old Corvette for the first time was going to be scary. We quickly got separated in Manhattan traffic, but somehow both of us got out of the Big City. I don't recall a thing about how we achieved this.

When I stopped at a traffic light in Briarcliff, New York, and put the clutch in—the clutch that took two feet to depress—to shift into gear, the pedal slammed all the way to the floor and stayed there. The car couldn't move an inch unless the clutch would come out. I think we (somehow) pushed it off the road, where I discovered a cotter pin that held the hanging pedal to the clutch linkage had popped off. [an aside: this became a chronic problem with this car: something was misaligned: I eventually "band-aided" it with washers and a bigger (?) cotter pin.] I put the factory cotter pin back in, and got the car to my home in Wappingers Falls, New York, where it would become my family car: my five-year-old son and four-year-old daughter sat in back under the split window.

An aside: this was 1965, and Ford had just introduced the revolutionary Mustang. I worked in an IBM laboratory as an electronics technician. Don, one of the four-year college-educated engineers, had bought a blue 289 Mustang coupe. And I, a "lowly" technician, showed up in a Big-Deal-At-The-Time silver CORVETTE...

Speaking of Mustangs: in all the time I drove the Corvette I never once raced it in any kind of "sanctioned" event. But...one day I ended up side by side with a 289 Mustang coupe at a traffic light. We gave each other "that look". When the light turned green, we both nailed it, and I don't think he was that surprised as I pulled away from him. But...I'm sure he was *really* surprised as the 14-foot fiberglass runabout I was towing passed him also. Gotta love that 300 horsepower 327...

The family adapted to the car. The kids got used to climbing in and out of the back (ummmm, no seat belts back there....). I never wore shoes in the car: in fact, a standing rule was anyone who got in the car had to remove their shoes...

We drove it on family vacations to Silver Bay on Lake George—I towed the 14-foot fiberglass runabout to the lake—in the southern Adirondacks, and to Montauk Point on Long Island. I put a ski rack on it and drove it skiing in New England.

We once drove to Daytona Beach, Florida: the kids were heroes... Somewhere in South Carolina I pulled out to pass a local beater car with South Carolina tags. It was on a long straightaway so I didn't have to downshift and nail it: just pulled out. As I was passing, the car swerved to the left right in front of me: no signal, no warning, no side road to turn into.

I locked up the brakes and steered left as much as I could, and—almost miraculously—screeched to a halt, engine stalled, and avoided the other car. Looking back, the only explanation I can come up with is that there are some really stupid people in this world, and the driver of the other car decided to teach the Corvette with New York tags "a lesson". I have no recollection of what transpired afterwards: if the idiot pulled off, or, if I caught up with him and this time downshifted to third and blasted by him... It was a very very ugly incident: Welcome to South Carolina...

I "customized" the first car I ever owned—a light green 1950 Plymouth fastback—removed the chrome from the hood and deck, lowered the back end, put on dual carbs and steel-tubing headers, and from there on customized every car I ever owned. Prior to the 'Vette I had a 1958 Plymouth Fury show car: hood louvers, pin-striping, chromed engine.

I removed all the "V's" from the front and back of the 'Vette, removed the front bumper, and installed off-road side pipes from a '67 a friend had raced: the greatest V-8 sound you ever heard, but, you had to be extremely careful getting out of the car so as not to singe the back of your legs on the pipes: ouch...

I did drive the car skiing, but had a standing policy not to drive it to work in the winter. One January day the forecast was for beautiful weather and I broke my rule. It was a beautiful morning on Meyers Corners Road, but there was a glaze of ice on one-half the road that you couldn't see. The posi spun the Corvette into the opposing lane: there was a mini van heading right at me. I steered into the skid, and the 'Vette smacked into the guard rail, pushing the whole fiberglass nose down...

I was sick at heart. I drove to work and walked into the IBM laboratory holding a piece of silver fiberglass... Back then it was almost impossible to find a body shop that worked on fiberglass. I finally found one, and they had the car a long time, but the rivets always showed along the front fenders, and they said they couldn't find Sebring Silver paint, so they painted it a Cadillac silver, that had a green tint to it.

This was the beginning of the end for the 'Vette. In 1972 I bought a "butterscotch" Pinto Hatchback, that eventually handled—Pirelli P-6's on all four corners— and sounded like a Porsche: dual carbs and steel-tubing headers.

The 'Vette was put on blocks in the garage and sat there, covered up: every year I said I was going to put it back on the road, but every year, for almost 50 years, Life Got in the Way...

Looking back, I owned this beautiful, extraordinary car for 55 years. But, only drove it seven years...

June 29, 2020
1,092 words

Since we were going to move out of New York, we had the Vette flatbedded to storage at a friend of a friend who lived close by. He was a good guy, and had quite a collection of beautifully restored cars; you could eat off the floor of his "museum". We paid $100.00 a month to store it. We eventually asked him to put out feelers about selling it, and he relayed several offers so us, in the $45,000-$55,000 range. I was disappointed with these figures, but, realistically, I had also been shocked at the deterioration of the car when I had finally given it a close look-over inside, under, and out..

We ultimately sold the Vette to a Really Good Guy from Pennsylvania for something like $56,000.00. He had been the most persistent potential buyer. An accomplished restorer, he said he'd be honored to own a split-window. He wanted it as a companion to his (hopefully) 2020 silver C8. I honestly pretty much ignored him for quite a while, but he persisted, calling every couple of months or so. I finally, sadly, agreed to sell it, because I felt the car deserved to be cared for, instead of just steadily deteriorating. He said he wasn't going to restore the car to showroom specs: he was going to restore it to the original 1963 *engineering specs*, and, he would keep us appraised of his progress. He recently sent photos of the meticulously restored frame/suspension/wheels/tires. WOW...

To be continued...???

Fiat 600

There are certain cars I just "like", and besides the '58 Fury most of them have been *small*. Back in the day, for whatever deep-down reasons, I "liked" the little Fiat 600; the smaller 500 did not have the same appeal. I found (probably in *The PennySaver*) a red Fiat 600 for sale in North Salem, New York, a snooty town over by the Connecticut border. I don't recall what year the car was, how much I paid for it, or how I got it home (that was, at the time, Little Falls Trailer Park in Wappingers Falls). It would be my then-wife's Eliane's car, and she would drive herself, and very young Ralph and Danielle around in it. In this Huge Monstrous SUV's day and age, a tiny, 600-cc car like this would be considered a death trap: no seat belts, air bags, no get-up-and-go, no nothing.

I recall putting NASCAR-like decals on the front fenders, and also recall it was a classic Fiat of the times: Fix It Again Tony; a real pain in the ass to keep the tiny three-cylinder (I recall the 500's were two bangers!!!) running; I was always tinkering with it. And, the doors and windows, and....

But, it might have been fun to drive, and probably very economical, gas-wise, and I guess it served its purpose, at least for a while. And, as the above tale about towing the '34 convertible home with a rope, the times were very different back then.

There are a couple of pictures of it somewhere in my "cars" photo album. I don't recall what eventually happened to the car; sold it, junked it...??? But I did buy a little white Fiat 600 for parts, to keep the red one running:

Fiat 600 (for parts)

I don't think there is even a picture of this particular car anywhere. I guess I also found it in *The Pennysaver*, and recall it was "local", probably somewhere in Wappingers. Again, no recollection of what year vintage it was, how much I paid for it, or how I got it over to the trailer park. I kind of remember it being parked somewhere in a common parking area (the red Fiat and the Corvette took up the two "allotted" parking places in front of the trailer). I don't really remember much about it, except it being used as a "parts car", and have no recollection whatsoever as to its fate when it outlived its usefulness to me.

1964 Dodge Dart two-door hardtop

This was my first wife's dad's car, and it was given to us (???), maybe after he died (much too soon, too "young" for such an "ahead-of-his-time" fitness-conscious man). It was a good looking car: a white two-door hardtop, red stripe down the side, 273-cubic-inch V-8. It would seem this was the car that replaced the two Fiats, a much bigger, classier, *safer* car.

Well, it wasn't all that long before I painted the Dodge's grille flat black (chrome was *out*, flat-black was *in* back then, and still may be now), **273 CU IN** was in big black letters on each side of the hood, the red stripe was orange, the hubcaps were off, and there must have been a dual exhaust system running through glass-packs, with chrome exhaust extensions on the tailpipes. And, most outrageous, a tall, giant flat-black "Superbird" wing towering over the deck lid!!! Made a statement... The car looked good, sounded good.

I recall the Dodge and the Pinto once ending up side by side at a traffic light on Route 9 in Wappingers. When the light changed, we both nailed it, and ran through the gears. I don't recall who "won"; I'm sure we had to back off pretty quickly, but it was A Moment.

I do vividly remember (I'll never forget this day) the time we took the Dodge out to Dover Drag Strip and entered it in G Stock Automatic, just for the hell of it. I hadn't drag raced in years. I took the air cleaner off, probably loosened the fan belt around the alternator, and put the smaller snow tires on the back, to effectively "lower" the real axle ratio: a lower ratio meant the engine would wind up quicker, and the car would accelerate faster (you didn't want this for daily usage: the lower the rear axle ratio, the worse the gas mileage/economy).

I used the push buttons on the right side of the dashboard to "manually" shift the car, and I qualified at 16.9 seconds through the quarter mile. ALL the rest of the cars in G Stock Automatic were 17-plus.... The little white Dodge was the fastest car in the class.

There were two obviously tricked-up cars in the class: a Chevelle, and a Ford, both, I'm sure, were "regulars" at the strip. I kept winning my heats, and eventually lined up with, I'm pretty sure, the Chevelle in the final heat. Off we went, and I was beating it, soundly. I punched the second gear button, and was still leading, when the engine simply lost power: in the excitement, I had kept the Dodge in second longer than I had in previous heats, and apparently the valves had floated. The Chevy surged by, and to everyone watching, it looked as if it had simply overtaken me, and won. But this wasn't the case: if I had punched the third gear button, the same time as I had in previous heats, the Dodge, the only car in the class in the 16's, would have won the trophy it truly deserved. To me, this was patently unfair, and I'll never forget this day at the Dover Drag Strip. To me, this is one of those things that prove there isn't some kind of All Benevolent God; a truly ABV "God" would not have let a shitty thing like this happen. Or, 9-11, for that matter. But don't get me going............

Again, don't know what ultimately became of this fine little car.

1972 Ford Pinto fastback

Ahhh, The Pinto. This is the car I bought to replace the Corvette on the road!!! Though these vintage Pinto's were much-maligned, this butterscotch-colored 2000-cc'ed tan-interior-ed hatchback was a pretty damned good little car (Interestingly Sis bought an almost identical car: same color, same engine, but I don't think hers was a hatchback). The 2000-cc engined Pintos were much better cars than the basic 1600-cc engined versions.

I soon put **Dodge** in big black letters on both flanks. Why??? I've always been a NASCAR MoPar fan—Plymouths and Dodges—and this made the Pinto NASCAR-like (but much to the chagrin of the local Ford dealership where I had bought the car, and brought it in for service while it was under warranty). I also put **2000 cc** in big black letters on both sides of the hood, again NASCAR-like.

Eventually the car was fitted with four big Pirelli P-6's, the front and rear suspensions were both tightened up, a dual-carb manifold and steel-tubing (???) headers, dumping into a pair of glass-packs were installed. It was one helluva performing, and handling, little car: "a Pinto that thought it was a Porsche".

I had fun with the Pinto, even autocrossed it once, but these cars were prone to rust, and the wheel wells began to rust, then the floorboards—I actually put something like aluminum NO PARKING signs in the driver's-side floor so I wouldn't be looking at the road flying by below my shoes...

The rust problem became so bad I bought a good-looking little red Fiat X1/9 to replace the Pinto on the road. For a while:

1974? Fiat X 1/9

Again, I have no recollection of how/where I found this car, how much I paid for it, etc. I had no interest in any of the Fiat 124 models: they were "boxy" to me. The X 1/9—known as "a poor man's Ferrari"—was classy, and this particular car exemplified this: red, with a black roof and black trim, mag wheels, and four exhaust pipes...Wowzer!!!

I did not modify this car in any way, unless having to take the driver's side door apart several times to get the window to work, or, getting the vanity tag **X RATEDX** count. I took the rusting-up Pinto off the road, and the X 1/9 became my everyday "poor man's Ferrari". But not for as long as I had hoped...

One day, on I-84 just this side of Danbury, coming back from Candlewood lake with a canoe on the roof (yes, a canoe on the roof...), the right front suspension pulled out of the belly pan and collapsed... It was definitely a good thing this happened on the right side, as I could pull off to the shoulder of the Interstate, rather than the left side, which could have pulled me into oncoming traffic. I managed to have the car flat-bedded home to Old Hopewell Road, and, amazingly, found someone who could weld the suspension back to the belly pan, and beef up (both sides, I hope) with heavy steel plates.

Well, needless to say I didn't really trust the car after this, and I put the Pinto back on the road, and put a For Sale sign on the Fiat. In time, a very young girl showed up with her parents, and was absolutely starry-eyed about the car; she had to have it, and convinced them to let her buy it. Anxious to sell it, I sold it to her... But, to my forever sorrow, without telling them about the wheel pulling out. Damn it, Ralph, YOU SHOULD HAVE... I had hand-written a note describing the whole wheel-pulling-out debacle, and after they took the car, realized that I had left it in the glove box... Maybe they never looked at it, but if they did, it would have served me right if they brought the car back and demanded their (the young girl's) money back, and/or punched me in the nose.

This was a lousy thing I did, and it pains me to write, and think back about it. The guy who welded the front end back together really beefed it up, so I hope the young girl got some use out of the "little Ferrari", but I still, and never will be able to, reconcile *not* fessing up about the front end.

1962 Chevy Impala two-door hardtop

This will be a quick story. Somehow Kath and I got wind of a really handsome white '62 Impala two-door hardtop with red stripes down the side. It was in good shape, and was a real looker, even though we didn't really have a need for it at the time. Kath had a good-looking maroon Ford Fairlane (???) and I was still driving the Pinto. We bought it, never really used it, then sold it...... when, where, how much, to whom???? Kath probably recalls....

1985 Honda CRX

Ahhh, my first of three (red) Honda Civics, all in a row. I was just starting to see Kathy at the time, and she lived in Red Hook, and I lived in Wappingers: a long "commute". The Pinto was getting weary, but I really didn't know what kind of car I wanted to replace it. We were up in Lake Placid, walking down the main street, when I spotted a little Honda, *with a bicycle inside it...* A perfect car for me.

I bought the red CRX at Friendly Honda, and now had a much more (actually perfectly) reliable car to visit Kath (and, ahem, for everyday use...). It was unique, a good-looker, economical, and, fun. I did eventually replace the stock exhaust system with a kind-of-tinny dual exhaust system. And then, Honda came out with an "Si" hot-rod version. I test drove one at Friendly, and floored it during the drive, and was absolutely stunned at how it accelerated; it was, truly, a "pocket rocket". It had all the good qualities of the '85, plus it...flew... I traded in the '85:

1986 Honda CRX Si

As I just noted, the Si was everything the '85 CRX was, and then some. I owned it for five years, and Kath and I were married during the time I owned it, but, strangely, I don't recall all that much about this great little car. At one point, I traded it in on the 1991 Si hatchback (Kath and I bought nearly-identical cars (hers had a radio, mine didn't...) at Friendly's on the same day):

1991 Honda Civic Si hatchback

I often observed that this was One Of The Best All-Around Cars I Ever Owned. And, after I had sold it, and before the new owner picked it up, I actually wept when I took it for my Last Ride in it... But this is getting ahead of the story.

It was good lookin', extremely fast—acceleration was almost scary—got 40 mpg, and was very practical: all kinds of "things" fit in the hatchback, and bikes and canoes were (fairly) easy to attach to the Yakima roof rack. Right now I can't think of much more to say except that it had 130,000 (maybe 230,000) miles on it when it reached the point where it was no longer practical (sensible) to put any more money into it, and I sold it.

1996 Dodge Neon four-door

We bought this purple Neon from Kath's Aunt Stella up in Pulaski, New York. One thing I recall right away was that it had, among other things, some plastic bags in the trunk, that I found useful to use around town, until I finally noticed that they had writing on the sides that said something like "stool softener"...

I put a good-looking set of mag wheels on it, and a muffler with a pair of good looking wide-spaced chrome exhaust tips. I had a lot of fun with this car, and we had some fine moments on curvey 301 around the reservoir in Putnam County.

One day there was some fluid in the driveway, and I pretty much assumed it was transmission fluid, as these cars had a reputation for "transmission problems". I brought it to what I thought was the most well-known, reputable transmission place in the area, over by IBM where 376 intersected with Route 9. It probably cost me quite a bit to have it "fixed", but the leakage showed up again shortly thereafter. I probably brought it back to them, and my recollection is they said it was an entirely separate "problem". Bullshit...

Long story short, I traded it in, along with Kath's beautiful white Supra, to a used car guy in East Fishkill. I had taken the mags and the pipes off, but he said he wouldn't take it unless I put them back on, so I did. He gave me peanuts for it (and for the Supra), but when I went back to his place sometime later there was writing all over the windows extolling the features of this car, and asking about ten times what he had given us for it. He was a tall, good-looking, charming man, but he personified the prick used car salesman. I understand you have to make a living, but you can also give people that you're buddy buddy with a break. On to the BMW convertible:

211

1996 BMW 328i convertible

I'd always wanted an E-36 BMW, with their jet-fighter-like Coke bottle "pinch" in the mid section. I even admired their black four-door sedans. I spotted the flashy red convertible in a used car lot as I bicycled back and forth to my job in IBM East Fishkill, and fell in love with it. I stopped in and asked about it, and eventually "test drove" it in pouring down rain. I brought it home, and I *wanted* it: period... Goodbye to Aunt Stella's Neon, and Kath's beautiful white Supra, that I often referred to as our "wedding anniversary" car. I did not dicker about the price of the BMW: I recall it was pretty fair, but still a bit hefty.

At the time, I figured, this was the last car I'd ever have to buy: after all, it was a **BMW**... The straight six was surprisingly powerful, and, the power was very smooth: no fuss, no noise, just strong, steady power. And what a looker it was: a **red** convertible... We took it to Uncle Bob Kiggin's funeral upstate, and I walked it up to 100 mph on the Thruway, with the top down and Sue and Sal in the back seat...

Then one day some kind of light came on on the dash and it cost me something like $750.00 to have some kind of sensor replaced. This became a too-often occurrence: every time a bird farted anywhere in four counties a sensor had to be replaced. The guy that replaced them called the "check engine" light the "check money" light. When he started making noises about the O2 sensors on the exhaust system, Kath said the car was "like a Greek God with brain damage".

It was off the road one entire summer, until I finally bit the bullet and had some kind of sensor replaced for more Big Bucks. It had tire problems: Gawd they were expensive, and had water pump problem symptoms. I spiffed it up and sold it back to the used car guy: he gave us peanuts for it: whadda guy... I (secretly) hoped it had as many problems for him as it had for us.

All in all, it was one of the shittiest cars I ever owned.

2006 Chevy Aveo hatchback

Ahh, the little white Aveo. Honda Civics were getting too big and fat, and I needed a car, and spotted this good-lookin' little white Aveo in the Chevy dealership by the Croton Diner, and stopped in a bought it. Like the Neon, I put a good-lookin' set of mags on it (don't really recall now whether I put pipes on it). And, we had some fine moments, until one day the front disk brake pads (or the calipers???) all fell off, and Chevy didn't think it was a big deal enough to back this up... Bullshit...

Again, this woulda/coulda/shoulda been a great car, except that it really was a Kia or something like that, and Chevy didn't put the time and energy (and $$$) into it make it a good little car: they were too busy selling enormous fucking Suburbans...

So, I was finally able to buy a Smart Car, here in the USA:

2009 Smart FourTwo Passion Coupe

As of right now, Monday morning, April 3, 2017, this is the Most Fun Car I've Ever Owned, particularly since I added the **SOLO** Performance exhaust system. Who would ever think this goofy little red car could sound better than a lot of late-model Corvettes???

I saw my first Smart Car in the parking lot at Trinity College in Dublin back in 1999, a year after they came out. I took a picture of it, and, I wanted one. It took ten years to get one. I opted for the Passion Coupe, with mags, Ferrari-like paddle shifters, and a (non-opening) dark plastic "sun roof". The paddle shifters became intuitive after my first ride around the block in the Smart Center Fairfield, where I bought the car. The ride home was hellish, as it had to be kept under 50 mph for a while, and this was about 30 mph slower than most of the Connecticut traffic around Fairfield. Kath finally tucked in behind me and maybe we put on the four-way flashers.

I love this little car. I really do. It goes like stink on stink (though I have *never* floored it), and consistently delivers around 45 mpg (topping out at 56.5, breaking 50 mpg (and getting over 400 miles on an eight-gallon tank)) this past summer. It makes people—from Mercedes drivers to school kids—smile, and I have to be constantly aware of people's potential reaction to the car. It's the opposite of the hoards of "cookie-cutter" cars out there, and "you can't rob a bank or have an affair when you're driving a car like this".

People often ask me (the same) three questions:

Do you feel safe in it??? It has a steel NASCAR-like roll cage. There's a U-tube video out there where somebody has set one of these up remote control and they drive it into a Jersey Barrier at 70 mph and neither the windshield, nor any of the glass, breaks..........

How is it on Interstates??? I tell them I get blown off the road all the time, but it has a parachute and it floats... Some people believe me... Actually the wind has very very rarely affected it: every once in a while, when even "normal: cars are being buffeted, but it's not something I have to be overly concerned about, or constantly aware of.

Is it electric??? No, it's a one-litre three-banger, in the rear. Smart makes an electric version, and I drove one, and was shocked at how it accelerated, but disappointed by its too-short range. It would be pretty much a city car.

I have had two problems with it: the oil pan developed a leak about a day after the (too short) warranty ran out. I made noises in Fairfield, and the Service Manager finally agreed to fix the leak for free.

Last year, I joined the Check Money Club. The check engine light kept coming on, and I brought it to Hopewell Auto and they told me what was causing it to come on, and they turned it off. After a few iterations of this, I brought it down to Fairfield and told them (as it turned out) exactly what the problem was. They said they had to "diagnose it" with their equipment: for $250.00.... Bullshit. And, their per-hour labor rates were, in a word, stunning... The car sat in the shop (I could see it on the TV screen) for several hours, as I sat in their boring (but very aptly named) waiting room. Nobody was working on it.

Finally my service rep came out and said it needed the parts Hopewell Auto had said it needed, but they didn't have them in stock and I would have to leave the car and come back. Well, it's a long bitch of a drive down to Fairfield (on the ride down I determined I would never ever buy a car at a dealership so far from home) on the Connecticut coast... They gave me a 2016 loner— they got chubby, and are not "cute" anymore—and I finally came back and it cost me an exorbitant amount of money for the two crappy things to be replaced. All in all, this left a very very bad taste in my mouth... I don't think I'll ever go back to Smart Center Fairfield.

I truly love this little car. It'll be eight years old pretty soon, and is just short of 70,000 miles. Since the check engine fiasco, I don't trust it like I used to. And, I don't like the chubby 2016's...

THE APPALACHIAN TRAIL...

Once upon a time I had a dream—to walk the whole Appalachian Trail. I don't think a helluva lot of people get to "realize" a dream—any dream. But, I realized this one—twice...

Between 1971 and 1975, when I was 34-38 years old, I walked the whole then-2048-mile Maine to Georgia Appalachian Trail. It was hard: it took me 151 days—about five months—grand total. I carried a pack that typically weighed 50 to 60 pounds, I weighed around 140, but I was as strong as an ox. There were many days I hated it: rain, bugs, exhaustion. I completed the Trail on July 19, 1975, atop the northern terminus, Baxter Peak, Katahdin. After I finished, people asked if I would ever do it again. My every-time response: "Only at gunpoint..."

In 1978 I began walking it again, as the instructor of an Arlington School District adult eduction class, a hundred-mile, nine-day (Saturday to the following Sunday) walk on the AT. The class eventually morphed into the Ralph's Peak Hikers club, and as a group we walked from ?????, Vermont to (I think) Duncannon, Pennsylvania. The Peak Hikers gradually went their separate ways, but the core—Jim Haggett, Pete Ricci, Charlie Goodrich, Don Cleverly, and I—continued to plug away. Jim became a marathon runner, and Pete and Charlie graduated to 7000-meter peaks, in Mexico and Central America. I continued to slug away, mostly solo, and 22 years later, on July 29, 2000, I completed the then-2,169-mile Trail a second time, again on Katahdin, a whopping Grand Total of 4,217 miles of on-the-Trail walking.

I feel it's my lifetime "Claim to Fame": to me the single most significant thing that sets me apart from the rest of the 13,999,999,999 people on the planet.

From "The Sixties", page 92, *WILD DUCKS FLYING BACKWARD, The Short writings of Tom Robbins*, Bantam Dell, 2005.

"In most of our lives, for better or for worse, there occurs a period of peak experience, a time when we are at our best, when we meet some challenge, endure some ordeal, receive some special recognition, have some sustained, heretofore unimaginable fun, or just feel consistently happy and free."

For me, this was on the Appalachian Trail in the mid-seventies.

BUT, Robbins goes on:

"There's a tendency then to become psychologically frozen in that glad ice, turning ourselves into living fossils for the remainder of our existence."

Yes, I have remained "frozen" in my "AT existence", but I feel it's not a bad thing (there are a lot of worse things I could be "frozen in", and the experience has evolved (58 countries in 23 time zones on six continents, etc), and a lot of good has come of it, and is still coming.

After I finished the Trail, I spoke about it, and showed my slides to over 10,000 people! I called the presentation "Summertime Dream". Here's my introduction:

IN ADDITION TO WALKING THE ENTIRE MAINE TO GEORGIA APPALACHIAN TRAIL *TWICE*— 4, 217 MILES—RALPH FERRUSI HAS ALSO:

TRAVELED TO 46 COUNTRIES IN 23 TIME ZONES ON 6 CONTINENTS.

TREKKED IN NEPAL TO WITHIN 12 MILES OF EVEREST.

CLIMBED TO 16,500 FEET ON KILIMANJARO, WHERE SEVERE HIGH ALTITUDE CEREBRAL EDEMA (H.A.C.E.) SYMPTOMS FORCED A HASTY RETREAT.

TREKKED ON THE INCA TRAIL IN PERU AND BOLIVIA, EXPLORING MACHU PICCHU AND LAKE TITICACA'S ISLANDS OF THE SUN AND THE MOON.

CLIMBED KOSZCIUSKO, THE HIGHEST MOUNTAIN IN AUSTRALIA —ONE OF THE FABLED "SEVEN SUMMITS"; CARRANTUOHIL, THE HIGHEST MOUNTAIN IN IRELAND; SEVERAL EXTINCT CARRIBEAN VOLCANOES; AND WALKED RIM-TO-RIM IN THE GRAND CANYON.

WALKED VERMONT'S ENTIRE 262-MILE MASSACHUSETTS-TO-CANADA LONG TRAIL.

CLIMBED EVERY 5000 FOOT SUMMIT IN THE NORTHEAST AND ALL 114 NORTHEAST 4000 FOOTERS, INCLUDING

> ALL 63 NEW ENGLAND 4000 FOOTERS,
> ALL 46 NEW HAMPSHIRE 4000 FOOTERS,
> ALL 46 ADIRONDACK 4000 FOOTERS,
> AND CANADA'S JACQUE CARTIER ON THE GASPE PENINSULA.

CLIMBED ALL 35 CATSKILL SUMMITS THAT EXCEED 3500 FEET <u>TWICE</u>, AND CLIMBED THEM ALL IN THE WINTER <u>TWICE</u>.

BACKPACKED AND BICYCLED THRU EUROPE NINE TIMES, HIKING AND CLIMBING IN THE ALPS AND THE PYRENEES.

WALKED NEW YORK STATE'S ENTIRE EXISTING 416-MILE GEORGE WASHINGTON BRIDGE TO LAKE PLACID LONG PATH, INCLUDING THE 135-MILE NORTHVILLE / PLACID TRAIL.

RUN A HALF MARATHON IN ONE HOUR, 28 MINUTES, AND 28 SECONDS.

BICYCLED OVER 6000 MILES A YEAR.

AND MAINTAINS A ONE AND A HALF MILE SECTION OF THE APPALACHIAN TRAIL ON STORMVILLE MOUNTAIN.

HE IS A PUBLISHED AUTHOR—*CATSKILL TALES AND TRAILS; UNCLE BEN, UNCLE BOB, UNCLE JOE, UNCLE PETE, P.D., AND POP*—AWARD-WINNING NEWSPAPER COLUMNIST, AWARD-WINNING ARTIST, TRANSCENDENAL MEDITATOR, AND HAS BEEN A VEGETARIAN SINCE 1974.

HE IS <u>NEVER</u> BORED... ... ...

Ode to the Appalachian Trail:
<u>Rediscovered in November 2020</u>

I returned to the AT
the other day.
It's in my blood,
what more can I say?

Georgia to Maine,
2000 miles long.
Sometimes I know
it's where I belong.

At its simplest,
a path through the woods.
On deeper levels,
It delivers the goods.

Mountains, towns, valleys,
it goes on and on.

Trail people its backbone,
its heart and its song.

Benton MacKaye thunk it,
in the 20's one day.
Volunteers keep it going,
Along its long way.

Trail angels, towns, magic,
evolved through the years.
Gotta love 'em,
all giving, all peers.

I first walked on it,
in '71.
When I got back,
I thought I was done.

The next four years,
I kept plugging away.
Little by little,
towards that Big Day.

Atop Katahdin,
In '75.
Triumphant and pumped,
really really alive.

In '78,
it was time to give back.
Playing it forward,
on the right track.

Two thousand and one,
Katahdin again.
Now time to help Pete,
on his end-to-end.

Two thousand and nine,
still Hooked on the Trail.
Four decades later,
it's been the Real Deal

2020:

Now I live in Maryland
those Glory Days miles away
Am I still "Elvis Trailsley"?
Right now it's hard to say

<u>ALDHA Gathering, October 2011</u>

In October 2011 I presented Summertime Dream at the 30th Annual Gathering of the Appalachian Trail Long Distance Hikers Association (ALDHA) at the Massachusetts College of Liberal Arts in North Adams, Massachusetts. Over the years I had presented this slide show to "over 10,000 people". As my presentation (unfortunately for me) coincided with that year's keynote speaker, "extreme adventurer" Andrew Skurka, I now can say I've presented my slides to approximately 10,020 people... I wrote a special introduction. Here it is:

It's 1974. There's probably a few of you out there that haven't been born yet. I'm standing here in front of you with brown hair down to my shoulders and a full beard, with a lot of hopes and dreams. One of those is to walk the whole Appalachian Trail.

I first set foot on the AT in 1971, forty years ago. According to the ATC, at that time only 92 people had walked the whole Trail. 12,236 have walked it as of Monday. From '71 to '74 I picked away at it, and had pieced together the whole Trail from Gorham, New Hampshire to Linden, Virginia—about 900 miles—on weekends, vacations, holidays: any chance I could get.

I was a section hiker, but we weren't called section hikers then, we were just hikers. There weren't Trail Names, nor Trail Angels or Trail Magic, though in the Shenandoah picnickers and tourists offered us food, and a family welcomed us into their home.

Guide books were very basic, and maps were, in a word, crude: no topo lines, no elevation profiles(though this might have been a blessing). There weren't hundreds of "I walked the Trail" books, and "I'm walking the Trail" websites; Ed Garvey's *Appalachian Hiker*, with its first-ever Mileage Fact Sheet, was the inspiration for my whole generation of hikers. Some of us kept written journals, and we'd call home when we were in town to let a few folks back home know we were still alive. No Internet, cell phones, etc, to let the entire world know when you changed your socks and underwear.

You were just out there, DOING IT.

Probably a decent amount of the Trail hasn't changed a bit since 1974, and some of it has changed a lot. The Trail was more rugged back then—switchbacks????—what are switchbacks??? And, Ray Jardine hadn't Gone Lite: our packs, with a full food load, weighed 62-65 pounds. We called them "lead sleds".

I carried a five-pound Nikon camera, and after I finished the Trail on July 19, 1975—the 311th person to complete it—I ultimately showed my slides to over 10,000 people. Back then I began my presentation with an overview of the AT—2,048 miles, Benton MacKaye—but most of you know all that. And, I told my audiences that the opening slides were taken all along the Trail. Most were, but some were taken in the Catskills and my front yard.

I won't remember the names of some of the people, or some of the mountains, gaps, or shelters—maybe you can help me out—though we all took pictures at MacAfee Knob... And, consider this: some of the bright young 20-year-olds in these pictures are now collecting Social Security...

The AT has changed me in many ways, and it still has a strong hold on me. I've been a maintainer for 33 years, and I now live 400 steps from the Trail atop Stormville Mountain, in New York; our back property line is National Park Service, the AT corridor. I've maintained the mile and a half of Trail behind the house for 21 years. You'll like the switchbacks I pick-and-shoveled in.

A final note: the taste of adventure instilled by the AT has led me to 54 countries, in 23 time zones, on six continents.

And, a technical note: when I had the 40-year-old slides put on a CD, some of the colors and saturation became a little bizarre.

OK, after the series of opening slides "taken all along the Trail"; let's head down to Springer Mountain, in June of 1974.................

Kath AT thoughts: October 2016

I stopped going to the gym and replaced my drive, treadmill, step-class, get dressed in the locker room, 4:44 am start with a walk on the trail to begin my day. The walk, not a hike, just a gentle stroll really, gets me centered and balanced. Participating in the natural world is a boost to my mental and physical well-being. In the summer I get to see the sun-rise either on my way out or back to the house. I come back to start my work-day with the smell of the woods, the sound of my steps, and the daily variation of the changing seasons.

I am not a through hiker or even a section hiker. I walk in the woods and on the AT to exercise my limbs and stabilize my mind. I have done longer hikes locally and in other states. When I see the white blazes my thought is always, I could walk home from here, very comforting and connected. The blazes keep me on track and trail while also allowing me the room to roam, I can always find my way by following the dots.

When there is snow, I ski and snowshoe as well. Most visitors to our house also get time in the woods, just a few steps away from many neighborhoods is the National Park Service gem, I take pride in having a country where we cherish the nature and invite all to share.

Little Claire And The Flamingos

Father's Day, Sunday, June 15, 2008, would have been a great hiking day: sunny and mild; perfect. But we had a list of house/yard chores a mile long, and we spent the entire day fixing, repairing, maintaining, cleaning, putting away, sorting out and throwing out things. Late in the afternoon, Kath decided that the old, goofy pink plastic Flamingos that we had had in the yard for years, just for laughs, had to go. Then she had an inspiration: "Why don't you take them up to the Trail??? Just for the heck of it. And, it will give you a chance to get away a bit, soothe yourself."

I took the six sun-bleached, faded Flamingos, some still attached to their metal "legs", some not, up to the AT, turned right (north), and walked uphill to where the Trail leveled out. There was a slightly higher, somewhat rocky point about 30 feet to the right of the Trail, and I artistically placed them there, some staring at the Trail, some staring at each other. I stepped back and admired my handiwork. Some of the "powers that be" in charge of Trail "rules and regulations" might not appreciate the humor and the irony, but I was sure the 2008 crop of thru-hikers, marching up the "long green tunnel" would love 'em.

I often encounter thru-hikers—it's pretty easy to pick them out—at the Mountain Top Deli, and I tell them I'm the Trail maintainer for the section they (northbounders) had just walked, but this year I also asked them if they saw any unusual wildlife up on the ridge. Nine times out of ten their faces would light up, and they would say, "The Flamingos!!!! I/we took a picture of them!" Kinda made their day, they'd write about it in their journals that night, and this was what it was all about.

Fast forward to 2009. I had walked over to the high viewpoint on Hosner, and was coming back where the Trail slabs the western side of the ridge for quite a while, and I encountered a young family heading south on the Trail. Bill, Amy, and three-year-old little Claire were heading to the Ralph's Peak Hiker's Cabin, for Claire's first overnight on the Trail. Claire's quite a hiker, but now she was perched high on Bill's shoulders.

They lived on Hosner Mountain Road, and often walked the local sections. Bill was a 1999 2000-Miler, and every summer they put signs up on either side of Hosner, inviting hikers to a picnic/barbecue in their back yard, right up the hill from the AT crossing. Bill wanted to become a maintainer, and asked me if I would keep him in mind if and when I ever decided, or had to, "let go" of "my" section. I was touched by his sincerity, and immediately felt he would be the perfect heir to the section that I had maintained, at that time, for almost 20 years. And, had become quite attached to.

They then told me the story of Claire's First AT Hike the previous September, when Claire was two years old. They had headed north from Hosner, up the switchbacks, past "Grand View", down into the Holler Where the Leprechauns Live, and up "north" Stormville Mountain. Claire was a natural-born-hiker, and was lovin' it. Then, she spotted the Flamingos, and, delighted, ran over to them, enthused and enthralled, as only an two-year-old can be. She was hooked on hikin' now: you could discover magic things, like pink Flamingos, in the woods. What a story. You've gotta love that AT Trail. Gotta love it.

I'd check the Flamingos periodically, make sure they were still gazing at the Trail, or each other, stand them back up if they had fallen over. Near the end of the 2008 hiking season, a flamingo disappeared. No big whoops, we knew this might happen, anyway. Then another vanished, until, ultimately, one day, there were no more Flamingos up on the Stormville Mountain ridge. It was, truly, kind of a sad day.

Eventually Ollie Simpson, tireless, remarkable local AT volunteer, reported that one or two were now residing at a couple of shelters north of Stormville Mountain. I confirmed that one was, indeed, guarding the entrance to the side trail to the Morgan Stewart. In 2009, rumor had it that besides the Stewart flamingo, several more were in residence at the Wiley, the Pioneers or the Ten Mile River Shelters. I haven't confirmed this. There certainly seemed to be a northbound trend—there has never been a report of a sighting south of Stormville Mountain.

Maybe someday one of them will get to Connecticut, or beyond. Someday, a thru-hiker may be holding one (or two) in their "Katahdin photo". You've gotta love that AT Trail. Gotta love it...

Thanks again, Benton MacKaye, for one Great Idea.

Thanks again, Bill, Amy, and little Claire, for reminding me there still can be magic out there in the woods.

November 24, 2009

Appalachian Trail Timeline

December 23, 1971: The first time I "officially" set foot on the AT. Walked from Route 9 by Graymoor to Route 9D north of the Bear Mountain Bridge and back.

1971-1974: Walked a contiguous 900 miles from Gorham, New Hampshire to Front Royal, Virginia on weekends, vacations, and holidays.

1974: Walked approximately 900 miles from Springer to Front Royal in two months.

1975: Walked approximately 300 miles from Gorham to Baxter State Park in about three weeks.

July 19, 1975: Completed the then 2,048-mile Trail on Katahdin. Became the 311th person ever to walk the entire Trail.

1976/1977?: Unofficially "adopted" the (since demolished) AT shelter near the northeast corner of Canopus Lake, Fahnestock.

1978: Became the official AT maintainer from Duell Hollow Road (Wiley Shelter) to the Harlem Valley State Hospital dump road. Often bicycled from Wappingers Falls to do Trail maintenance.

1978: Began re-walking the Trail as the teacher of an Arlington High School Adult Education class. The classes walked approximately 100 miles of Trail on the week of the Fourth of July, and the hikes became known as "Nine Days". The classes eventually evolved into Ralph's Peak Hikers club, continuing the nine-day tradition, and as a club we eventually walked the AT from Glencliff, New Hampshire, below Mount Moosilaukee to Duncannon, Pennsylvania.

Early 80's?: Declared a small cinder block cabin on property the National Park Service had acquired on Hortontown Road as a "Trail Shelter", that became Ralph's Peak Hikers' Cabin.

1983/1984: The club builds the Morgan Stewart Memorial Shelter south of Depot Hill Road, thanks to club member Fred Swincicki obtaining a $2,500.00 IBM Community Service Funds grant. The shelter was built with old-fashioned hand tools in Bob Haas's garage in Hopewell Junction, from plans of a shelter I had seen in Pennsylvania. The walls use intricately interlocking square oak logs When completed, it is dis-assembled and transported to the prepared Trail site in pieces.

198?: The club dissolves, and Jim Haggett, Pete Ricci, Don Cleverly, Charlie Goodrich, and I keep walking nine-days for a few more years, then go separate ways. I keep plugging away.

1988: The Telephone Pioneers Shelter is built on a steep hillside south of West Dover Road (and the Dover Oak), using the same intricately interlocking logs design as the Morgan Stewart. Most of the heavy pieces are helicoptered in.

1990: I assumed maintenance of the 1 ½ miles of AT on Stormville Mountain between Hosner Mountain Road and New York State Route 52.

July 29, 2000: After 22 years, I finished the then 2,169-mile Trail a second time, on Katahdin, a Grand Total of 4,217 Trail miles.

20??: I'm featured in a segment of the New York State Department of Transportation film *Better Than Before*, filmed just north of Ralph's Peak Hikers' Cabin. Bette Midler is also featured in the film.

2009: I'm filmed sawing out a blowdown just north of Hosner Mountain Road, and on the Bear Mountain Bridge, in the Mid-Atlantic Highlands portion of the National Geographic Society's *America's Wild Spaces, the Appalachian Trail* film. Brian Armstrong, the film's director, invites Kath and I to the World Premier of the film in Grosvenor Hall in the Society's World Headquarters in Washington DC. It receives a standing ovation.

Sunday, August 3, 2009: Kathy and I accompany Pete Ricci to the top of Katahdin, as he finishes the whole AT after 27 years, the first—and up to now only—member of the Peak Hikers to finish the Trail. It was a tough, 11-hour round trip.

2012/2013????: I'm filmed by "Sasquatch", a 2000-Miler amateur film maker, while doing Trail work on Stormville Mountain. This film captures the nuts-and-bolts of the everyday 2000 miler experience better than any AT film I've ever seen.

May 23, 2017: The first time, in a 46-year AT involvement, that I've put together a "timeline"....

From *The Appalachian Trail, Celebrating America's Hiking Trail*

From the *Foreword* by Bill Bryson, pp. 8-9:

"I can unhesitatingly say that I have never been so tired and wet and cold and stiff and bedraggled as I often was along the A.T.....But I also never, anywhere, experienced more transcendently sublime moments than I did in our long summer of toiling up and down mountains."

From a Page 68 quote from David Brill, 1990, *As Far as the Eye Can See*:

"I doubt that any other event of my life will choke me with as much emotion, fill me with as much pride, or define more clearly who I am than my summer on the Appalachian Trail."

March 20, 2018

Appalachian Trail Quotes

Richard Judy, author of *Thru: An Appalachian Trail Love Story,* commenting on David Hiscoe's 2018 *Take the Path of Most Resistance*: "So many end-to-end hikers have rattled off memoirs adding to a slush pile of genuinely forgettable accounts of daily drudgery."

January 12, 2019

Planting Seeds: Trail Magic Becomes A Two-Way Street

Last spring Marie, a friend of a friend, asked me if I'd like to take some of her 4-H kids for a walk on the Appalachian Trail. I've walked the whole Trail twice—4,217 miles—and the "AT" is in my blood, etched into my fiber, my very soul. I agreed to take the kids for a short walk, but deep down I wasn't really sure I'd like to spend a day in the woods with a bunch of modern-day, spoiled, whiny, electronic-gadget-minded rug rats.

Several months later, the Big Day finally arrived. It rained… Back to Square One. The next day the weather cooperated, and I arrived at the trailhead 15 minutes early, curious as to who would show up. A dark grey minivan pulled in, and Sue got out and introduced herself, four-year-old Jacob, and six-year-old twins Sarah and Derek, all blond haired, bright-eyed, and full of energy: good kids. This just might be fun. Three more minivans pulled in, and the headcount rose to ten kids—five girls, five boys, ages 4–15—and four moms—Sue, Katrina, Marie, and Allison—all polite, enthusiastic people.

Geared up and ready to roll, I gathered them up and asked if anyone had ever been on the AT. 15-year-old Brooke shyly raised her hand, and between the two of us we explained the AT was a hiking trail, but one of the things that made it unique was it was 2000 MILES LONG. To emphasis this to the kids, I said if we started walking it today—July 20th—we would, walking just about all day, every day, not finish *until Christmas*. I'm not really sure if this impressed them, but, it sure impressed me! I explained the white, blue, and double Trail blazes, thru-hikers, and how one man, Mr. Benton MacKaye, had made a very positive difference in the lives of millions of people.

Off we went, like a herd of turtles, our goal, Nuclear Lake—a pristine lake, with a terrible name—about a mile and a half north. I asked Marie to lead us at first and said anyone else could take turns leading if they wanted to—just follow the white blazes.

Marie's a teacher, and she began pointing out small trailside natural wonders, like Indian Pipes, as we walked and Brooke—the apple doesn't fall far from the tree—chimed in, spotting things I wouldn't have noticed in a million years, including a tiny grey caterpillar on a log. The kids gathered around, wide-eyed. Jacob, the youngest, said, "Can I touch it?" I gently let it crawl unto my finger, then onto his. He was fascinated, awestruck, by this simple act. I was fascinated by his fascination.

Later, ten-year-old Noah caught a toad, and they all gathered 'round, wide-eyed and curious. They were enthralled by frogs in vernal pools. Brooke demonstrated how to make an acorn cap a (loud!) whistle. I didn't get the hang of it (I practiced at home later, as promised, and mastered the technique), but several kids did. The woods were full of wonders, and whistles, and I was as delighted to be sharing them—learning about them— with these kids as they were discovering them. For them, and now for me, it was about the journey, not the destination.

When we arrived at the lake several kids—and some parents—dashed to the shore line, where they took off their shoes and waded in the clear, cool, shallow water. As we settled in for lunch, several of the boys skipped rocks.

My one-word description of the day: delightful. A group of well-behaved, curious, enthusiastic, respectful kids, and four great Moms. Back in the parking lot, we immediately started kicking around ideas for another trip on a different stretch of Trail, and, the possibility of an overnighter at one of the nearby shelters with some of the older kids.

As deeply ingrained as the Appalachian Trail—and its culture— is to me now, it occurred to me that at one time I had never heard of it: I had no idea what it was or what it was all about. Today, seeds had been planted. Some of these kids may be future "2000-Milers". Or, who knows, maybe some of the Moms....

702 words

Taking a Step Back

I grew up in a small house on a 100X100-foot lot in a small town. There was a small brook running through the lot, and in the woods beyond the lot there was a dirt path running through the woods alongside the brook. I spent a lot of happy hours walking through the woods on that path, down and back to the street it ended up at about a quarter mile away.

There's also a dirt path through the woods up behind the house I've lived in for the last 28 years. It's a very long dirt path, but, when it comes right down to it, it is, in essence, a dirt path through the woods. I've spent a lot of happy hours walking on this dirt path up behind the house, and every once in a while I come across a tree that has fallen across the path. I dutifully return with my bow saws and Home Depot (Made in India) axe and clear the tree from the path. I've been doing this for various parts of this path for 40 years.

Over the years, various clubs, conferences, government agencies (and even a "conservancy") have sprung up, making ever-increasing rules and ever-elaborate regulations and restrictions concerning what I can (but mostly what they've deemed I *cannot*) do when I find a tree laying across the path.

If I followed these rules, regulations, and restrictions to the letter and made all the now- "necessary/required" phone calls and filled out all the paperwork it would probably take a month to do something that would take me about 15 minutes to do if I just walked up to the dirt path and did what had to be done. I would ***never*** think of doing this...

My Appalachian Trail Favorites
1971-1975, 1979-2000 First Pass

Shelter: Cooper Brook Falls, Maine

Trail town: Hot Springs, North Carolina

AMC hut: Greenleaf, New Hampshire

Mountain: Lafayette, New Hampshire

Lake: Nahmakanta Lake, Maine

River(s): The French Broad, the Nolichucky

Hostel: Bob People's Kincora

Outrageous Trail Name: "Toxic Sugar Butt"

Highway Intersection: Cloverdale/Troutville, Virginia

On the Trail railroad station: Metro North, Pawling, New York

(Outrageous) spring: Potaywadjo Spring, Maine

View of Katahdin: From Nahmakanta Lake

Memorial Garden: Geraldine Messerich Memorial Garden, Ralph's Peak Hikers' Cabin, New York

State: Pennsylvania :)))))))))))))

Food and Drink

Pizza: Danny's, Stormville, New York

Bakery: Worthington's, New Jersey

Trail food in the 70's: Peanut M&M's

Sandwiches: Mountaintop Deli, "Lily of the Deli", Stormville, New York

Right on the Trail soda machines: Maryland

Unfavorites

Brushy Mountain(s), Virginia

The much-too-steep South Slope of South Kinsman, New Hampshire

Worst false summits: northbound up Mount Success, Maine

July 4, 2020

My Appalachian Trail Favorites
1971-1975, 1979-2000 Second Pass

Outfitter: Bluff Mountain Oufitters, Hot Springs, North Carolina

Motel: Mull's Motel, Hiawasee, Georgia

Inn: Bear Mountain Inn, New York

Monastery: Graymoor, New York

Church: Father Charles Holy Family Catholic Church, Pearisburg, Virginia

Boarding house: Keith Shaw's, Monson, Maine

General store: Caratunk, Maine

New England Inn: the Fife n' Drum, Kent, Connecticut

Major bridge: Bear Mountain Bridge, over the Hudson River, New York

Yuppy Trail Town: Kent, Connecticut

College town: Hanover, New Hampshire

View of Manhattan: Bear Mountain Tower/West Mountain Shelter, New York

360-degree views: All of those BIG Southern balds

"Trail of the Future": Eddie Walsh's incredibly designed trail, north slope of Bear Mountain, New York

Outstanding ATC Headquarters, Harpers Ferry, West Virginia people: Jean Cashin, Laurie Potteiger

Swimming hole: Nuclear Lake, New York

Small beach: on the Housatonic River, Connecticut, just north of the Ten Mile River bridge

Big beach(s): Pine Grove Furnace, Pennsylvainia; Canopus Lake, Fahnestock State Park, New York

Trail maps: the New York-New Jersey Trail Conference's highly-detailed full-colored topo maps

Great double blaze idea: New York-New Jersey Trail Conference *staggered* blazes

Blazes: George Muller's Hosner Mountain, New York blazes

"Lyin' guidebooks: Too many...

Single's bar: Just kidding......

Food and Drink

Ice cream: the "Ice Cream Lady", Vernon Valley, New Jersey; Pine Grove Furnace, Pennsylvania's "Half Gallon Challenge", the ice cream stand at the north end of Damascus, Virginia

Trail shelter to order Chinese take-out from: Ralph's Peak Hikers' Cabin, New York

Overrated???

MacAfee Knob photos...

July 4, 2020

The Last Mountain

Back in the day I used to—just about literally—run up, and down, mountains: 3000-, 4000-, and 5000-footers in the Catskills, Adirondacks, Vermont, New Hampshire, Maine, Europe, the Caribbean. I lugged 50-60 pound backpacks for years, day after day, on the AT, the Long Trail, etc, etc.

The times they have a'changed: it's been a while—quite a while—since I've been on a mountain of any consequence. Not that long ago Kath, Ralph, and I bagged Catskill peaks pretty regularly, winter and summer. Thinking about it, it's been quite a while since we've bagged a Catskill peak. Surprisingly, the last 3500-footer I bagged was Table, with Ralph III and Pete Ricci, on Wednesday, July 31, 2013: *three and a half years ago!* The last 67'er was 3,420-foot Stoppel Point, on the Escarpment Trail, on March 13, 2016.

I don't "hike" anywhere near as often as I used to. I do try to get out on the AT up on the ridge for walks, but when I walk the mile over to Hosner, and back, it just about always beats me up much more than I feel this relatively "easy" walk should.

So, lately I've been thinking about when I'll "climb my last mountain". I recall reading in the ADK 46'er quarterly, "PEEKS", quite a while ago a description of the legendary Grace Hudowalski's—ADK 46'er #9—last climb. My recollection is she specifically chose Esther—basically, a bump on a ridge sticking out from Whiteface—as her very last climb, as it had been the very first 46'er she had ever climbed.

So, I wondered what peak I would choose for my Very Last Climb. Hmmm. I can't imagine, nowadays, banging out peaks like Friday and Balsam Cap; I'll probably never set foot on them again. My recollection is the first 3500-footer I climbed was Wintenberg, with Howie Roth, a long, long time ago. The current route up Wintenberg from Woodland Valley is not one of my favorites, and, it's a pretty rugged climb: I doubt if I would care to reenact my original climb.

But, most likely, if I had to choose a Last Peak to climb it would be in the Catskills. I mentally ran through the list of 3500-footers, and there really weren't many peaks that I would now care to slog up for this weird occasion. Most likely I would choose an "easy" 3500-footer like Balsam Lake, or, Windham High Peak; though nowadays even easy Windham has kicked my ass more than I care to admit.

So, considering how "difficult" it is for me to even do "easy" walks anymore, and, considering the current "unstable" state of my health in some important aspects, I just might already *have* climbed my last peak....

Stoppel Point??? Not exactly a Blaze of Glory. Shit.............................

January 15, 2017

Cairn Memories: In Defense Of Cairns

Prepare to arise, all ye zealous, self-appointed cairn-police/cairn-bashers/cairn-busters. Be outraged, foam at the mouth, scatter Little Johnny's innocently- and proudly-arranged little pile of rocks, near the "official" big pile of rocks marking the actual summit of what may perhaps have been the very first 4000-foot pile of dirt that he had ever in his young life climbed.

Cairns: I love 'em: many of them serve as unmistakeable, hard to miss trail markers. Some mark the "true" summit of trail-less (and trailed) peaks, reassuring us obsessive "gotta-find-the-very-very-very-highest point", saving a lot of angst, anxiety, and thrashing about. Many serve no purpose at all: just-for-fun, just-for-the-hell-of-it, make-ya-smile: pure whimsy, in this getting-all-too-serious day and age. Cairns always make me smile when I come across one (or more) unexpectedly on some stretch of trail, or road. I often add a rock.

How could you not be impressed by the legendary Guy Waterman's eye-catching, works-of-art, architectural wonders on the Greenleaf Trail up the west slope of Lafayette from Franconia Notch in the Whites??? I had the honor of meeting Guy up there one long-ago day, and was deeply impressed not only by the man, but by his cairns.

And, I dare say I might not be writing this, and a few of you might not be around to be reading this, if it wasn't for all those cairns, maybe less than twenty feet apart, high above treeline on the Presidential Ridge. There were a few zero-visibility white-out days when if it wasn't for those cairns that— to get maybe a wee bit too maudlin and dramatic—I may have stumbled around, until, exhausted, I became just another Mount Washington/ Presidential Range grim statistic.

There was that time in Northern Ireland, heading for the Devil's Causeway, when we came upon a quarter-mile or so of ingenious cairns, lining the road along the rocky coast. We were compelled to stop and add our own creations. I, in a burst of creativity/originality, attempted to build mine "upside down", and it ultimately toppled over. I rebuilt it more conventionally.

Then there's that huge cairn atop Popolopen Torne in the West Hudson Highlands south of West Point Military Academy built by West Pointers and service men in honor of service men Missing, Wounded, or Killed in Action. It moved me—an Honorably Discharged US Army Field Artillery Radio Sergeant—deeply, and made me proud. I added a rock.

We've been assured by cairns on the Everest Base Camp Trail in Nepal, on the Marangu ("Coca Cola") Route on Kilimanjaro, and on the West Highland Way in Scotland, not to mention on the high southern "balds" and above timberline in the Whites, Presidentials, and Maine's Mahoosucs on the Appalachian Trail.

Then there's that much-maligned little cairn on the old roadbed west of the Devil's Acre leanto on Hunter that marks the left turn up the faint herd path that points you in the general direction of the elusive Leavitt Peak (formerly Southwest Hunter) canister. It has never "ruined" or in any way shed a negative light on any of my Southwest Hunter quests using this approach. Rather, I have always been thankful that someone had been thoughtful enough to place it there to assist/help/guide future peakbaggers. Thank you, whoever you are.

I've built several cairns on the mile-and-a-half stretch of AT on Stormville Mountain in Dutchess County that I've maintained since 1990. Hikers add to them, and every once in a while other cairns pop up.

And, just for the fun of it, my wife Kathy and I have built a half-dozen eye-catchers along the low stone wall marking the front of our property. Guy Waterman would've loved 'em..

Ralph Joseph Ferrusi
    #2023
    Catskill 3500 #122, #34W
    Appalachian Trail 4000-Miler (2000-Miler #311)
    38-year AT Maintainer
    Northeast 114er
    Author, *Catskill Tales and Trails*
    Cairn Builder.................

612 words

WAR/THE MILITARY

Land Mines in Vietnam

I just finished author/Vietnam vet Tim O'Brien's 1975 *If I Die in a Combat Zone Box Me Up and Ship Me Home*. He devotes Chapter Fourteen, *Step Lightly*, to the horrors of North Vietnamese land mines: Bouncing Bettie's, booby-trapped grenades, and directional-fragmentation, M-14 antipersonnel, and Soviet/Chinese antitank mines.

He wraps up the chapter:

After the war, he [the Vietnam vet] can begin to be bitter. Those who point at and degrade his bitterness, those who declare that it's all a part of war and that this is a job which must be done—to those patriots I will recommend a postwar vacation to this land, where they can swim in the sea, lounge under a fine sun, stroll in the quaint countryside, wife and son in hand. Certainly, there will be a mine or two still in the earth. Alpha Company did not detonate all of them.

December 4, 2018

Lieutenant General Hal Moore on "War"

I'm a huge fan of General Hal Moore. Years ago I read his *We Were Soldiers Once, and Young*, about the November 1965 Ia Drang battle in Vietnam. I'm now reading *We Are Soldiers Still*, about his return to the Ia Drang in the mid-'90's where he met with the North Vietnamese officers who were his opponents in the Ia Drang. Here are some of his comments on "War":

"Most wars are cruel and costly mistakes whose causes are rooted in the failure of diplomacy and poor judgment in national leaders. It is far easier to get into a war than to get out of one. The outcome is seldom what those who championed a war, any war, envisioned when first the bands began to play and soldiers began to march."

"War is absolutely the last card any national leader should play, and only when every other alternative has been exhausted."

"[Any] questions [raised] demand answers and careful thought *before* the war drums are sounded and the dogs of war let loose."

December 5, 2017

I Was A Soldier Once, And Young

I'm flying to Washington, DC on a Hudson Valley Honor Flight on Saturday, April 13, 2019 as a "Post Korean War/Vietnam Era" veteran.

Whenever I see a guy wearing a World War II, Korea, or Vietnam cap I shake their hand and thank them for their service. If they are Vietnam vets, I also say "Welcome home." Recently I was surprised to see a guy with a Vietnam *Era* cap.

I served in the United States Army National Guard from 1959-1965: between Korea and Vietnam. I contacted the Honor Flight people and asked if I was eligible for a flight. They said yes, and sent me an application.

I wasn't a gunner on a B-17 or B-24, and didn't land on a beach at Guadalcanal or Iwo Jima. I survived six weeks of Regular US Army Basic Training in Fort Knox, Kentucky, trained in a Signal Corps school in Fort Gordon, Georgia, and once fired a 50-calibre machine gun at "enemy" tanks and trucks from a ridgetop in Camp Drum, New York.

But...on Saturday, April 13th I will walk tall and proud in Washington DC, as an Honorably Discharged Radio Sergeant, 156th Field Artillery, USANG.

NG22002843: A Soldier.......................

March 10, 2019

9/11

2007-2015 I wrote yearly 9/11 columns. This 2009 column was rejected as "not appropriate", because it included a long quote from Sean Michael Flynn's *The Fighting 69ᵗʰ—One Remarkable National Guard Unit's Journey from Ground Zero to Baghdad*.

The words I quoted are absolutely *the* most poignant words I have ever read about 9/11. Here's the rejected column:

It's easy to take our hiking and walks in the woods for granted, but as the country song says, "freedom don't come free", and 09/11/09 just might be a good time to think about this.

As you are pulling on your hiking boots this weekend, trying to decide whether to climb Windham High Peak, or Panther, or Breakneck Ridge, or go for a stroll around Dennings Point, give some thought to the thousands of other American men and women, pulling on their boots, in some God-forsaken, hostile, far-away place on the other side of the world, defending your freedom and taken-for-granted but not-exactly-God-given "right to hike". Or think back to the firemen, policemen, or National Guardsmen who pulled on their boots, some for the last time, on September 11, 2001.

The following passage, Page 32, Chapter 2, Book 1—"Minutemen"—of Sean Michael Flynn's "The Fighting 69ᵗʰ—One Remarkable National Guard Unit's Journey from Ground Zero to Baghdad"—relating a 09/11/01 incident at the ruins of the World Trade Towers brought tears to my eyes, and may give you pause. This paragraph wasn't the only time this superbly-written book effected me this deeply. Later descriptions of incidents and events at the wreckage of the World Trade Center and in Taji and Baghdad elicited similar, deeply emotional responses. Ultimately this book made me extremely proud of these American "citizen soldiers", proud to be an American, and proud to be a New Yorker (and former National Guardsman: Radio Sergeant Ralph Joseph Ferrusi Jr.).

The back cover of the book states: "Read it. Give it to people you love. It's about our country."

I have...
I did...
It is... .....

"2: MINUTEMEN

[New York Army National Guard 69th Infantry Regiment Battalion Commander, Lieutenant Colonel Geoffrey James] Slack stared at the ground, squinting through the shroud of ash and smoke to get a better look at what he had just stumbled across. Next to his dust-covered boots was a shoe that still contained a foot. He crouched down and blinked tears over his dry, burning eyes to make sure of what he was looking at. There was no mistaking it. Though he had already encountered dozens of horrific sights, nothing else he had seen at the World Trade Center defined what had happened earlier that morning more completely than that shoe. He reached out with his left hand and picked it up. It was a light blue pump, and though her foot was sheared off through the ankle, Slack could picture the woman who had put it on that morning. She had driven to the train for the commute into Manhattan on the Long Island Rail Road. It was a crowded ride, but she managed to get a window seat and stared into the bright September day, isolated in her own thoughts about work, an overdue oil change for her car, and her beautiful children, who would have already finished their breakfast and begun the trip to school. When she got into the city, she rode the subway to the World Trade Center and bought a banana and a bottle of juice at the newsstand before riding the elevator to her office high up the tower. Then she and thousands of other people—innocent civilians, people sitting at their desks, having a cup of coffee, going to their offices—were murdered by some filthy terrorists who had deluded themselves through a twisted psychology into thinking that what they were doing was a noble act. It wasn't noble. It was murder—senseless, pitiful murder. Slack needed to do something, but what? He wanted to help, but how? After several moments of struggling with feelings of uselessness, he decided that all he could do for the moment was to try to give that woman back some dignity and respect. Slack rose from his crouch, opened the right cargo pocket of his camouflage uniform, and gently slid her foot and her shoe—slid her—inside for protection until he could find someplace proper to lay her down again."

9/11, Vindicated

2014, a different editor printed the following 9/11 column, with an abbreviated quote. I didn't realize at the time it would be my final 9/11 column for the newspaper.

My column has been around since April 2004. The first 9/11column, a visit to the 9/11 flag on the Appalachian Trail on Shenandoah Mountain in East Fishkill appeared September 8th, 2005. We've revisited the flag twice since, on September 7th the following year, and last year, on September 5th, noting how it—but hopefully not what it stands for—is fading away. There's been a 9/11 column every year since '05. We've visited the 9/11 Memorial at Graymoor Monastery down by Peekskill (09/11/08) and the Lagrange Sunrise Rotary Memorial on Stringham Road (09/24/09). On 09/08/11 we visited the then-unfinished United 93 Memorial near Shanksville, PA, then returned to the now-completed memorial on 09/06/12. The 2012 Memorial Day column visited the 9/11 Memorial at the Pentagon, and the 2012 Fourth of July column visited the National September 11 Memorial in Manhattan.

This year we've going to experience 9/11 from a surprising, extraordinary perspective via a review of Jim Defede's 2002 *The Day the World Came to Town; 9/11 in Gander, Newfoundland*; visit the still-smoking ruins via an excerpt from Sean Michael Flynn's *The Fighting 69th—One Remarkable National Guard Unit's Journey from Ground Zero to Baghdad*, then listen to Garrison/Cold Spring's's own MotherLode Trio's—Stacy Labriola, Patti Pelican, and Terry Textor Platz—haunting 9/11 tribute.

Gander: "We're all Americans tonight." September 11, 2001, America's entire airspace, for the first time ever, was CLOSED. Period. No if's, ands, or buts. All aircraft arriving over the north Atlantic had to return to their point of origin or, past the point of no return, land in Canada. Tiny Gander, Newfoundland had an ex-military airstrip that could accommodate jumbo jets. 38 jetliners, with 6,595 passengers and crew—some with exotic cultural/religious needs—landed there. Gander, and neighboring villages, opened their doors, and hearts, to the "plane people", welcoming them to their homes, and accommodating them at the Lions Club, Knights of Columbus,

American Legion, schools, fire houses, community centers, churches. Every business in the area donated/contributed—thousands of dollars worth—from toys for the kids and prescription drugs, to 4000 *toothbrushes*. Animals on the planes were fed and cared for. The last plane left on September 17th. A very readable, moving, inspiring account.

Manhattan: [New York Army National Guard 69th Infantry Regiment Battalion Commander, Lieutenant Colonel Geoffrey James] *Slack stared at the ground, squinting through the shroud of ash and smoke to get a better look at what he had just stumbled across. Next to his dust-covered boots was a shoe that still contained a foot...Though he had already encountered dozens of horrific sights, nothing else he had seen at the World Trade Center defined what had happened earlier that morning more completely than that shoe...It was a light blue pump, and though her foot was sheared off through the ankle, Slack could picture the woman who had put it on that morning. She had driven to the train for the commute into Manhattan on the Long Island Rail Road...she managed to get a window seat and stared into the bright September day...she rode the subway to the World Trade Center and bought a banana and a bottle of juice at the newsstand before riding the elevator to her office high up the tower. Then she and thousands of other people—innocent civilians, people sitting at their desks, having a cup of coffee, going to their offices—were murdered by some* [misguided fanatics] *thinking that what they were doing was a noble act. It wasn't noble. It was murder—senseless, pitiful murder. Slack opened the right cargo pocket of his camouflage uniform, and gently slid her foot and her shoe—slid her—inside for protection until he could find someplace proper to lay her down again.*

MotherLode Trio's 9/11/01 Memorial *Sometime Lofty Towers* (Sonnet #64 by William Shakespeare, track 8 on their *MotherLode Trio* CD) stirs the soul. Listen to it on Facebook: https://www.facebook.com/pages/MotherLode-Trio/104496156265344

Lieutenant Colonel Geoffrey Slack

I've just started re-reading Sean Michael Flynn's *THE FIGHTING 69TH, FROM GROUND ZERO TO BAGHAD*. After I'd first read it, I'd noted on a piece of paper in the front of the book that "this ranks way up on my Best Book I've Ever Read list".

Did I ever recommend it to you??? Have you already read it???

Lieutenant Colonel Geoffrey Slack, Commander of the Fighting 69th, is a Tommy Franks kind of leader/soldier/warrior. In the front of the book, he is quoted as saying, immediately after 09/11/01, "I'm going home to decompress. I'm going to clean up my equipment. I'm going to make contact with my chain of command, and I'm going to get ready to go. Because right below the pain I feel is a burning fucking desire to kill something. And somebody needs to give the 69th a chance and that somebody is going to get a belly full."

Fuckin' A.......................

HudsonValley Honor Flight Mission #5, September 27, 2014

My Dad, Corporal Ralph Joseph Ferrusi, served in the Philippines in World War II. Uncle Pete was a decorated corpsman in the Battle of the Bulge. Uncle John was a Navy Chief Petty Officer. Three older cousins also served in the Pacific: Joey was a Seabee, Ron was on an LST in the Navy, and Sonny was in the Army.

Saturday, September 27, 2014 I walked the walk on Hudson Valley Honor Flight (HVHF) Mission #5 as a volunteer Guardian for 88-year-old City of Poughkeepsie resident retired Master Sergeant Frederick Kratzer, 43-year active/reserves World War II Navy/Army/Air Force veteran. It was a deeply-moving, super-patriotic, Proud-to-be-an-American day. Here's what this extraordinary day felt like, boots on the ground:

Honor Flights fly World War II vets on charter flights, at no cost, to the World War II Memorial in Washington DC. Each vet is accompanied all day long by a volunteer "guardian". The Honor Flight Network was co-founded by Earl Morse, a physician assistant and retired Air Force Captain and Jeff Miller, a small business owner from Hendersonville, North Carolina. The first Honor Flight took place in May 2005: six small planes flew 12 veterans to Washington.

Back in 2012, Steve Nicoli, proud resident of Walden, NY had a great idea. He and Brian Maher became co-founders of HVHF. Patricia Maher and Becky Boone are also founding members. The Inaugural HVHF, Mission #1, took place June 2012.

A September 10th (very thorough) Guardian Training session emphasized the safety, comfort, and well-being of the vets (average age 90+) would be our Number One Priority. Many of them would be wheelchair-bound. We were to treat them like the heroes they were, as if they were family. I was given Freddie's phone number, called him right away, and we were on the phone 53 minutes; he had a lot of stories... Freddie and I met for the first time at a two-hour HVHF "Meet and Greet" September 14. He had more stories.

The Big Day began at 7:00 am in the ShopRite parking lot in Montgomery. It was 50-some degrees, clear skies; a great day for flying: 85 vets, aged 85 to 103 (US Marine/Rhinebeck resident Ruth Milliot); 31 Army, 32 Navy, 16 Air Corps, 3 Marines, 3 Coast Guard, one British Army(!). The Honor Flight people were super-attentive, as they would be for the next 16-17 hours.

ShopRite provided coffee, doughnuts, muffins: ShopRite has nationally donated *$1.6 million dollars* to veteran causes. Bravo!!!

We boarded four big Leprechaun buses, and were escorted to Stewart by 180+ motorcycles. Hundreds of cheering people were lined up to greet the vets at Stewart. Speeches were made, the service hymns and God Bless America were played/sung, then we were off between cheering crowds to a USAir charter A321 Airbus. Freddie and I were the first on the plane. TSA check??? Show your HVHF name tag, get checked off: "Welcome Aboard, sir."

The whole ceiling of the Airbus was decorated with strings of red/white/blue stars and streamers; the flight crew wore red/white/blue Hawaiian leis, a big American flag decorated the galley. Brown-bagged donuts/muffins (Otis Spunkmeyer Chocolate Chip...) awaited on each seat. As we were taxiing to take-off, the pilot announced the Collings Foundation P-51C Mustang—the Mustang, the B-17G *909*, and the B-24H *Witchcraft* were over at Dutchess County Airport—was going to do a low-level fly-by along the runway. WOW!!! And, as we taxied, local fire engines sprayed arches of high-pressure water over the plane: VIP treatment.

The flight was quick; we were given Honor Flight priority at Reagan. Nearing the gate, the ground crew guys smiled and waved American flags. Dress-uniformed military personnel—Army, Navy, Air Force, Marines—greeted us at Arrivals, then we passed through more huge flag-waving, cheering crowds to four big chartered buses. The road along each side of the buses was lined with dress-uniformed military personnel, and as the buses pulled away they all saluted.

It was 85-degrees in DC, not a cloud in the sky. Arby's-supplied box lunches—big, thick sandwiches—were passed out. We were police-motorcycle-escorted through the Capitol, lights flashing, sirens wailing, zipping through red lights and intersections. Wow!!! VIP's!!!

There were several other Honor Flights at the Memorial: Tennessee (yellow Honor Flight t-shirts), upstate New York (red). We were dark blue. "What do you want to do, Freddie???" "I don't know, what do you want to do???" There was *so* much going on, all patriotic, and, peaceful. We wandered around the Memorial, taking it all in; there were a lot of photo-ops. Several folks were dressed in 40's-vintage clothes, and at one point I passed General Douglas MacArthur, khaki Class-A's, aviator glasses and all. I reached over and shook his hand; "Thanks for being here, general."

Finally, it was on to Arlington National Cemetery, and the very precise, very impressive Changing of the Guard. Running late, we did a double drive-by of the Marine Iwo Jima Memorial, then headed to a white-linen/stemware dinner at Doubletree Crystal City, where a retired Four-Star General spoke.

What a day, what a day. We were all getting a bit tired, but the overall energy of the event kept the adrenaline going. Freddie held up *very* well.

We arrived back at Stewart around 10 pm, and were directed through a door to a large reception area. I was astonished it was jam-packed, at this somewhat late hour, with people, families and young kids, waving flags and chanting "USA, USA, USA". Made ya proud. Very proud...........

We finally spotted Nancy, who had come to drive Freddie home, in the crowd. Freddie thanked me for escorting him, and said "You can go now Ralph." I said, "Not until I see you sitting down in Nancy's car, my friend: it's my duty..."

When I finally walked out the door, heading to my own car, a young family—husband, wife, two young kids—were on the sidewalk, and all four of them thanked me—Ralph Joseph Ferrusi Jr, Honorably Discharged Radio Sergeant, 156th Field Artillery, NYSANG—for *my* service. I thanked them all for being there, at eleven o'clock at night, for the WWII vets.

Saturday, October 10th, HVHF Mission #9 will depart from Stewart International Airport, and Saturday, November 7th, HVHF Mission #10 will depart Westchester County Airport. For more info, or to volunteer, contact HVHF at www.hvhonorflight.com, 845-391-0076.

February 11, 2015
1174 Words

This first appeared in John Vargo's Boating on the Hudson and Beyond *September 2015 issue.*

HudsonValley Honor Flight Mission #22, April 13, 2019

On September 27, 2014 I flew to Washington DC on Hudson Valley Honor Flight "Mission # 5" as a "guardian for World War II veteran Master Sergeant Freddie Kratzer. He was quite a guy, and we both enjoyed the phenomenal experience. We're still in touch: occasional phone calls, Christmas cards.

Every chance I get—tipped off by their Army/Navy/Marine/Air Force/ Coast Guard/Sea Bees caps—I thank veterans for their service, and I always say "Welcome home" to Vietnam vets. A while back I saw a guy with a "Vietnam Era" cap: I'd never seen this before. I served in the US Army National Guard from 1959 to 1965: after Korea and during Vietnam.

I contacted the Hudson Valley Honor Flight and asked if I was eligible for a flight, even though I hadn't flown in B-17's or B-24's, or had landed on a beach on a Pacific island.

They said yes, and sent me an application.

On Saturday, April 13, 2019 I flew to Washington DC on Hudson Valley Honor Flight "Mission # 22" as a "Cold War" veteran. Spencer was *my* guardian. It was raining like hell at Stewart International when we left. It was a beautiful, glorious day when we arrived in DC. Whadda day it was!!!

My Saturday, April 13, 2019 words at the "farewell" dinner in Washington, DC

Marianne, the Honor Flight head nurse (there was at least one nurse on every bus) bought my "Uncles" book well before the flight, and I told her I would autograph it for her. She brought it to DC, and, quite amazingly, I signed it at the Vietnam Wall: certainly my most memorable book signing.

She then surprised me by asking if I would say a few words at the "farewell dinner" in DC at the airport Marriott. I said I would think about it.

At the dinner, one of the HVHF volunteers, Carol Smith, who knows Kath, came over to me and asked if I was ready to talk (for "two minutes").

Ya gotta go for the moment...so, I stood up in front of a huge ballroom full of vets and volunteers, and, after checking the microphone, put on my "speakers voice", and talked about *them*, not me..........

Several people afterwards said that I "nailed it", a couple of women said I (almost) moved them to tears, and when I got back on the "Blue Bus" (one of five buses) a lot of the guys on the bus congratulated me....

Here's (approximately) what I said:

First I introduced myself as Ralph Joseph Ferrusi *Jr.*, Honorably Discharged Radio Sergeant, 156th Field Artillery, then proceeded:

My Dad, Corporal Ralph Joseph Ferrusi *Sr.*, served in the Philippines in World War II.

Fourteen family members—Dads, uncles, cousins—served in World War II, and we have four Purple Hearts in our extended family.

This is my second Honor Flight: I flew on Mission #5, September 27, 2014, as a Guardian for World War II vet Master Sergeant Freddie Kratzer. Five years later, I'm here as a Post-Korean-War/Vietnam Era veteran.

I was asked to say a few words about today's experience. I have become a "semi-famous" author—books, newspaper columns, magazine articles— with over a half-million words in print.

I cannot think of words to describe today.

The veterans—the "Blue t-shirts"—and the guardians—the "Grey t-shirts"—have been acknowledged all day long, from the time we arrived at

Stewart International in Newburgh this morning. I would now like to thank the "Red shirts": all the "behind the scenes" Hudson Valley Honor Flight staff, and volunteers, for everything they have done for us today.

One last thought: I have always been very proud of my military service.

But, today is the very first time I have been *honored* for my service.

Thank you.

POLSKA...

Time was running out for our World War II Memorial visit. I was standing by NEW YORK when a woman walked right towards me wearing a red t-shirt with "Polska" on it in white lettering. I assumed she was from Poland, and greeted her in Polish with my two best Polish phrases: "Zshen doe-bray, yok-shi-mosh???" "Hello, how are you???".

She looked at me blankly: she was from the midwest: an Athletic Director escorting a debate team... I said that I only remembered three "everyday" words in Polish: "zshimnaw": cold; "goognah": shit; and "doo-pah": ass.

She said she only remembered some "bad" words, and said—in Polish—asshole, fuck, and, m**********r.........

Gotta love these chance meetings at a World War II Memorial with someone wearing a red t-shirt with "Polska" on it...............

April 18, 2019

HEALTH/MEDICAL

Vegetarianism, Meditation, Fitness, And, Cancer

I consider myself very fit and have taken great pains to keep myself in the best physical condition I can since my mid-thirties: hiking, biking, canoeing, cross-country skiing, snow shoeing lawn mowing, leaf raking snow shoveling, gathering/sawing/splitting firewood. I was "a runner" for quite a while, and ran competitively; I was *fast*: lotsa trophies and plaques. I figured the less I weighed, the faster I would be. I recall subsisting on "a glass of water and a slice of lettuce" per day. At one time, at 5' 11", I got my weight down to 117 pounds (there are pictures somewhere: I was skeletal).

I dinged my lower back a while back, working on a stone wall along the upper driveway at 34 Kim Lane on a cold, damp April day. I went to chiropractors to get it fixed, and one of them, Tom, who also belonged to the Hudson Valley Velo Club, the local bike racing club (oh yeah, I raced bikes for a few years: lotsa trophies and plaques) told me about a series of stretches I could do to keep my back in good shape. Every morning since then I've done a series of six stretches for my back. They've worked: if I forget to do them, my back lets me know some time during the day...

Vegetarianism is a big part of my fitness. I feel I eat a very good diet: no dead animals, fish, or fowl (I don't get on this bandwagon very often, but it is very important to me that I don't eat other living creatures...), lotsa fresh veggies, fresh fruit (though not as much). It's a very rare day that Kath and I don't have a good-sized salad with dinner. And, I've cut way way back on sugar: no pies, cakes, cookies, soda (real juices instead). Ice cream is a treat every once in a while (a couple of times a year, not counting visits to Ocean Pines).

Ah yes, and on the "mental" side of fitness, I've meditated 20 minutes twice a day, since the Seventies. And, I read a lot.

So....it was a big shock to me when, on Tuesday, February 25, 2014, around 4:00 PM, Doctor Tom Grimaldi, a Mid-Hudson Medical Group urologist, told me I had prostate cancer (Johnny Rit died around 2:00 AM the same day).

When I walked into Dr. Grimaldi's office that day, I did not expect to get this news: I was stunned; pole-axed. Me, *cancer*??? After all the time, energy, and effort I'd put into years and years of "clean livin'"??? Shit...................................

Monday, January 30, 2017
Some Really Unexpected, Really Shitty News

Michelle from Caremount called and said my "EKG shows some subtle changes" I asked her what they were, and she said "T-wave changes in 3 F." I asked her what that meant [in English...]. She said that it "could be a blockage in the heart." I said (or definitely thought) something like "Holy Shit!!!". I told her I had an appointment with a cardiologist, and she asked when it was. I told her it was near the end of February (I had an appointment with Fatos Rugova, MD—recomended by both Dr. Gerringer and Kath—on Monday, February 17th). She said to wait a minute, and came back and said this was not an emergency, but I should move up the appointment. My appointment now is this Friday, February 3, at 1:15 PM at 30 Columbia Street, in Poughkeepsie.

Carpal Tunnel Release:

Highway Robbery in The World's Last "Great Super Power"

In early October 2017 I woke up in the middle of the night and my left hand, out of "the clear blue sky", "was numb". I didn't think much of it, and figured this would go away:. Hope Springs Eternal. Surprise, surprise, it didn't, and eventually escalated to very extreme pain, that kept me awake for hours, night after night, but, subsided during the day. Definitely neurological, it soon reached a point where something had to be done about it.

Figuring it might be a pinched nerve in my neck or upper back, we first went outside the mainstream medical system. After two trips to a licensed massage therapist and three to a chiropractor brought some temporary, but no long-term real relief, we had to bite the bullet and go "mainstream". And, by now, mid-December or so, the night pain had escalated to something like 15 on a scale of 1 to 10.

First step, in late December, was a very reputable hand surgeon who had treated Kath years ago. His diagnosis: Carpal Tunnel. But, he couldn't fix it as he was retiring at the end of the year: in a week or so. He recommended another hand surgeon. And, I think he recommended getting a neurologist's opinion to confirm the CT. These appointments took time...

Both the neurologist and the recommended hand surgeon said carpal tunnel, but the surgeon said I'd have to see my primary physician to say that in his opinion I'd survive the surgery.... It was now late-January. Early February I spent several mind-numbing hours in a dreary hospital waiting room for "pre-surgerial testing", and a week or so later had surgery—The Whole Nine Yards Just Like On TV—on February 9, 2018: just about four months to the day after my left hand went numb in the middle of the night: zippity doo dah, U.S. Medical System.

So what did this cost, in time, mileage, and money???

Time and mileage:

Two visits to the LMT, three to the chiropractor.

Seven visits to four doctors—two surgeons, a neurologist, and my primary— plus a radiologist, an anesthesiologist, and a PA.

Two hospital visits.

Several pharmacy visits.

About 634.6 miles on the road.

Money:

As of now, Medicare and Me have run up a tab of about $3,057.50.

The worst of it: the neurologist dinged us an astounding $750.00, for, basically about five minutes of his exalted time, and one pertinent sentence: "Yes, it is Carpal Tunnel".

The first visit to the recommended surgeon was $250.00, resulting in pretty much the same sentence. Two visits—about 15 minutes, and two five-word expert deductions—equaled a cool One Thousand US Dollars:

One hour: $4,000.00.
One day: $32,000.00: not a bad day's pay.
One year, $8,000,000.00: that's Eight *Million* Dollars................

And it only took *four months* to figure it out and do something about it: a health "care" system to be proud of????????

March 2, 2018

Happy Birthday, Sis!

April 16, 2003. I called my sister from the Atrium hotel in Krakow to wish her a happy birthday. She was delighted to receive a birthday call from Poland. She asked me how I was doing. "Fine, Sis." This is the only time I have ever lied to my sister.

April 17, 2003. Lying, flat on my back in an Intensive Care Unit bed in the Szpital Uniwersytecki w Krakowie: full-time oxygen, IV dripping into my left arm. Diagnosis: emboliae arteriae pulmonalis – pulmonary embolism.

STOP.

REWIND.....

November 2002. We receive a surprise note from our 10-12 year old nephew Brian Kosilla. He is selling magazines for his school class trip. My wife Kathy orders a subscription to <u>Arthur Frommer's Budget Travel</u>.

January 2003. Intrigued by some of the low cost, week-long trips in the "Best Bargains" section of the magazine, Kathy suggests that we fly to Poland for a week in April, on the cheap: Krakow and Warsaw. We've never done this kind of trip before: typically, we spend 2-3 weeks, exploring wherever we go "in depth": parks, alleys, back streets, markets, little restaurants and bistros.

I am reluctant, but Kath convinces me, and we book the trip. A week before we leave, a big tree falls on me. It doesn't land on my head, or break a leg or some ribs. It just bangs up my midsection – no big deal. Our second evening in Krakow, I feel a bit faint, and very lightheaded. That night, intense right side pains develop.

We get to a clinic, and then to a pulmonary specialist, who says, in broken English, "Get to an Emergency Room, queekly." The ER sends me upstairs, to the Cuckoo's Nest, and I'm Jack Nicholson, and most of the nurses are Nurse Ratched: except they don't speak a word of English, and they aren't as nice.

Neither does the axe-murderer in the bed next to me in Room 2, who has the most God-awful racking, wheezing, bubbling, burbling cough that I have ever heard in my life – please, please, please that whatever it is that he has is not contagious – and who wanders around the room and the halls, most of the night, mumbling and muttering to himself in Polish, accompanied by his cheap (but loud) plastic radio, that he sings along with to American rock and roll and Polish religious music.

Neither do the dieticians. How do you say, "I'm a vegetarian." in Polish? Who cares, Jack… Neither do the doctors, any of the other patients, any of the visitors, the priests. Thank God Kathy does.

Most of the nurses are mean to me – very mean. Some of them are downright nasty. It's not because I am an American; they treat the old Polish guys the same way. I am awakened every morning at 6:00 AM with a needle in the gut, and usually without a "Good morning." I am jabbed with a variety of needles in a variety of places every day, without any explanations.

I do not get decent nourishment, or fluids. I am served, basically, potatoes, some bread, and some cheese. I have no access to water that won't kill me. I am not being cleaned or washed, or getting clean bed clothes.

The language barrier with the docs is horrific: "Vee must draw blood. From your hand." Oh my God. Thankfully, he meant "wrist"; still not exactly a barrel of laughs.

And just when I thought things couldn't get much worse, Easter weekend rolled around. Easter isn't just a Sunday in super-Catholic Poland. The whole country shuts down for 4 days, minimum. In the world outside the szpital, this is a wondrous, special time. Things got a little tough in the Hotel California. My temperature soared to 104 degrees Fahrenheit, and there were only a few members of the "B Team" around, and not only didn't they speak English, these people barely spoke Polish.

On Easter Sunday, I was dehydrated, weak, and slipping fast. Kathy finally arrived, and I almost deliriously implored her to contact the Pentagon to have a C-130 Hercules dispatched to get me the hell out of here and whisk me away to anyplace in Western Europe, where at least there was a chance that someone spoke English, and might hook me up to a life-saving IV. The C-130 never happened, but Kath did manage to find a (handsome) young Polish doctor, who spoke about 3 words of English, and who, after some negotiations (I had to convince him that it was HIS idea, not mine), had me hooked up to an IV. Saved. For the time being...

I seriously began thinking of tying bed sheets together and rappelling down the side of the building to the streets three stories below. I honestly investigated this, but discarded this plan because I was rational enough to realize that even I if I survived the rappel, I had no clue how I could possibly navigate from the hospital through the Jewish Ghetto to Kathy's hotel. I had no money, spoke about 10 words of Polish (hello, goodbye, please, thank you, ass, shit, hot, cold, red, green...), and was still wearing the same insane-asylum striped hospital pajamas that I was issued when I was admitted several long days ago. Nope, not a Good Plan.

This was a Very Scary Experience, and I realized at times that it would take every bit of my wits and experience to get me reasonably strong and reasonably healthy, so that I could be discharged and somehow get back home safely. To accomplish this, I had to have some "real" food, WATER, get cleaned and washed, get some real, clean clothes, and some mental stimulation to get me through the 22 hours when Kathy was NOT there with me.

Here are some of the Good Plans that Kathy and I came up with. Kathy had moved to a nearby hotel in the Ghetto, and walked over every day, sometimes twice a day. These visits were lifesavers, and I eagerly anticipated them, as I was bedridden for most of my stay. Kathy brought me fruit, yogurt, and bottled water, and, some cookies and chocolates, on occasion... She brought in a bar of soap, and a razor, and found a plastic bucket and I was able to finally wash and shave, and she somehow managed to find out where the clean pajama tops and bottoms were, and I finally changed my bedclothes. She found a London Times and an English language National Geographic, and paid an enormous amount of zlotys for them, but I finally had something to occupy my mind, rather than stare, bed-ridden, at the plain gray walls and ceilings. I read the print off of the pages.

All the while I was in the hospital, Kathy was phoning (very very difficult to deal with) and emailing (much, much better) the folks back home from Internet cafes to let them know what was going on. The email and the Internet were lifesavers. Kath also emailed my physician back home, and he reassured her that the treatment I was receiving was the correct protocol. She also made an appointment for the day after we arrived back home.

The doctors had said that I could be in the hospital for as long as two or three weeks, but once I started feeling better, and was allowed to roam the halls and walk to the bathrooms, we kept on their case about getting out. We finally convinced them that I was well enough to at least be an outpatient at the hotel, and I finally escaped, after nine days in ICU. FREEDOM!!! We had no idea how much all of this was going to cost, and whether or not my USA insurance was going to cover it. Before I was discharged, Dr. Bochenek came in with The Bill: 9 days in ICU, MRI's, Ultrasounds, oxygen, IV's, medications, mashed potatoes: $1,234.88. Kath and I just looked at each other. Dr. B asked, in broken English, if this was a lot. "No, it's OK."

There were some (three, of dozens) wonderful, caring nurses. One of the dieticians made a real effort to get me some decent vegetarian food. Both of my fellow patients in Room 5 hugged and kissed Kathy when I left. The docs really did what they had to do, and they did all of it right.

But, when I finally walked out of there, into the Ghetto, I wanted to jump up and down and click my heels – I was *free*, and, alive. The day after I was discharged we rented bicycles and rode the beautiful bike paths along the Vistula. This may sound a bit nutty, and it was, but I am extremely athletic, and enormously fit. This is one of the reasons why I recovered so rapidly. Krakow was just beginning to turn springtime green, and it <u>is</u> a great town. We spent three days exploring it (together...) before we flew to Zurich, then home.

And, by the way, it was the tree that loosened up the embolism... ....

November 25, 2003

October 2016

On October 12, 2016 I noted that Dr. Mike Gerringer had informed me that I had "dense calcification" in my coronary arteries. He prescribed 20 mg of Lipitor (Atorvastatin).

I currently take five pills every day: two prescription blood pressure pills, an aspirin, and B-12 and Gingko Biloba for memory. Now I'm up to six.

In the last 40 years I've done my God damnedest to live a health, active life: diet, and exercise, both physical and mental: 41-year vegetarian and daily meditator. Physically fit, not fat, no big belly. Stretch daily to keep my back limber. Massage therapy four times a year. Read, do puzzles to exercise my mind/brain. Brush and floss, morning and night. Get 8-10 hours of sleep most nights.

But, I'm losing the battle, Big Time: I have cancer. High blood pressure. My coronary arteries are densely calcified. I have constant dental problems, and just about constant physical/health problems: *something* is just about <u>always</u> "wrong" with me.

259

Recently, I've "lost"—amongst several other "lesser" things—my car key ($350.00) *and my wallet*: these mental lapses are very very disturbing to me.

All of the above makes me very angry, and frustrated. I consider myself "The unhealthiest healthy person I know."

And, I am scared shitless about my coronary arteries...............

A Thousand (Or So) Things You Don't Know About Heart Attacks, or, Open Heart Surgery

Before/Background

Friday, May 15, 2020, 11:05 PM, I had a heart attack. I was 82 years, 8 months, 3 days old. I had been in top physical condition for 50 years—a half century—and had been a vegetarian for 45 years: a lot of salads, greens, broccoli, garlic, olive oil.

May 19th, around 7:30 AM I had a seven-hour open-heart quadruple bypass. I was anesthetized for 10 hours.

Here's the Reader's Digest version of what I knew about heart attacks before May 15th: You had a heart attack. You were taken to a hospital in an ambulance; red and blue lights flashing. You either died, or you lived. After the surgery, with your new pipes, you ran a marathon the next day. BULLSHIT....

Here's what I knew about open-heart surgery: ZERO. Zilch. I was an excellent health/fitness Poster Boy. From my mid-thirties I was a James Fixx generation avid competitive runner. 10K's in the low forties—PB 38:36—a half marathon in 1:28:28. Early on I learned to *always* start on the front row, and I ran with the lead pack for about half the race. I had one helluva finishing "kick". I felt that the less I weighed, the faster I would be. I subsisted on a slice of lettuce and a glass of water a day. At 5' 11" I weighed 124 pounds: I have pictures somewhere: a *lot* of ribs showing. I had rooms full of trophies, plaques, ribbons.

Somewhere along the way I bought a good multi-speed bicycle. In the same amount of time I could slog out a decent training run, I could ride 15-20 miles on the bike: new, broader horizons. I was hooked. I did "century" rides, and began racing: road races and criteriums. I had rooms full of trophies, plaques, and ribbons. Bicycle racing was the hardest thing I've ever done: my eyes watered, my nose ran, and, I DROOLED. Yes, I drooled...

I then discovered "hiking", and soon gobbled up all the thousand-foot mountains in the mid-Hudson Valley. Howie Roth, my then-IBM manager, introduced me to the 3000-4000 foot Catskill mountains, and, casually mentioned the Catskill 3500 Club: 34 peaks that exceed 3,500 feet elevation. Turn me loose!!! I eventually found out there were 114 4000 Footers in the Northeast: off I went...

Some of the 4000-footers in Vermont, New Hampshire, and Maine were on the then-2,048 mile Maine to Georgia Appalachian Trail. I eventually walked it TWICE: 4,217 miles over the ruggedest terrain on the Eastern Seaboard. I was invincible. Until May 15, 2020, 11:05 PM...

I was awakened by horrible pains radiating down both biceps. I had never experienced anything anywhere like this before. The pain would not subside, no matter what I did. I felt a tightness in my chest and broke out in a drenching sweat. "Should I call 911???" "YES!!!"

The phone didn't work...

June 21, 2020
495 Words

Hospitals → Surgery

I put on the pair of ratty work jeans I'd worn all day and "put my teeth in": I have upper and lower partials. I walked barefoot out to the front porch and was hoisted into the ambulance. Laying inside, I very quickly wondered why they don't put shock absorbers on ambulances: every little crack/crease in the road slammed and jarred me.

I was put in Room 11 in the ER: a small, cheerless room with one small window in the door at the very end of a very long hall. I was wired up, and, because of 2020 "no family allowed" restrictions was left there all alone at midnight, isolated, scared to death, in pain, and exhausted. It was beyond awful: the worst part of the whole hospital experience. After a horrific hour I was ready to rip off all the wires and stagger down the long hall to try to find out what the *%@#* was going on. A doc—a good guy—finally came and said I was going to be admitted. I asked him to call my wife.

I was taken to a cheerless semi-private room. "Archie" was on the other side of the curtain, then "Captain Bill", a United States Marine Corps officer. Both were "good company". The RN's were taking gallons of blood out of me, and on the third try an "enzyme" that was a heart attack "marker" zoomed up from single digits to high teens double digits and a doc "dropped the H bomb" on me: I had indeed had a heart attack. Back to another shock-absorberless long ambulance ride to a regional hospital that did heart surgery.

I will mention one thing here: with all the 2020 virus crap going on I think the general public's impression of hospitals is that they were grey, gloomy, cheerless dungeons. On the contrary, both hospitals were bright, cheerful, upbeat. All of the staff wore motorcycle-like helmets with full face shields, and with a few minor exceptions were helpful, positive, polite, and informative. I felt I was in a good place, and, in very good hands.

Right now I don't remember much about the 3-4 days between the heart attack and the surgery, except my surgeon—an upbeat, nice guy—and his PA's—I remember Sam, and Dr. Joe—ran me through, in great detail, what was going to happen: before, during and after, pretty much step by step. My anesthesiologist also spoke to me, and emphasized NOT TO TOUCH under any circumstances the ventilator that would be down my throat when I woke up.

The Big Day came, and I was wheeled into pre-op. I was scared shitless. Amazingly, they allowed my wife to visit for a few minutes before I went into surgery: NICE...

There were a lot of people in the OR, all upbeat and "laughing and scratching" among themselves: this was very reassuring. At some point, as I was lying on my back on the operating table (?), a pretty young RN introduced herself and said she was going to "shave my groin"...from this point onward, any kind of "modesty" went flying out the window. Three or four female RN's were close by during this "procedure". I don't remember a single thing after this until I woke up ten hours later in Recovery.

My recollection is the first thing I did when I "came to" was to give two thumbs up to whoever was there. Then there was the horror of the ventilator down my throat: the gagging sensation was awful, but I remembered NOT TO TOUCH anything. I kept wanting to "go back to sleep", but a voice told me to fight this: the longer I could stay awake, the quicker the damned thing that was gagging me could be removed. I battled. I don't recall how long it took, but do recall the blessed relief when it was gone.

June 21, 2020
652 words,

ICU → Discharge

Somehow I ended up in a big, bright, "cheerful" private room with a big window in ICU, with several really nice RN's, looking after me 24 hours a day. But, here comes THE BIGGEST THING THEY DON'T TELL YOU, and I fully understand why.

Day 1 after open heart surgery will be one of the worst—if not *the* worst—day of your life. You will have suffered monstrous trauma—physical, mental, and emotional—most likely beyond anything you have ever experienced before. You'll be scared, scarred, horrifically bruised, confused, and in pain from your sternum having been sawed right down the middle. You'll have about 16 tubes, wires, and pipes attached to various parts of your body. They'll be a very annoying, extremely sensitive tube inserted in your "groin", and two big plastic "drain tubes" in your chest.

You'll be virtually trapped, on your back, in a hospital bed. Any kind of "normal", taken-for-granted movement will be, impossible. Getting "comfortable": hah!!! The sheets, blankets, hospital gown, or your PJ's will become your worst enemies, snagging, sticking to you and binding in your crotch. Due to the head-up tilt of the hospital bed, you will slowly, slowly slide down against the bottom of the bed, and it will take two RN's—"1-2-3"—to yank you back up.

You'll be groggy/dopey for a week or so from the heavy dose of anesthesia. RN's will be drawing gallons of blood from you, day, morning, and night. *All* the nights were longgggg. I pretty much was in constant pain, and when it shot up to two or so out of ten Tylenol was the pain killer of choice. Seven or eight out of ten brought on the Big Guns: morphine, or oxycodeine. And, when deemed necessary, nitroglycerine... At some point, the tube in my "groin"—I was told it went all the way into my bladder—was removed, and this was a blessed relief.

Considering the weakened condition I was in, I did not, in any way, desire to be discharged until the docs felt I was good and ready. I was informed that I would have to, to use the technical term they did, "poop" before I could be discharged.

An aside: at seemingly random times—day or night—for no rhyme nor reason, the Beatle's "Here comes the sun, dooten do do" would be played on the PA system. I was eventually informed this occurred any time a virus patient was discharged. Priceless..............

At some point I was moved to a room in PCU. Not to get into the gory details, I really missed the big, bright, cheerful ICU room, and the exceptional care I received there. And, even though it was really only a couple of days since the surgery, I reached a point where I Wanted To Get Outta There. The ugly red/yellow gunk draining out of my chest into big plastic buckets alongside the bed out of my sight had to reach a certain point of "clarity": this would be the indicator that I would be "good to go".

Every morning, they'd check the gunk: nope. Then one morning I was unexpectedly told I had "passed", and could be discharged within an hour or so!!! WOW!!! Freedom!!! But first, I had to be "disconnected"........................

544 words
June 21, 2020

Discharge → Home: The Long Road to "Recovery"

I hadn't given a single thought to "being disconnected". It turned out to be a longer, more complicated process than I would have imagined: "the sixteen tubes, pipes, and wires". I had two tubes (it seemed like four) attached to the inside of each wrist. I had a tube in the right side of my neck that I couldn't see, and barely knew was there: it went right inside of my heart, in case of an "emergency". And then there were the two big, plastic drain tubes in my chest, to say nothing of all the wire connection points here and there. The RN said she was going to remove two wires *connected to my heart*, and it was going to feel "weird". It DID... I was finally wheelchaired out to an Exit door.

I don't recall being overly excited or euphoric about "going home": I attributed this to the lingering "dopy-ness" from the anesthesia. I walked up the front steps into the house, and then the fun began. Until you've had your sternum sawed in half, you don't give a single thought to how the whole front of your upper body pivots, with each little move you make, around this critical point. This single thing became the biggest focal point of "recovery".

I was just about totally helpless, and relied pretty much 100% on my wife to accomplish even the simplest things. It exhausted me to read..... Kath had to single-handedly do what four RN's—night and day shifts—and two "techs" did in the hospital: a LOT of work, time, and energy. She has excelled.

Pillows, and getting to sleep. In the hospital I had four "Dollar Store" little white pillows. At night, one would end up behind my head, one at my right side, one at my left side, and, one between my legs. I had no idea until I got home how crucial these were to resting, and, maybe, to getting some (very elusive) sleep. The longggg first night at home we went from the bed, to the sofa, to the lift chair, to the bed, to the sofa; attempting to find the right combination, and "sweet spot", that would allow me to fall asleep. It was a long, long night, and in the morning, lying on the sofa, there were 23 pillows of various shapes and sizes scatterered around the living room. This became a long, hard battle, until we found a three-pillow combo that worked in bed.

And, relearning getting in and out of bed with the sawed-in-half sternum took forever. And, sleeping on my back: if you are among the .00001% of humans who normally sleep on your back, you're "golden". If you are the vast majority of side/belly sleepers, you're screwed.... This has become one of My Biggest Problems.

Other things: The only "pain" med we had at home was Tylenol. No morphine, oxycodeine, nitroglycerine. I have had a huge decrease in appetite: no desire for salads, wine, beer, alcohol, ice cream, or, pizza... I've lost about 20 pounds: I do not recommend an open heart/quadruple bypass as a way to lose weight. I'd become much more sensitive to hot/cold. I was enormously reluctant to use a walker, but a visiting RN said it would make for a faster, safer recovery. Me, "Mr. Walked the Appalachian Trail Twice" used a walker, and, a lift chair. And, at night peed in a "urinal". I doddered around like a 90-year-old.

And, whine, whine, one of the fistfuls of pills I'm required to take is photosensitive: stay outta the sun...

Being told in early June that I'd be "back to 'normal'"—I've *never* been *normal*—in August, or, my God, November—autumn—was not reassuring.

It took a while, but I figured out how to get in and out of bed, and finally had sufficient Range of Motion to dress myself, and amazingly tie my own shoes!!! And, set the table and wash dishes. Progress. Sleep is still disgustingly elusive.

Looking back, I've concluded the heart attack—tightness in the chest, cold sweat—and the surgery—"the ten best hours of sleep you'll ever have"—were relatively straightforward compared to the interminable long, long road to Zippity Do Dah "recovery".

Today's the First Day of Summer. Tune in in November when I climb Kilimanjaro.....

Thanks for listening....

726 words
June 21, 2020

January 11, 2021: considering all of the above, here's my Very Profound Thought this Monday morning: My heart didn't *attack* me: it warned me that *it was on the brink of failure.* Heeding this warning is the reason I am sitting here writing this today...

Some Heart Attack Information To Ponder

Often, the main side effect of a heart attack is death.

A "typical" heart beats about one hundred thousand times a day. This comes out to an astounding thirty five million times a year. This all happens so subtlety we are not at all aware of it in our daily life, until the very intricate process that must occur for it all to go right, *breaks.*

Considering the above, it really is quite amazing how rarely the shit hits the fan.

If you survive your first "heart attack", you will realize your "vincibility": from this point on, time will not ever again feel like a given.

Heart failure/cardiac death is the most likely way most of us will die. It kills around 325,000 Americans every year, and is the largest cause of "natural death" in the USA.

Think about all this the next time you're punching down a big hamburger and fries.

Or, don't...

December 21, 2020

29 YEARS AT 34 KIM LA...

Wednesday, September 4, 1991, we closed on 34 Kim Lane (the street sign says "Kim La"...), a "dream house": a striking A-frame, perched—very privately—high up on Stormville Mountain, surrounded by evergreens, two fireplaces, loft, great "rustic" finished basement, lotsa stone/wood inside, three decks, kidney-shaped pool.... Kath and I both owned small "starter houses". To me this place was straight out of The Lifestyle of the Rich and Famous. I never thought, or dreamed, I would actually live in a place like this.

Kath and I, married in '89, were living in my small house at 276 Old Hopewell Road in Wappingers, and were looking for a place of our own. Aleta Husted had found the Hopewell Road house for me 'way back, and I contacted her. Aleta knew her stuff. My recollection is that 34 Kim Lane was the last –of four—houses she showed us that day. At some point, she casually mentioned that the Appalachian Trail was right behind the back yard... She knew her stuff...

I also recall it was a miserable day, raining. I know I was awed by the house, but about the only things I remember about our first tour inside the house was a young boy, downstairs watching TV—he ignored us—and not being able to look at the garage because a big dog was barking right on the other side of the inside door to the garage.

I recall the asking price being $250,000.00: a quarter of a million dollars!!! I never dreamed I'd be living in a quarter-million-dollar house. I guess we "made an offer", but were soon informed that the house "had been sold to a young couple". So near yet so far: I was devastated. We then heard the young couple's parents wouldn't let them buy the house, or something like that, and we could have it for their negotiated price of $225,000.00!!! WOWZER!!!

Floyd, the owner, was very nice, and let us store "stuff" in the house before we moved in. I'll never forget when he said "Wait'l you see the first snowfall..."

Oddly enough, he had closed the pool before we moved in, even though it was early September, with almost a month of "pool time" still to be had. We figured he was just saving us some hassle. More about this later...

Since this place is such a big slice of my life, I'm going to look back at it, from The Early Days to now, 24 Years Later. Hang on, it's going to be a more complete story than I originally anticipated:

The Early Days

I don't remember much about right after moving in. We had family over, the first snow fall was probably magic, we lit fires in the free-standing fireplace in the living room, drank decent Saint Emilions...

Spring came, and we pulled the cover off the pool and started it up. When the water pressure built up, we found out there was a leak in the main inlet line... Unfortunately, this was a portent of things to come. We plugged up that line, and used a line right next to the skimmer that had been used for a "self cleaning" gadget as the inlet line.

The 10,000-gallon pool—the leaky line notwithstanding—was spectacular, filling a perfect setting in the side yard right outside the dining room picture window. We had family and friends over, poolside, and had a "House Warming" party. As the years went by, we lived The Good Life. We both had full-time jobs, fuel oil was reasonably cheap, and we could keep the thermostat reasonably high, and not worry about all the heat escaping through the basically un-insulated A-frame roof and the big glass sliding doors. Clearing the snow and ice off the driveway was a pain, but early-on it was worth the time and energy.

Home Improvements

The house was about 25-years-old when we bought it, and eventually it seemed that a whole bunch of things were beginning to wear out all at once: the roof, the decks, the driveway, the front walk. Kath commented, wisely, that she would never buy a 25-year-old house again.

The Original Front Walk: The original front walk was a straight, narrow cement walk, leading to a small set of cement stairs to the front door. There was a dinky roof over the front landing. Kath visualized a graceful, S-curved UniLoc red brick walk, leading to graceful, curving red brick front steps. Chuck Beverly, a talented young guy artisan, did a great job implementing this. Ralph and I (he was The Gaffer, as Pop would have put it, and I was the Gopher) designed and built a much longer, wider roof over the landing, supported by two tall 6X6's.

The Roof: Ralph and I also put on a new architectural-shingled roof. Again, he was The Gaffer, and I did a lot of the grunt work. Every nail was pounded in by hand, and the flashing is copper. The non-A-Frame roof had a few dinky round vents in the soffits. We had Jim, the Mid Hudson Handyman right around the corner on Route 52, install 18 brown, 12"X2" aluminum vents, so the attic could breath a lot better.

The Decks: The wooden deck behind the kitchen and the wooden deck alongside the pool were deteriorated and looked like hell, and we had them both replaced with red UniLoc brick decks. A branch fell off the big Norway Spruce to the right of the house one winter, and smashed the side of the front deck—which was getting pretty beat anyway—and Ralph and I replaced it with a sturdy Trex deck. The original deck was supported by three measly 4X4's right in the middle. Our new deck is supported by EIGHT sturdy 6X6's. You could park a truck on it; Good Job...

The Driveway: The driveway is about 300 feet or so long, and is very steep. It deteriorated over the years. I kept patching it, but it got worse and worse and worse. It was hard enough keeping it clear in the winter without having to deal with the cracks and holes. We finally bit the bullet and had it repaved. $11,000.00. Ouch...

The Pool

Ahh, the pool. A stunning, kidney-shaped 10,000 gallon in-ground pool, that filled the area alongside the dining room perfectly. There were flood lights along the side of the house, that made it magic at night. In the summer, we enjoyed poolside dinners at The Best Outdoor Dining Area in the county.

The downside(s):

The Liner: we had no idea how old the liner was when we first moved in, but over the years it too began to age and deteriorate. Every once in a while a pinhole would poke through the liner, and water would drain out at a horrific rate, and Keith, the frogman would have to come over and find it and patch it. For $250.00 a shot... Once just about the whole damn pool drained, and we had to have a big tanker come over and refill it, for big bucks. I always worried about leaks in the liner, and the first thing I would do just about every morning, summertime and even in the winter when the pool was closed and covered, was look out the dining room window to see if the level of the water in the pool had dropped.

Chemicals and maintenance: the pool, to me gobbled up an inordinate amount of my time, and our money. It was only open four months of the year, from mid-May to mid-September, but required weekly maintenance, and, sometimes, just about daily attention. The weekly maintenance involved keeping an eye on the chlorine Smart Sticks in the skimmer, shocking the pool and adding algecide, plus brushing and vacuuming the liner, sides and bottom (I actually did not vacuum every week; it was tedious and time-consuming).

I bought the chemicals at Rainbow Pools on Route 82 when required, and this was about every two weeks all during the season, and each trip seemed to cost about $200.00. So, it was costing approximately a thousand dollars a year for chemicals.

Closing, and opening the pool every year were Big Deals. I painstakingly cleaned the pool every September before covering it up for the winter, but just about every spring, when we uncovered it, it was a mess; rotting leaves and vegetation always seemed to get under the cover. Most of the time the water was green, one year it was absolutely greenish BLACK. I never thought it would ever be clear again. The only time I ever didn't worry about the pool was when it was finally frozen solid in the winter, but even then the snow would eventually build up and push the cover down, and every year it looked like the water was leaking out and I worried about it.

Problems: Just about every single year there seemed to be one problem or another: pin holes in the liner, leaks in one or another line, equipment failures. The main drain at the bottom of the pool began leaking, and I plugged it up, so the only outlet was through the skimmer, which was now right next to the only inlet. I once had to dig up this inlet line because it had been installed over the edge of a big rock, and finally sprung a leak over the years. The skimmer eventually began leaking, and I sealed it. We had to replace the pump, and the big DE filter. The liner began ripping, and I glued big patches over the rips.

The End: Over the winter of 2013-2014 it not only looked like the water was disappearing from the pool, but soon became obvious that it really was disappearing. When we took the cover off in the spring, there was only a little bit of water down in the deep end of the pool. The now-very-faded liner was dry and wrinkling badly, and there really wasn't any way to find the leak. We had a guy from NeJame, who had built the pool, and people from Rainbow come over to see what could be done. Bottom line, pretty much, it would cost $18,000-24,000 to fix it; it would have to be just about totally rebuilt. It would cost about $2000.00 to fill it in. We were not actually swimming in it very much at all anymore, so it seemed to me a very very outrageous amount of money to spend to rebuild it.

Kath and I cut out the liner and rolled it up in sections and brought it to recycling. I began sledge hammering the reinforced concrete around the edge, and Ralph and I did all the dirty work getting out the steel braces and galvanized edge of the pool. HARD, DIRTY WORK. We asked the town if we could heave all the debris into the hole, and they said it was OK by them. We contacted [Kevin Zemmirolo] and he brought a big back hoe up and dumped about 46 tons of fill into the hole, carefully tamping down each dump truck load. He got most of the fill from Package Pavement, right around the corner on Route 52. He did a really good job.

It hadn't rained for a long time, but right after Kevin brought a couple of loads of (much more expensive) top soil over in the afternoon to finish the job, it began pouring out, and I was stunned, watching the top soil, and the fill, running off down the hill. I ran outside barefoot and put 4X4's and built up dirt dams to keep all the precious, and expensive dirt from washing away. We had plans to artistically finish off the area, but quickly planted several hundred dollars worth of grass seed to keep the area from eroding. The grass seed never really caught on in the hard-packed shitty soil, and as of today, October 1, 2015, the patchy-grassed "side yard" really doesn't look all that good.

Every once in a while this summer Kath said she misses the pool, but I'm really glad it's finally gone... I never really wanted it in the first place; it just came with the house. It was a pain in the ass for me to keep up, and I *always* fretted about it, whether it was open, or closed. And, it bit me in the ass, right up to the very end.

Buttoning Up

When we first moved in, we were both working full-time, and fuel oil and electricity were relatively cheap. We kept the thermostat at "normal" temperatures in the winter, and burned wood in the free-standing fireplace in the living room mostly for "ambiance"; it had a blower that would kick in, but most of the heat from the fire went right up the chimney. The A-framed living room ceiling was pretty much un-insulated, and the living room was always chilly. The fireplace made it more liveable, but it was impossible to keep this big area warm in the winter.

As the years went by, fuel oil and electricity prices rose, and we began taking measures to make this house, which was basically a sieve as far as energy-efficiency was concerned, as energy efficient as we could.

Most of the following energy-efficiency ideas were Kaths:

(I will point out here that a gadget that nephew Wade originally bought for his parents, and that I was so impressed by also bought one—a hand-held Radio Shack digital laser thermometer—was a *huge* help in just about all of the following improvements. You point the red dot this thing throws out somewhere, and it gives you an instant reading of the temperature of what you are pointing at. I went all around the house, up and down, taking readings, and finding out where heat was escaping, and cold was getting in, then taking measures to keep the heat in, and the cold out. Couldn't have figured out a lot of the following without it.)

Windows: We had modern, energy-efficient windows installed in the kitchen, main bathroom, both bedrooms, the loft, and downstairs. They said the windows would reduce our heating bills something like 25%, but to me, since the windows made up something like 55% of the total outside walls of the house, I felt this was over-optimistic. At any rate, they do look better, work better, and help the overall cause.

Drapes/curtains: The house has three big double sliding doors, and a big "picture window" in the dining room. We have double insulated drapes on all of them, and insulated curtains on the four bedroom windows and the main bathroom window. In the winter I open these on sunny days to let radiant heat in, and close them every night to keep the cold out. In the summer I close them during the day to keep the heat out...

Attic insulation: When we moved in, and for quite a while, the attic had one layer of crappy, beat up "pink stuff". I eventually put in a good, brand-new, fluffy layer of "pink stuff" between the joists (???), and eventually followed this up with another layer perpendicular to them. There is now a very thick layer of "pink stuff" up there. It's gotta be "helping the cause".

Energy-efficient light bulbs: We've replaced just about all of our incandescent bulbs with modern, "long-lasting" energy-efficient bulbs. And, we're pretty careful about leaving them on unnecessarily.

Draft elimination: Kath had a company come over that found and sealed up all the drafts and leaky areas in the house. It cost a fair amount of money, but they did find, and seal up, a lot of drafts that I never knew existed.

Storm glass on front door/panel beside the front door: Getting into the swing of things, I measured the small window above the front door, and the tall plastic panel beside it, and had storm windows made up for both of them.

New *insulated* garage doors: We had our old, wooden, unreliable garage doors replaced by windowless insulated doors. The guys that installed them did an excellent job, and they have made a measurable difference in keeping a lot of cold outside air from sneaking past the basement inside garage door.

Downstairs fireplace insert: After we first moved in I recall only lighting a fire in the down stairs brick in-the-wall fireplace once, and it filled the basement with smoke, so it just sat there, unused for years. We had a Very Efficient insert installed (for Big Bucks), and the guys promised us it would, essentially, heat the whole house, and we'd be walking around in t-shirts and shorts upstairs, all winter. It had a fan that kicked in after a while, but about the only thing it heated was about five feet in front of the glass door.

NO heat was getting upstairs. One day, on a whim Kath lit some incense, and we found out why: the cold air from the A-frame living room was plunging down the basement stairs, overpowering the warm air that was trying to get upstairs. We installed (seasonal) insulated drapes along the living room sideboard to block the cold air, and bought a couple of "muffin fans" to blow the warm air up, and this has helped this cause. The insert now contributes a bit to warming up the house; at least it's pretty toasty downstairs, some of the time.

Firewood: When we first moved in I would harvest and stack a rack of firewood for the free-standing living room fireplace. Since we've had the insert, I try to get three racks of wood, and we usually burn two stacks each winter. Dragging dead trees down off the ridge behind the house, sawing, splitting, and stacking it are hard, back-breaking, dirty work, and then hauling it downstairs and stacking it on the small rack is no barrel of laughs either. To me, in the Old Days when houses were small and had low ceilings and modern oil burners had not been invented, and when burning wood was just about the only way to heat a house, this was the way to go. Nowadays, fill the fuel tank up with fuel oil and turn the thermostat up to 60 and, zippity-do-dah....

Living in a 60-degree house for seven months of the year: Finally, with the high cost of fuel oil, and in the interest of "There's Only One Pie, It's How You Slice It" (having more of the pie for nice overseas vacations, for one thing) we keep the thermostat at 60 degrees (sometimes sneaking it up to 62) from November to May... Seven months: this is unpleasant to say the least, and, uncomfortable. But, I do my damnedest to hang in there with it.

Thoughts While Splitting Firewood At 34 Kim Lane On A Cold, Damp, Dreary October 2016 Morning

A down-the-street neighbor called yesterday afternoon to inform us that our last remaining original neighbor from 26 years ago, had died.

He had the same cancer I have—a cancer I was told was "very slow growing", and that it was OK to "keep an eye on it every six months". He was (about) 83; not very healthy looking at all, but healthy enough looking that I was very surprised to hear that he had died.

I asked the down-the-street neighbor what he had died from. He said the cancer had suddenly spread, and that his health had deteriorated very quickly, and he had died "in a couple of weeks".

Kath and I had moved to 34 Kim Lane in 1990, still practically on our honeymoon. The 1974-vintage A-frame was striking: it was a dream house. We had good neighbors across the street, to our left and right, and even way up on the ridge behind us. It never entered my mind that 26 years later *all* of them would be gone.

Across the street moved out, on-the-right disappeared: gone without a trace, or, a goodbye. A For Sale sign appeared by the up-on-the-ridge's mailbox, then disappeared. Down-the-street told us a new family had moved in. Then told us our last original neighbor had died...

24 Years Later

I love this place; we've lived here 24 years, more time than I have lived in any other place. The winter of 2014-2015 was an absolute bitch—unnecessarily cruel—the worst that I, and many other area residents, remember. I spent an inordinate amount of time battling the snow and ice on the driveway. Sometimes it took three days to get it passable, and it seemed to snow (or rain and freeze) just about every other day. I'd just get the damned driveway clear—hard hard work, long long hours—and it would snow or rain again; back to Square One. We did not want to deal with a winter like this again, and for the first time ever we talked seriously about getting out of here. Preferably to some place where no one has ever heard of a snow blower... Red tile roofs, palm trees???

Raking Leaves, November 2015

For the past several years or so (definitely since I heard that deer ticks survive the winter in leaves) I've raked just about the whole yard, starting with the pachysandra patch down by Kim Lane, then all the way up the left side of the driveway, then the pachysandra patches (pachysandra is a pain in the ass to rake) at the top of the driveway, then the whole area above the back yard, all the way up to the tree line. I rake the leaves unto a big heavy-duty tarp, then dump them over the "downhill" side of the driveway, where hopefully they'll eventually become soil and help the cause.

This whole operation takes days and days, and is hard, but satisfying work, and, good exercise; to me, it's better than riding a bike to nowhere or walking somewhere I've already walked hundreds of times.

This year, while I was out raking (or maybe it was when I was sawing and splitting firewood), Kath said something that was 'way up on the Melancholy Scale: "This will be the last time you ever do this. Next year it will be the new people's job"................

"Feedback"

We've had about ten "showings" of our house. They're a pain in the ass: "prepping" the place, going somewhere to "hide" for an hour or so while strangers roam around your house, then, not receiving any "feedback". Only one of the ten made an offer: that means 90% of the strangers, for whatever reasons, did not "like" this beautiful place enough to want to buy it.

Here's what I think may be some of their reasons:

The driveway isn't steep enough.

The neighborhood is too quiet: there's not enough traffic.

The nick in the paint of one of the kitchen cabinets is too small.

The house was too clean and uncluttered.

The inside of the house has too much wood and stone.

MISCELLANY

Lists

Countries...

I love to travel; explore the world. Mom and Pop used to take us on a family vacation every year. We'd set out in the black 1937 Plymouth four-door sedan (with "suicide" back doors...), or, later, in the light blue 1949 Dodge four-door sedan. We went to Letchworth and Watkins Glen State Parks, Santa's Workshop on Whiteface Mountain, Franconia Notch, the "Skimobile", and the Flume in New Hampshire. A seed was planted.

As a young married couple/family we went to Silver Bay on the northwest shore of Lake George, and Montauck, Long Island. We might have ended up in Canada at some point. Mexico??? Not a chance, amigo...

In 1971 we flew to France: Paris, the Mont Saint Michel, Saint Tropez. Hoo Boy, Europe. A foreign country, across the ocean. A bigger seed was planted. Over the years, we eventually ended up in Italy, and Switzerland. Three European countries, but who's counting??? Years and years later, I began; counting, *collecting*:

Some people (maybe *a lot* of people) are compelled to "collect: things: stamps are the first thing that come to mind, and doesn't Jay Leno have quite a collection of "exotic" cars??? Years ago I knew somebody that collected barbed wire, and someone who very seriously collected *bricks*...

I've never really thought of myself as a collector, but at some point I started noting—and counting—the countries I had visited. There are something like 230 countries on the planet. I don't really want to visit them all—some (Somalia comes to mind) are really shit holes—but I must admit that I am compelled to get to as many as I can. Below is the current list, but I must admit whenever I tell anyone how many countries I've been to, I say "58"; I always add one for good measure, or, just in case...

Oh, and by the way there are a bunch of 1/24 scale NASCAR Dodges stashed away in a box somewhere in the house. Not that I have been collecting them, mind you...

Africa (3/3)
    Kenya
    Morocco
    Tanzania

Asia (4/7)
    China
    Nepal
    Thailand
    Turkey (11/12)

Australia/New Zealand (2/9)
    New Zealand (03/06)

Central America (5/14)
    Costa Rica (11/07)
    Nicaragua (11/07)
    Panama (11/08)
    Belize (05/09)
    Guatemala (05/09)

Europe (37/51)
    Andorra
    Austria
    Belgium
    Bulgaria (05/26/18)
    Croatia
    Czech Republic (11/12/05)
    Denmark (08/28/17)
    England (United Kingdom)
    Estonia (09/02/17)
    Finland
    France
    Georgia (former Soviet Union)

Germany
Gibraltar (United Kingdom!)
Holland   (09/07/17)
Hungary
Iceland   (01/14)
Ireland
Italy
Luxembourg
Monaco
Montenegro
Northern Ireland (United Kingdom)
Poland
Portugal
Romania   (05/30/18)
Serbia   (05/28/18)
Scotland (United Kingdom)
(09/13)
Slovak Republic   (12/05)
Slovenia
Spain
Sweden   (09/03/17)
Switzerland
Wales (United Kingdom)
USSR
Vatican City

Island Nations   (8/59

Antigua
Barbados   (09/10)
Dominica   (09/10)
Montserrat
Nevis
Puerto Rico
Saint Kitts
Saint Lucia   (08/14)

North America	**(3/62)**
Canada	
Mexico	
USA	(09/37)
South America	**(2/65)**
Bolivia	(1996)
Peru	(1996)

Places I would like to get to in the future

Africa: South Africa, Nambia, Botswana, Zimbabwe, Swaziland???

Asia: all of the "stans": Turkmenistan, Kazakhstan, Uzbekistan, Kyrgyzstan, Tajikistan, "because they're there... India, Vietnam.

Central America: Honduras, El Salvador: "Get It Done!"

Europe:
> Western Europe: Lithuania. Latvia, Belarus.
> Eastern Europe: Macedonia, Albania, Moldova, Bosnia.
> Northern Europe: Norway.

South America: Brazil, Argentina, Chile, Uruguay, Paraguay.

Created: December 10, 2004
Last Revised: June 7, 2018

While we're at it, let's do Border Crossings

I never really thought about all the international border crossings I've done until we were canoeing back into Vermont from Quebec on the Northern Forest Canoe Trail. We had canoed into Canada from the US on Lake Memphremagog—this was a much-anticipated Big Deal, having never crossed an international border in a canoe before—and several days later were approaching the Vermont border on the Missisquoi River. I really didn't think of this as any kind of big deal as Kath and I had already done a lot of much more "serious" border crossings in our international travels.

There was a highway bridge crossing the river that to us represented "the border", and we pulled in to shore on the Canada side, and I simply got out of the canoe and walked up to the road and to the border station, prepared to tell the border people our "canoeing back into the US" story, figuring we weren't the first canoeists they had ever encountered on this famous "international" canoe trail.

Well, they did treat it as more of a Big Deal than I ever would have dreamt, almost to the point of "**STOP** where you are sir and put down that canoe paddle".... Shee-it.... I finally convinced them that I (we) was (were) indeed innocent Northern Forest Canoe Trail paddlers simply trying to get back into the US so we could drive home and resume our normal middle-class American lives, but the whole experience was very weird to me.

At any rate, it made me think about—and make a list of—21 (06/18) border crossings that I could remember doing:

Belize/Guatemala
Costa Rica/Nicaragua
Kenya/Tanzania
Peru/Bolivia
France/Italy
France/Germany
France/Luxembourg
France/Switzerland
France/Andorra
France/Monaco
Spain/Portugal
Spain/Gibraltar
Czech Republic/Slovak Republic
US/Mexico
US/Canada
Italy/Austria
Italy/Hungary

Italy/Slovenia
Ireland/Northern Ireland (???)
Bulgaria/Serbia   (05/18)
Serbia/Romania   (06/18)

I'm sure this isn't a complete list, and I feel it's pretty impressive: North America, South America, Africa, Central America, and over two dozen countries, so I maybe can forgive myself for being a bit "cavalier" about "simply" crossing back into Vermont from Quebec: in a canoe....

And, we might as well do states I've been to

As of March 4, 2013—36 states visited.
Bold are "haven't"
14 are Appalachian Trail states.
6 were new on the 2004 Wade Road Trip.

1) Alabama—2004 Wade Road Trip.
2) Alaska
3) Arizona—Grand Canyon rafting trip.
4) Arkansas
5) California—returning from Honeymoon.
6) Colorado—start of Yampa rafting trip.
7) Connecticut—AT state.
8) Delaware—on the way to OP.
9) Florida—with Mom and Pop on vacation.
10) Georgia—AT state.
11) Hawaii
12) Idaho
13) Illinois—landed in Chicago en route to Minnesota.
14) Indiana—en route to Detroit 2007.
15) Iowa
16) Kansas
17) Kentucky—Army basic training in Fort Knox.

18)   Louisiana—2004 Wade Road Trip.

19)   Maine—AT state.

20)   Maryland—AT state.

21)   Massachusetts—AT state.

22)   Michigan—Detroit 2007.

23)   Minnesota—flew out to visit Donna, high school girlfriend.

24)   Mississippi—2004 Wade Road Trip.

25)   Missouri

26)   Montana

27)   Nebraska

28)   Nevada—2004 Wade Road Trip.

29)   New Hampshire—AT state.

30)   New Jersey—AT state.

31)   New Mexico—2004 Wade Road Trip.

32)   New York—AT state.

33)   North Carolina—AT state.

34)   North Dakota

35)   Ohio—en route to Detroit 2007.

36)   Oklahoma

37)   Oregon

38)   Pennsylvania—AT state.

39)   Rhode Island—on the way back from Maine 1975.

40)   South Carolina—on the way to Florida.

41)   South Dakota

42)   Tennessee—AT state.

43)   Texas—2004 Wade Road Trip.

44)   Utah—Yampa rafting trip.

45)   Vermont—AT state.

46)   Virginia—AT state.

47)   Washington—Landed in Seattle on our way to Nepal

48)   Washington DC—visiting the Capitol.

49)   West Virginia—AT state.

50)   Wisconsin—wedding in Milwaukee.

51)   Wyoming

Movie Scenes/Songs

Les Mis...: Ann Hathaway, *I Dreamed a Dream.*

Zero Dark Thirty: Jessica Chastain, "I'm the motherfucker who found him..."

Fly Away Home: Mary Chapin Carpenter, *Fare Thee Well, My Own True Love*: Anna Pacquin and the geese.

Titanic: Celine Dion, *My heart will go on.*

Chariots of Fire: Vangelis and the opening scene, filmed on the beach at Saint Andrews, Scotland.

Strictly Ballroom: *Time After Time.*

Ghost: The Righteous Brothers, *Unchained Melody.*

I Walk the Line: Joaquin Phoenix/Johnny Cash, *Folsom Prison Blues.*

Evita: Madonna, *Don't Cry For Me Argentina.*

Apocalypse Now: *The Theme from the Valkyries:* Robert Duval, "I love the smell of napalm in the morning"

Thelma and Louise: *Lucy Jordan.*

Easy Rider: "And wander through the forest, where the trees have leaves of prisms, that break the light in colors, that no one knows the names of".

The Last Waltz: Neil Diamond, *Dry Your Eyes.*

Top Gun: Kenny Loggins, *Fly Me to the Danger Zone.*

I'LL BE ME: Glenn and Ashely Campbell, *Dueling Banjos.*

Ricki and the Flash: Meryl Streep, [Bob Seeger song].

Not in a movie, but: the Mother Lode Trio's *Sometime Lofty Towers*.

Tuscany, Andre Rieu: Suzan Erens, Carmen Monarcha, Carla Maffioletti, *The Rose*

Live In Dublin, Andre Rieu: *Chianti Song*

Susan Boyle, *I Dreamed a Dream,* Britain's Got Talent

Frank Sinatra and Steve Kazlauskas (Echoes of Sinatra, A Celebration of a Man & His Music): *Summer Wind; My Way; New York, New York*

The ReDucED ShaKeSpeaRE CoMpanY: *The Complete Works* of **WILLIAM SHAKESPEARE (abridged): Adam Long, Reed Martin, & Austin Tichenor:** Othello as a rap song:

("Here's a story of a brother,
by the name of Othello.
He liked white women.
And he liked...green Jello."

"And Iago loved Desi,
like [???] loved Venus.
And Desi loved Othello
cause he had a big...sword.")

To be continued...

Close Encounters With The Rich And Famous

I'm probably pretty safe in saying that many (most???) people go through life without having any contact whatsoever with anyone "rich and famous". Not me:

I passed Paul Simon walking the other way on a Manhattan street one Halloween.

I saw Carly Simon getting out of a cab in front of Grand Central Station.

I sat right next to Robert Joffrey, front row center, at the Joffery Ballet in City Center.

I met Rick Danko, Richard Manuel, Garth Hudson, and Levon Helm in a room in the Plaza Hotel after they had performed at Madison Square Garden with Bob Dylan.

I've shook hands with (pretty much in the order of occurrence):

Gorgeous George, after his wrestling match at Peekskill Stadium, in Peekskill, New York.

Richard Petty, at Bridgehampton Raceway on Long Island. I was so starstruck that I, to my eternal mortification, called him "Dick"...

Phil Liggett and Paul Sherwin, acclaimed Tour de France commentators, at a gas station somewhere in France during the 1992 Tour.

Kevin Bacon, outside the venue in Pine Plains, New York before he performed with the Bacon Brothers.

Colonel Francis Gabreski, 56th Fighter Group, World War II's leading P-47 Thunderbolt ace, at a Warbirds air show, Dutchess County Airport, New York.

Willie Nelson, while he was standing on stage after performing at the Mid Hudson Civic Center in Poughkeepsie, New York.

J. Robbie Robertson, at Rick Danko's funeral in Woodstock.

"Miscellaneous":

I've encountered two Appalachian Trail "luminaries": Earl Shaffer—the first person acknowledged to have walked the whole Maine-to-Georgia trail in one shot—on the AT on Hosner Mountain on his third thru-hike, when he was 78-years-old. I observed that he really wasn't having that much fun. And Ed Garvey, author of *Appalachian Hiker*, that jump-started my long-time Appalachian Trail involvement, at the AT's yearly meeting in New Paltz, New York, date unknown.

I've delivered hay to Kevin Bacon's farm—*Bacon's Acres*—in Connecticut, and Mary Tyler Moore's farm near Millbrook, New York.

And finally, I met Ernest Hemingway (and Hadley and Bumby) on the Rue Mouffetard late one night in Paris (Just kidding with this one, though this area, behind the Pantheon, is one of my Paris faves).

Les Mis, and movies...

I haven't seen many professional plays, but I have seen Les Miserables performed several times, on Broadway, and at West Point's Eisenhower Hall, for example. I've also watched several Les Mis films, and the live performances, and the films, never fail to move me deeply.

I've seen many strong Jean Valjeans, and Javiers, but Ann Hathaway's *I Dreamed A Dream* in what I think of as the "Liam Neason" Les Mis is one of the strongest performances I've ever witnessed in a film. I could watch it over and over.

And speaking of strong film performances, Jessica Chastain's angry "explosion" at her CIA (???) boss and the "I'm the motherfucker who found him" response to James Gandolfini are also at the top of my cinematic moments list.

And, the beautiful cigar-smoking French woman in *Apocalypse Now Redux* letting the Martin Sheen character know she was "available" by just, very subtlety, moving her eyes was, well, memorable...

"Favorite All-Time Movie": *Thelma and Louise*.

"Favorite All-Time Make-You-Feel-Good Movie": *Fly Away Home*". A very-young Anna Pacquin is superb, and Mary Chapin Carpenter's *10,000 Miles* at the end of the film is perfect.

Food and Drink

I've had some fancy meals in some fancy restaurants all over the world: North America, South/Central America, Europe, Asia (can't remember any memorable meals in Africa), but when it comes right down to it, my all-time favorite food is *pizza*; plain old cheese/tomato pizza. Favorite topping is onions, sometimes eggplant. I used to say that I've never had a bad pizza, but that was before we went to Venice...

I recently made some very basic "gorp"—dry roasted peanuts and M&M's, about 50/50—for an Adirondack canoe/camping trip, and kept wolfing the remains down after we got home, until it was all gone...

The Eight Greats

Back in the early 80's Kath and I bought, and drank, a bottle of each of what I thought were the Eight Great Bordeaux of the Classification of 1855:

Ausone,
Haut Brion,
Latour,
Margaux,
Petrus,
Rothschild,
Lafite, and
Cheval Blanc.

I then bought a bottle of each—vintages late 70's-early 80's—and paid about $150-250 apiece. Kath (finally) convinced me to uncork one of them, our Cheval Blanc, to celebrate the Millenium. It was good... Afterwards, Danielle looked it up on the Internet, and it was valued at something like $2500.00!!! The Petrus was valued at $4000.00...........

The seven bottles are still stashed away in our unused downstairs bathroom, the closest place in this house that has a fairly constant cool temperature. But, they have become "white elephants": since they were not stored at a constant 55 degrees or so, to me they have all "gone bad": even "super" Bordeaux don't last 40 years or so stored in a downstairs bathroom...

Kath still wants to drink them. I still don't. Not many middle class people have a collection like this, undrinkable as it may be. So, we dusted them off, I made a list of them, and put them back on the rack in the bathroom. Here's the list, with dates:

> 1977 Chateau Ausone (Saint Emilion),
> 1983 Chateau Haut Brion,
> 1983 Chateau Latour,
> 1983 Chateau Margaux,
> 1983 Chateau Petrus,
> 1980 Chateau Mouton Rothschild,
> 1981 Chateau Lafite Rothschild, and
> 1970 Chateau Cheval Blanc (Saint Emilion): uncorked December 31, 1999...

We also still have one each of the following "non-Greats":

> 1982 Chateau Priure-Lichine,
> 1984 Chateau Palmer,
> 1975 Chateau Montrose, and
> 1986 Chateau Beychevelle.

The Seven Dwarfs

Dopey
Grumpy
Sneezy
Doc
Bashful

Sleepy
Happy

Numbers

19: for whatever mysterious reason, "my number".

NG22002843: My National Guard serial number. I once thought it added up to 19, but it doesn't.

830062: my IBM man number: it adds up to 19.

195: Centre Street. It has a "19" in it.

199: The New York State route Kath lived on when we met: 199 also adds up to 19.

July **19**, 1975: The day I first finished the Appalachian Trail.

1936, 1963, 1972: Cars I owned: a 1936 Ford, a 1963 Corvette, a 1972 Pinto. All their year numbers add up to 19.

43: Richard Petty's NASCAR number.

3: Dale Earnhardt Senior...

327, 289, 351, 426...: Automobile engine cubic inches.

1111: "The Angel's hour".

1234: The second best digital clock numbers, besides 1111.

24601: Jean Valjean's number in *Les Miserables*.

909: The name of the Collings Foundation B-17G.

122: I'm Catskill 3500 Club #122. When Pop was in the Montrose VA, he was in room #122 in the Catskill wing. This is utterly bizarre.

Principal 1998 New York Yankees

"The Team of the Century": 125 wins

Manager

Joe Torre

Pitchers

David Cone
David Wells
Andy Pettitte
Orlando Hernandez
Jeff Nelson
Mariano Rivera

Catchers

Joe Girardi
Jorge Posada

Infielders

Tino Martinez
Chuck Knoblauch
Derek Jeter
Scott Brosius

Outfielders

Paul O'Neill
Bernie Williams

Ricky Ledee
Shane Spencer
Chad Curtis

Others

Darryl Strawberry
Tim Raines
Chili Davis

Friday, October 29, 1999

The scene: a dingy subway platform somewhere in lower Manhattan. The train rumbles and rattles into the station, and screeches to a halt.

The door opens and I automatically step inside without really looking around. Three men swiftly surround me, one in front, two behind. The man directly in front of me YELLS at me:

> *"It's long!"*
> *"It's deep!"*
> *"It's outta here!"*
> *"It's another home run for Scott Brosius!"*

Then he high-fives me. I'm wearing a New York Yankees shirt. So is he, and so are the two guys behind me.

Friday, October 29, 1999: the New York Yankees parade in Manhattan's "Canyon of Heroes" in front of about 3.6 million fans...

<u>My Mona Lisa</u>

The month of May, 2016 I had an art exhibit at the East Fishkill Community Library: "The Early Works: '72-'75". Six oil painting and a drawing, in the styles of DaVinci, Botticelli, Monet, Degas, Modigliani, Picasso, and, Hopper.

The library has monthly art exhibits on the long wall across from the main counter. Back in the middle of 2015 I asked if I could have an exhibit. I was put on a list.

Back in 1973 I had painted a full-scale Mona Lisa as a Dutchess Community College Art History course term project. My recollection is it took about a week to paint, and I only used 14 colors. The painting was a remarkable likeness. It came out as well as it did because I didn't know I *couldn't* paint it. I got an "A".

It had, essentially, been stashed away in a closet or two for something like 43 years. After it was presented to the Art History class, it had never been publicly displayed. I honestly thought it would create a bit of stir: a real hoot to have *the* Mona Lisa hanging in the East Fishkill Community Library for a month.

I originally planned to exhibit just the Mona Lisa, but decided to surround her with some other paintings I had done during the mid-70's: the "Monet", "Modigliani", "Picasso", and "Hopper" were all from an oil painting class at Dutchess. The Degas was a ballerina pencil drawing. I had painted the Botticelli—a head and shoulders of Simonetta Vespucci, the model for Botticelli's *Venus Rising From the Sea*—from an ad in Elle magazine for shower gel or something like that. I prize this small painting, and really hesitated to bring it the library.

Along that line, I had to sign a release that the library would not be responsible for any damage to the paintings. It did occur to me that it might be possible for the Mona Lisa to be attacked, or, stolen......

I made two improvements to the Mona Lisa before bringing it to the library: I glazed it: this brightened it up, and made it look more "Renaissance". The frame was a dull golden-brown, and I gilded it to make it richer looking. These two improvements really enhanced its "authenticity".

The Big Day came when I was to hang the exhibit. I thought I would be doing this after hours, when the library was closed to the public, but as it happened, I had to hang the paintings after 10:00 AM on a Monday morning, right after the library opened. It was raining...

When I brought the Mona Lisa in, I expected some of the staff, who I have interacted with for years, to react. They didn't... There were three older people using the library computers that are next to the wall where the exhibits are displayed. I wrestled the Mona Lisa up onto the wall, half expecting some kind of "Holy shit, there's the Mona Lisa" reaction: it isn't everyday a pretty damned bona-fide Mona Lisa is displayed at a small library somewhere in Small Town USA. Nothing... It occurred to me this might make a good video: an "artiste" hanging up the Mona Lisa right behind an older woman pecking away at a computer, oblivious...

I glanced at the woman's computer screen: *she was buying underwear*........

I hadn't realized what a pain in the ass—and how much work it would be—to hang the paintings: to space them, get them straight, etc. It took an hour, maybe more. I broke a sweat, and was getting tired of the hassle. And in all that time, no one showed the slightest interest at all. Finally I stood back and looked at them. It was a remarkable selection of paintings, most of them pretty good. But, it was very very strange—actually, quite unsettling—seeing *my* paintings up there on the library wall. As familiar as they were to me—I had created them—all of them, excepting the Botticelli, had been stashed away for years, like the Mona Lisa. Done hanging them, I left the library. Nobody seemed to notice.

At first I had decided against having a "Meet the Artist" reception, but changed my mind. The library scheduled it for Friday, May 6, 2016, 6-7:30 PM. Sue and Roy and Sal and Vin and Kelly; neighbors Laura and Ed; hiking friends Duke and Margret; and three other people came. I recall a woman related to the Hopper/Route 9 scene; she had worked at a store in one of the malls.

I visited the library a few times during the month; no one was ever paying attention to the paintings. I always checked my Comments book, hoping someone had gushed on and on, but excepting family and friends, there were hardly any other comments.

I took the paintings down at the end of the month. The Mona Lisa and Simonetta are up in the loft. The other paintings stacked in a closet in the loft. I'm not sure where the Degas is.

Afterwards, I mentally referred to the exhibit as my "Fart in Church" exhibit; my feeling is, overall, it went over like a fart in church..............

January 15, 2016

The Library Announcement

Local author/columnist Ralph J. Ferrusi painted a full-scale* replica of Leonardo da Vinci's *Mona Lisa* as a Dutchess Community College Art History 101 term project in 1973. It has been stored in various closets for over four decades, and this will be the first time it has ever been publicly exhibited.

It took less than a week to paint it: 43 years ago it *never once* occurred to Ferrusi that he *couldn't* paint it....

Over a two-year oil painting "career", Ferrusi created 22 paintings—the exact same productivity as Vermeer—and also painted in the styles of Botticelli, Monet, Modigliani, and, Edward Hopper.

Then, he bought a Nikon camera, and went to Paris..............

*except—if memory serves me right—for reasons I cannot now fathom, it's about 3/8 of an inch short on the vertical.

February 18, 2016

"Jackson-isms"

Catherine and Blair Jackson are friends that go 'way back. We recently visited them in Asheville, North Carolina, and I mentioned to Blair that it was noted in an Asheville tourist magazine that "Asheville was the Paris of America". Blair immediately commented that "Paris was the Asheville of Europe"!!!

Other "Jackson-isms" from over the years:

"And what kind of [ice cream, etc.] would you like???": "Someofeach."

A take-off on the Polish raise-your-wine-glasses salute "Nostrovya": "Nice Driveway"....

November 16, 2017

A 1997 "Status Report"

We entered a local canoe race on Sunday. A "Good Old Boy" race, where the men are all brawny and have really bad teeth and look like they would have been shoe-ins for bad-guy extras in **_Deliverance_**, and RACE, and where *their* women all stand around looking like county/western singers and wear embarrassingly tight jeans and watch the kids and make sandwiches for The Men who are RACING.

Kath and I were the Number 1 boat, and came in second of five in our heat. 3 of the boats were Good Old Boys, and the boat that beat us was an 18 ½ foot Alumacraft "cheater" boat. We were the third boat to finish in each stage of the race (there were two stages, with a hot dog and beer break in between). We were first in our class out of 8 boats after a tough hour and 41 minutes of racing, 15 minutes up on the second place boat. We were 5th overall out of 46 entries; all 4 of the boats ahead of us were racing boats. They had a local band at the SportsMEN's club afterwards, and more hot dogs and beer. It was a really good time. They gave us a foot and a half tall trophy for First Place, but they didn't tell the assemblage that a WOMAN came in fifth overall......."

October 26, 2017

IBM and Alessandro Botticelli

Just about anytime someone mentions IBM I have a very negative knee-jerk reaction from all the later years I worked there as an increasingly square peg in a round hole.

Recently, it occurred to me to try to put some positive spins on my years at IBM: the first thought was they did pay 100% for my college education: seven years (all at night) at Dutchess Community College, Liberal Arts Degree, Humanities. The one course that impressed me the most (and just about the only course I can remember anything about right now) was Art History.

Ultimately I ended up in Florence (Firenze) in the 70's, hair down to my shoulders, full beard, cut-off jeans, red bandana, walking the streets *barefoot* (!) and actually oil painting in the small room in the pensione I stayed in.

Kath and I returned to Firenze recently, and the biggest priority for me was the Botticelli gallery in the Uffizi. I worked my way through the swarm of

Japanese tourists and finally stood right in front of *The Birth of Venus/Venus Rising From the Sea*; it was a couple of feet away from me. Behind me, across the gallery, was *Primavera*: Springtime. Thanks, IBM...

I knew (from my Art History course???) that Botticelli's model for Venus was Simonetta Vespucci, the Most Beautiful Woman in Firenze, who died at the age of 23 from consumption.

I painted my own detail of Simonetta Vespucci in 1973 from a (body lotion???) ad in a copy of *Elle* magazine. In the late 70's (early 80's???) I met Simonetta, now a vegetarian, in Jimmy's Steak Ranch in Poughkeepsie, New York. She soon moved in with me, and we "lived together" for a year or so. I also at this time—holy shit!!!—met Flora, from *Primavera*, in a class at Dutchess. She was married, and lived in Red Hook, New York...

I don't recall any of us bringing up "The Good Old Days in Firenze", but, thinking back, I really really should have pursued this...

January 4, 2018

"Fabulous"

I'd say my parents kept an eye on my teeth when I was a kid. They probably pretty much made sure I brushed them morning and night: "Go Brush Your Teeth!" And school nurses probably looked into our mouths every once in a while, pretty much checking that we indeed *had* teeth.

But once I was out of school, and had a car, taking care of my teeth was not as big a priority as driving around, and, girls. I drank soda, ate candy, cookies, cakes, and pies. I probably brushed my teeth twice a day, but, I didn't start flossing until much later: actually too much later. The damage had been done. My neglected teeth were, in a word, terrible.

So, over the years I have had more "coming from behind" dental work— cavities, crowns, root canals, posts, extractions—than anyone should have in a lifetime. I went to the dentist often, mostly early-morning appointments.

And, though a long-time vegetarian/"health food nut", I started treating myself to breakfasts at Dunkin' Donuts: egg and cheese on a croissant and a Cappuccino. I was a stranger in a strange land in Dunkin' Donuts. The regulars would zip in, get their coffee and donuts, and zip out. I sat down and savored my "forbidden treats".

One morning I walked in and a chubby young kid was behind the counter. He looked about 16. He asked me how I was, and I knee-jerked "OK, how are you?" He said, "Fabulous." I was stunned. Here he was, behind the counter at Dunkin' Donuts, dealing with all these zip in-zip-out people all day every day, and he just said "fabulous"?

I had no idea at the time this would be, for me, one of those rare, positive, Life Changing Experiences. From that day forward, just about any time anybody asks me how I am, I respond, "Fabulous". I'm Paying It Forward, just like the Haley Joel Osment movie.

And, it works: I was in the Garden Department of Home Depot a short time afterwards, and the check-out lady asked "How are you today?" When I said "Fabulous", she kind of looked at me like I was crazy, but after she checked me out and I turned to leave, she said, "Have a fabulous day." WOW!!!

I've often told my story of the chubby young kid at Dunkin' Donuts, and very often people "get it". And, maybe *they* Pay It Forward.

July 29, 2021

Global Warming, or, Naturally Occurring Cycles???

For whatever reasons, I count the number of times I cross-country ski each winter. I don't count the number of times I hike, or canoe, or bicycle each year (though I do fastidiously record the number of miles I bicycle each year), but I am compelled to count the number of times I ski. Recently I went back through my engagement calendars (where I keep my counts) and documented them, from the first time I recorded them for the 2007/2008 winter to the 2014/2015 winter, and, did some tabulations.

A local newspaper recently tabulated snowfall depths from 2011-12 to 2015-16. I found these figures very interesting, and I thought they would pretty much correlate to the number of times I've skied each winter, but, surprisingly, they don't. I guess a lot depends on how desperate I am to ski; if there's a lot of snow, I can ski as often as I want to. But, if snow is scarce, I often ski on "crumbs": on very little, or very marginal, snow.........

2011-12: **20.5 inches**

2012-13: **38.9 inches**

2013-14: **64.1 inches**

2014-15: **60.7 inches**

2015-16: **13.2 inches**

OK: about two feet, around three feet, OVER five feet, five feet, then...about a foot......

The question is, is the lack of snow—and skiing opportunities—last year, and so far this year, due to global warming, or naturally occurring cycles???

Here's my ski counts:

Season	First Ski	Last Ski	Count
2007-2008	01/15/08	03/03/08	16
2008-2009	01/01/09	03/05/09	33
2009-2010	12/25/09	03/13/10	**40**
2010-2011	12/14/10	02/26/11	30
2011-2012	**10/28/11!!!**	03/02/12	**13**
2012-2013	11/08/12	03/21/13	26
2013-2014	11/12/13	03/21/14	27
2014-2015	11/14/14	03/25/15	35
2015-2016	01/13/16	**04/06/16**	19
2016-2017	11/20/16	01/24/17	10

As of the 2015-2016 season I've managed to ski during six months of the year, from October 28th in 2011 to April 6th in 2016, and have skied an average of 26.6 times a season. The beginnings vary from October to January, but all but two seasons have ended in March. As of today, 01/23/17, the 2016-2017 hasn't been promising...

My Obituary

RALPH JOSEPH FERRUSI, JR.
SEPTEMBER 12, 1973–

March 11, 2009
March 30, 2009
January 31, 2014

He was a good man—strong, honest, a gentleman—just like his Dad.

He loved the outdoors, the mountains, and travel to faraway places.

He always tried to do the best he could with what life threw at him—with the cards that he was dealt.

He wasn't always successful: he was a lousy father, and a lousy husband—not because of any innate meanness or stupidity—he did the best he could—he could just never figure it out.

He *was* a good son, and a good brother.

And, damn, could he climb mountains, and ride a bicycle.

And, write a hiking column...........

Music I would like played (03/08/09):

Country Roads	John Denver, track 7
Windsong	John Denver, track 9
Holly Holy	Neil Diamond, track 7 (???)

Clothes (03/09/09, between 3:00 and 4:00 AM)
Updated 01/31/14:

Blue blazer
Nice (brown???) top: *not* a turtle neck or mock turtle neck

Black Jockey underwear (NOT the JAKES—I never liked them)
Faded blue jeans
Black dress socks
Brown Florsheim shoes

Don't let them do something weird with my hair!!!

EPILOGUE

I began writing this on Sunday, April 19, 2015. I always figured 80,000 words or so would be a good to-be-published goal. On Wednesday, June 30, 2021, after adding several pieces from the "My Computer" folder on the flash drive that I had backed up my original old Gateway "desktop" computer, I ended up with 86,197 words.

Gulp...time to bite the bullet and call iUniverse. There is some pretty good original writing in here, some serious, some pretty funny.

Ralph Joseph Ferrusi, July 2, 2021

September 1, 2021
88,569 Words...

April 19, 2015

...

September 1, 2021
88,569 Words